CORREGIDOR

CORREGIDOR

The Rock Force Assault, 1945

Lt. Gen. E. M. Flanagan, Jr. USA (Ret.)

PRESIDIO

*For the valiant soldiers of the Rock Force—
paratroopers and amphibians—who
overcame great odds of enemy, terrain,
and weather to free Corregidor*

*"I'm proud I'm allowed
To be one of the crowd."*

Line from 503d Regimental Combat Team song.

Contents

Acknowledgments

Writing about a military operation which took place over forty-two years ago requires a great deal of search: search for records, for men who were present at specific times and places; search for maps of the area, for photographs of the action; search for authentic remembrances of things past, untainted by nostalgic stories passed around at annual reunions.

Without General George Jones's cooperation and assistance, I could not have even begun the search for records, reports, and former members of the 503d. In fact, I could not have written the book without his help. He sent me monographs written by some of his officers who attended service schools just after the War; he remembered and wrote about many significant incidents covering the entire life and battles of the 503d; he referred me to officers and men who were key members of the regimental combat team; he called me a number of times with additional suggestions and references; and most important of all, he reviewed the entire manuscript and made valuable comments and corrections before I sent the manuscript to the publisher. His help was inestimable.

As usual, the editor-in-chief of Presidio Press, Adele Horwitz, was my mentor and guide. She drew on her vast editorial background to lead me through the manuscript, editing and correcting on the way. To her, I owe a great deal of gratitude.

Many other men who were part of "The Rock Force" contributed markedly to the final version of this book. I have listed them alphabetically because I cannot with any degree of accuracy list them in any order of priority.

Donald E. Abbott, the executive officer of E Company, 503d, sent me his draft manuscript of his jump, his subsequent actions, and E Company's operations on "The Rock."

Colonel Robert M. Atkins, USA, Retired, sent me his monograph and a number of letters; he was particularly helpful in tracking down and identifying the present status of many members of the 503d.

Colonel John H. Blair III, USA, Retired, wrote an excellent monograph at the Infantry School shortly after the War. It was entitled: *Operations of the 3d Battalion, 503d PIR on Corregidor.*

Warren W. Elfrank, who was a 1st Lieutenant in the 161st Engineer Company with the 503d, sent me a tape of his experiences on the Rock, detailing his experiences and those of his men on the jump.

Edward T. Flash, who was a platoon leader in F Company of the 503d, sent me the lesson plan for a class he taught at the Infantry School on the subject of airborne operations in the Southwest Pacific area, with special emphasis on Corregidor. He also sent me letters detailing specifics of the actions in which he was a participant.

Colonel Henry W. "Hoot" Gibson, with whom I served at Fort Sill a few years after the War, wrote me a long letter outlining the part played by his battery, B Battery of the 462d, in the Rock attack; he also wrote that when he was a boy his father had worked for the Navy at Cavite and that he had gone to Fort Mills, Corregidor, to participate in swimming meets with boys who lived on Corregidor.

William Hennessey, who was a 2d lieutenant in B Battery of the 462d, met with me for lunch at the Parris Island Officers club where he filled me in on his and B Battery's part in the operation.

Joseph L. Gray, who had been a lieutenant in B Battery of the 462d, sent me a paper outlining his recollections of the Corregidor operation and also sent letters from Sgt. Thomas L. Shutt and Park Hodak, both ex-members of B Battery of the 462d.

Major James J. Helbling for his thesis in the 1971 Class at

the Command and General Staff School wrote a paper entitled: "Combined Assault-Fortress Corregidor."

Weldon B. Hester, who had been the Red Cross Field Director with the 3d Battalion of the 34th Infantry, sent me many letters enclosing copies of articles from his vast collection of magazine articles, newspaper clippings and official reports, all dealing with the conduct of the war in the Southwest Pacific, with particular emphasis on Corregidor. One important document was BG S. L. Howard's report on the employment of the 4th Marines from September 1941 to May of 1942. Mr. Hester also sent me items from the Manila Press, printed while the newspaper was under the control of the Japanese.

Captain Hudson C. Hill, while a student at the No. 1 Advanced Course at the Infantry School at Benning, wrote an outstanding monograph on "The Operations of Company E of the 503d at Wheeler Point, 23 February 1945."

Dr. Logan W. Hovis, Battalion Surgeon with the 3d Battalion of the 503d, wrote me letters detailing the operations of the 3d Battalion.

Carl Kuttruff has done a great deal of research on a special pictorial project of the assault on Corregidor.

Lt. Colonel John H. Lackey, who commanded the group of C-47s which dropped the 503d on Corregidor, wrote an excellent staff paper at the Armed Forces Staff College entitled: "The Rock Operation."

Karl H. Landes, PhD from the university of Berlin in 1930 came to the United States in the same year, and enlisted in the Army in 1940 at Edgewood Arsenal. He went to jump school in 1941 and later transferred to the 503d. Because of his engaging personality, he became known to every man in the 503d as "Doc" Landes. He wrote me a number of fact-filled letters covering the operations of the 503d from Stateside through Corregidor.

Ron Lee, a S/Sgt in the 3d Platoon of I Company 503d wrote a splendid letter about his platoon in combat on Corregidor.

Lester H. Levine, a major at the time, wrote an outstanding monograph while at the Infantry School advanced course. It was entitled: "Operations of the 503d PIR in the attack on Corregidor."

Frank H. Linnell, now a retired brigadier general, wrote his monograph on "The Retaking of Corregidor" while a student at the Amphibious Warfare School, Marine Corps Schools, Quantico, VA in 1948.

Rev. Msgr. John J. Powers wrote concerning some of the details of the Corregidor operation with which he was familiar.

Irving Sellinger wrote a number of letters and sent a brief chronology of the 503d. He also included some 39 of the 503d's wartime songs ranging from "Powdered Eggs" to "The Golden Gate Bridge."

Captain Magnus L. Smith wrote his monograph, while at the Infantry Officers Advanced Course, on "Operation of the Rock Force in the Recapture of Corregidor."

Lt. General John J. Tolson wrote a number of letters explaining in detail the organization and history of the 503d.

Dick Williams, the photographer with the 503d on the Corregidor operation, sent many photos of the assault and subsequent battles. He also sent me a detailed account of his work with the 503d. I am especially indebted to him for loan of his outstanding photos of the assault on Corregidor.

Introduction

"CORREGIDOR, fortified rocky island (2 sq mi) in the Philippines, at the entrance to Manila Bay. Under U.S. control from 1898, it fell to the Japanese in May 1942 when Gen. Jonathan Wainwright surrendered after four months of fierce fighting. Recaptured in 1945, it is now a WW II memorial."

With those fifty words, the *Concord Encyclopedia* sums up tersely and unemotionally the varied and tumultuous history of the island fortress that guards the approaches to Manila Bay. This book is a story of those fifty words, with emphasis on three words: "Recaptured in 1945."

The 503d Parachute Regimental Combat Team, reinforced by the 3d Battalion Combat Team of the 34th Infantry Regiment, 24th Division, made up the "Rock Force," which assaulted Corregidor (The Rock) on 16 February 1945. Two-thirds of the parachute regimental combat team jumped onto the small island, defying the Japanese commander's firm conclusion that a parachute assault could not take place on the island because there were no suitable drop zones. He was almost—but not quite—correct: the drop zones used by the 503d were, in fact, barely suitable, but the 503d parachuted onto them anyway. The regimental combat team's (RCT) jump casualties were relatively high, but not as high as the regimental commander had first predicted. But given the nature of the DZs—small (the bigger was 325 by 125 yards); rubble-strewn, from all of the U.S. Air Corps and Navy's prejump softening-up bombing and strafing; wind-blown by a constant breeze that flowed across the island (a wind so strong that it would have canceled training jumps in the States)—the jump injuries were relatively minor.

To attack a small, heavily fortified island defended by elite troops with a phobia about surrendering is a risky operation. But war is, by its very nature, filled with risks. Daring, courage, danger, and gambles are commonplace in war; soldiers practice those virtues hourly.

The successful commander is the one who studies the situation, assesses his forces and the enemy, analyzes the terrain, considers the weather, and then weighs all of the factors and makes a decision. If there were no risk involved, there would be no war; it would be a peacetime maneuver. A soldier wins a medal for taking a risk; a unit wins a battle.

Just so at Corregidor. The commander evaluated all of the factors bearing on his decision and decided that he could land on the island by parachute troops and thus achieve one of the most important principles of war—surprise. And with surprise, he was able to secure a foothold with relatively few troops. By parachuting onto the forbidding high ground, he was able to secure the controlling terrain and dominate the island, which, in turn, permitted him to defeat in detail a much larger, more heavily fortified, more deeply dug in, more ingeniously camouflaged enemy force.

Certainly the 503d did not achieve the victory unaided and unsupported. The 3d Battalion Combat Team of the 34th Infantry landed amphibiously on the island a couple of hours after the initial drop of the 503d. The Air Corps and the Navy provided countless sorties and surface ship attacks in support of the Rock Force. Thus, the recapture of Corregidor was in every sense a joint operation; it could not have been accomplished by one service alone.

Military history is replete with battles won by intrepid, clever, decisive commanders against great odds and seemingly insurmountable conditions. But the Rock Force attack against Corregidor on 16 February 1945 must go down as one of the most daring, well-planned, and superbly executed operations in the annals of the U.S. or any other army. The rugged terrain, the fanatical enemy, the strong defenses, the concrete and steel fortifications stacked the odds in favor of the enemy. Yet the Rock Force achieved success through its daring plan of attack; sound implementation of the battle plan; the bravery, discipline, and training of its soldiers; and the wholehearted support of the other services.

This, then, is the story of the Rock Force.

CORREGIDOR

CHAPTER I
Corregidor Won

Corregidor and some 7,100 other large and tiny islands (only 400 of which are inhabited and only 460 of which are larger than one square mile) make up the Philippine Island archipelago. The Phillppines came under the tutelage of the United States as a part of the settlement of the Spanish-American War.

That war was fought in naval and ground battles thousands of miles apart. Theoretically, the ostensible and much-publicized objective of the United States in the war was the liberation of Cuba from Spanish control, a hegemony that had been established while the Spanish were building their worldwide empire in the fifteenth and sixteenth centuries.

By 1895, the Cubans had had their fill of autocratic Spanish rule. In that year, Cuban revolutionists rose up against the Spanish, and the resultant turmoil, unrest, and destruction caused heavy losses to American investments in the island. Beyond that, however, the United States, which was committed at that time to the building of the Panama Canal, recognized the strategic and commercial importance of Cuba as an independent nation, or better, a protectorate of the United States and, therefore, sided with the revolutionaries against the Spanish.

Two events triggered and inflamed the emotion of the United States toward Spain: one, with unbelievably bad timing for its international relations with the United States, the Spanish minister to the United States, Depuy DeLôme, wrote a letter that criticized and disparaged President McKinley, calling him "a weakling—a bidder for the admiration of the crowd" and "a would-be politician." After its publication in the Hearst and Pulitzer papers on 9 February 1898, public indignation in the United States boiled high over the insult to the President and thus to his nation. With the subsequent fanning of the flames of war by the press, the people of the United States leaned more and more toward war with the Spanish. DeLôme's resignation did not calm the fury.

The ultimate catalyst for causing the United States to take action against the Spanish was the mysterious explosion on and the subsequent sinking of a U.S. battleship, the USS *Maine,* in Havana Harbor on 15 February 1898, with the loss of 2 officers and 258 sailors. "Remember the *Maine,* to hell with Spain!" very shortly became the battle cry of the newspapers and thereafter the people of the United States. A great many influential citizens now demanded that the United States retaliate against the Spanish. "There'll be a hot time in the old town tonight" became another people-rouser. Newspapers throughout the country demanded war.

After the *Maine* exploded, a disaster for which neither the Spanish nor U.S. investigators could fix responsibility, the United States summarily demanded that the Spanish withdraw from Cuba. To emphasize that demand, on 22 April 1898, the United States ordered Rear Adm. William T. Sampson to blockade Cuba. As expected, the Spanish did not withdraw from Cuba but declared war on the United States on 24 April. The United States followed suit and declared war on Spain the next day.

Prior to the declaration of war, Commodore George Dewey, commander of the six-ship Asiatic Squadron of the U.S. Navy, was in Hong Kong taking on provisions and coal in preparation for a quick run to the Philippines, where he knew there was a Spanish fleet. War with Spain would make every Spanish possession an objective. On the day the United States declared war against the Spanish, the British forced Dewey to leave the neutral port of Hong Kong. On that same day, the Navy Department sent Commodore Dewey a cablegram that stated: "Commence operations at once, particularly against the Spanish fleet. You must capture vessels or destroy." (Given today's layered military command-and-control structure, one must admire the brevity, directness, and clarity of this order.)

On 27 April, Dewey ordered his squadron to sail for the Philippines. On that same day, Adm. Patricio Montojo Pasaron, commander of the seven-ship Spanish squadron in the Philippines, moved his ships from Manila Bay to Subic Bay because he felt that with his ships and the shore batteries surrounding Subic, he could defeat the larger American force. At Subic, he sank, futilely, three of his vessels to block the eastern channel but then found, belatedly, that the shore batteries were not operational. He returned to Manila Bay on 28 April.

On 30 April, Dewey, by now off Luzon's west coast, made a reconnaissance of Subic Bay but, of course, did not find the Spanish ships. That night, he sailed south. Early on 1 May, Dewey and his squadron sailed into Manila Bay. He was aboard his flagship, the USS *Olympia*, at the head of his squadron. His ships steamed past Corregidor, which the Spanish used as a lighthouse base, signal station, and checkpoint for ships entering the bay.

Commodore Dewey continued boldly at about eight knots on his course into Manila Bay within range of the onshore Spanish guns at Cavite and very shortly under the guns of Admiral Montojo's ships, which were backed up in the bay near Cavite. Dewey's squadron followed behind his flagship in column "keeping their distance excellently," he wrote later.

In his autobiography, Dewey described the attack on the Spanish fleet early in the morning of 1 May:

> The misty haze of the tropical dawn had hardly risen when at five-fifteen, at long range, the Cavite forts and Spanish squadrons opened fire. Our course was not one leading directly toward the enemy, but a converging one, keeping him on our starboard bow. Our speed was eight knots, and our converging course and ever-varying position must have confused the Spanish gunners. My assumption that the Spanish fire would be hasty and inaccurate proved correct.
>
> So far as I could see, none of our ships was suffering any damage, while in view of my limited ammunition supply it was my plan not to open fire until we were within effective range and then to fire as rapidly as possible with all of our guns.
>
> At five-forty, when we were within a distance of five thou-

sand yards, I turned to Captain Gridley and said: "You may fire when you are ready, Gridley."

From then until shortly after noon, Dewey's squadron steamed back and forth past the Spanish fleet, closing the range on each successive run. His ships' guns fired rapidly and accurately. By the time the attack was over, the eight ships of the Spanish fleet, including Montojo's flagship, the *Reina Cristina*, had been sunk or scuttled in the bay. Dewey had not lost a single ship or a single sailor.

"The order to capture or destroy the Spanish squadron had been executed to the letter. Not one of its fighting vessels remained afloat," he wrote. In his diary that night, Dewey recorded the day's action rather succinctly and concisely, with just a hint of modest understatement: "Reached Manila at daylight. Immediately engaged the Spanish ships and batteries at Cavite. Destroyed eight of the former, including the *Reina Cristina* and *Castilla*. Anchored at noon off Manila."

Dewey's impressive victory against the Spanish fleet in Manila Bay did not, however, gain him any control over Manila. In a few days, the shore batteries of Cavite fell to the commodore, but Manila itself remained in the hands of the Spanish. Dewey had only seventeen hundred men of his own, barely enough to man his ships. Therefore, Dewey, not a man to remain idle, blockaded the port, encouraged Emilia Aguinaldo (whom he had brought with him from exile in China) and his Filipino insurgents to surround the city, and requested from the U.S. government a land force large enough to take the capital of the Philippines.

While awaiting the arrival of the ground forces, Dewey, by now an admiral (date of rank, 7 May 1898), had more than enough crises on which to expend his considerable talent. English, French, and German ships arrived in the bay ostensibly to protect their nationals from the insurgents. But the real reason, Dewey suspected, especially for the Germans, was to be on hand to pick up any territories of the islands that, in the event the Americans decided not to control the Philippines after the departure of the Spanish, might be up for grabs. Dewey handled the violations of the blockade by these interloping ships with firmness and patience. And once it became clear that the United States was not going to abandon the islands, the third-nation ships departed.

That was just one of Dewey's problems out of the way. His biggest concern was that he was still afloat in Manila Bay with no way of taking Manila.

The War Department was very slow in shipping Army forces to the Philippines for a very good reason: at the outbreak of the war, the U.S. Army was in a deplorable state—a condition in which it found itself at the outbreak of every succeeding war in the twentieth century. The Regular Army of 1898 numbered slightly more than twenty-eight thousand men, scattered on many small posts across the country. The troops were well trained individually, but they were not trained to fight in large units. There were no organized units larger than a regiment. The Army had no mobilization plan, no doctrine for joint arms operations, no functioning high command, and few officers who had even seen a unit as large as a brigade, let alone commanded one. In addition, in spite of the long period of strained relations with Spain before the war, the War Department had no plan for military operations in Cuba, or anywhere else, for that matter.

The National Guard was in a far more lamentable state—if that were possible. It was composed mostly of infantry units with a strength of one hundred thousand men. The soldiers knew little beyond close-order drill and small-unit administration. Their equipment was obsolete, and even that was scarce. The organization of the National Guard varied from state to state, and, in effect, there were as many different kinds of National Guard units as there were states. The adjutants general of the various states were extremely jealous of their prerogatives and highly suspicious of any move to bring the National Guard under the control of the Regular Army. Besides all that, there was some question of the legality of sending National Guard units abroad. So the federal government acquiesced and decided that the National Guard units could remain in their states under the control of the various governors.

Lt. Gen. Nelson Miles was the commanding general of the Army at the outset of the war; Russell A. Alger was the secretary of war. Unfortunately, they were hardly on speaking terms, a situation which did little to enhance the combat readiness of the Army. Alger had been a general officer in the Civil War and considered himself fully competent to run the Army without the assistance of General Miles.

Their antipathies toward one another resulted in two divergent plans for mobilizing the Army and the "volunteers" for combat service in Cuba. General Miles advised the secretary to concentrate the entire Regular Army and enough volunteers to make a small force of eighty thousand men at Chickamauga Park, Georgia, where it could be "equipped, drilled, disciplined and instructed in brigades and divisions and prepared for war service." The secretary turned down that sound advice; instead, he ordered the cavalry and the artillery to Chickamauga and the infantry to New Orleans, Tampa, and Mobile, thereby effectively negating any possibility of combined-arms training and the development of divisions and larger units.

Alger, backed by a rabid Congress and a warmongering public, called for up to 267,000 men to enter the Army. Because the war had been so highly touted by the press and because of the inflamed passions of the people against Spain, about a million men offered their services for what they thought would be a big picnic in the lush tropics of Cuba. But by the time they were subjected to camp life in the south, their views changed radically.

In the camps there was total confusion. The volunteer officers were without even rudimentary military training; supplies and arms were short; sanitation conditions were disgraceful; food was tainted; medical care was unbelievably bad; and weapons, such as they were, were obsolete. Men by the thousands lacked such basic items as underwear, shoes, and socks. Those who were fortunate enough to receive uniforms were startled to find that they were woolen uniforms, suitable for winter campaigns on the plains, but hardly for wear in the south or in Cuba in the summer.

Not only did the War Department have no plan for operations in Cuba, neither did it know the strength, disposition, or capabilities of the Spanish or the insurgents who would become its allies once U.S. troops were deployed in Cuba. There was no plan for nor training in amphibious warfare, an obvious necessity when combat operations must take place across the water to a landing on an island. Accurate maps of Cuba were essentially nonexistent.

There was only one saving grace for the U.S. Army—the Spanish were even more inept and ill prepared.

The Navy was far better trained and equipped for wartime operations than was the Army. The Navy had, for a decade, been modernizing and constructing ships for its fleet and for training its sailors. Therefore, when it was ordered to blockade Cuba, the Navy could immediately dispatch Adm. William T. Sampson and his fleet to secure the northern approaches to Cuba.

Adm. Pascual Cervera commanded a Spanish fleet of four armored cruisers and six torpedo boats. On 29 April, he sailed from the Cape Verde Islands in a westerly direction. But because no one in the U.S. command knew where he was headed, the United States succumbed to unreasonable panic along the eastern coast, and the Navy Department ordered the Navy to split its Atlantic Fleet and use one part to protect the eastern seaboard and the other to blockade Cuba. Thus, in the only successful maneuver on his part in the war, Cervera was able to accomplish two things: he split the fleet and eluded Sampson's ships off the northern shore of Cuba. Cervera sailed unmolested into Santiago Bay on the south side of Cuba. There his luck and intelligence failed; for reasons known only to him and Madrid, he bottled up his fleet in the confines of the narrow Santiago Harbor. Sampson and his fleet easily blocked the entrance. Cervera's selection of Santiago had another offshoot advantageous to the United States: it gave the U.S. Army an objective—Santiago. But it would be some time before the disorganized and basically not-combat-ready Army could get there.

Meanwhile, however, Sampson dispatched ashore a force of his ship-borne Marines and ordered it to seize Guantánamo Bay. After a minor skirmish with the Spanish, the Marines placed the U.S. flag on Cuban territory. This action was the first on Cuban soil involving Americans; the Marines and the flag are still there.

Admiral Sampson was now faced with his major problem: how to defeat the Spanish fleet even though it was checkmated in Santiago Harbor. He was hesitant to run the narrow channel into the five-mile-long harbor because of a fear of mines and the supposedly formidable Spanish coastal defenses on both sides of the entrance to the harbor. He tried to knock out the batteries guarding the entrance with a naval bombardment; he tried to block the exit from the harbor by sinking the collier *Merrimac* across the channel. Neither scheme succeeded. Finally, he decided that he had only two courses of action: he could either force an entrance with his ships, or he could call on the U.S. Army to defeat the batteries at the harbor's gate. He elected to call for the Army. Little did he suspect the difficulties he would bring on himself and the Army.

The U.S. Army, still ill-equipped for tropical operations, untrained in joint and amphibious operations, and located at Tampa, a city whose port had only one pier and one single-track railroad, was, nonetheless, eager to get into the action. After all, it was a very popular war in the United States, "a splendid little war." On 11 June, the Army ordered the embarkation of V Corps under a 62-year-old, 300-pound commander, Maj. Gen. William R. Shafter.

The embarkation of the seventeen thousand men in Tampa was as confused, chaotic, and poorly planned as had been the training, equipping, and concentration of the force in Florida. The loading, which should have taken about eight hours, took four days. V Corps had no plan for combat loading and no staff on hand to supervise it. The men, supplies, and equipment were loaded haphazardly aboard various ships, with no thought to the possibility that their disembarkation in Cuba might be opposed at the beaches or docks. The officers commandeered trains, appropriated equipment consigned to other units, and even suffered fights of their men with other units on the piers in an effort to board the transports. Nonetheless, in spite of the scenario that might have been the plot for a latter-day movie comedy starring the Three Stooges, the convoy finally got underway on 14 June; on 20 June, it reached a point off Santiago.

General Shafter and Admiral Sampson held a joint conference as soon as General Shafter arrived and could board the admiral's flagship. Sampson wanted Shafter to take direct action and land his forces just to the east of Morro Castle, the fort guarding the eastern side of the harbor and about five miles south-southwest of Santiago, and then attack and destroy Morro Castle and the Spanish batteries on the west side of the harbor's mouth. If the guns were silenced, Sampson reasoned, his ships could sweep the mines at the entrance to the harbor and move in to attack Cervera's fleet, which was locked up inside. But, unlike today's command-and-control arrangements for amphibious and ship-to-shore deployments, Admiral Sampson was not in command of the debarking troops, and General Shafter could do exactly what he wanted to do when he felt ready to do so.

Knowing how incompetent his command was, well aware that the ships were not combat loaded for a landing against even the slightest resistance, and somewhat awed by the sight of Morro Castle rising 230 feet above the sea, General Shafter disregarded Admiral Sampson's request and opted for another solution: he took the advice of General García, the commander of the Cuban insurgents ashore, and landed his force at Daiquirí, eighteen miles to the east of Santiago Harbor.

In spite of the obvious disagreement between the general and the admiral, Sampson had his ships shell the landing area heavily, and General Shafter's troops began to stumble and wade ashore. The landing was perhaps even more incompetent than the loading. Fortunately, there were no Spanish troops in the area. If there had been, they could have had a field day against the disorganized mobs of troops and undoubtedly could have prevented a landing. But the Spanish were equally unfit, unprepared, and poorly located. U.S. units got ashore as best they could, with or without their equipment. Many captains of chartered merchant vessels transporting the troops refused to take their vessels near the shore, backed off, and attempted to flee the area. The Navy rounded them up and forcibly shepherded them back to the landing docks and beaches. The cavalrymen had no idea of how to get their horses ashore, so they simply threw them overboard and let them swim to the beach. Unfortunately, some of the horses did not know the way to the beach and headed out to sea. Finally, one enterprising cavalryman tied the horses together and led them ashore with a boat.

General Shafter finally succeeded in landing about six thousand troops the first day and began his march to the west toward Santiago. Three days later, Brigadier General Lawton, one of his subordinate commanders, reached the town of Siboney, about nine miles to the east of Santiago, and captured it without difficulty.

Thereafter, Shafter used Siboney as the debarkation point for the rest of his command. Siboney thus inadvertently became his base of operations.

About twelve thousand Spanish troops defended Santiago in forts and entrenched lines that encircled the city to the north, east, and south. (The harbor was to the west.) The most important of these defenses were along a series of ridges, known collectively as San Juan, to the east of the city, and a fortified village to the north, El Caney. Shafter decided to attack El Caney first, block reinforcements to Santiago, and cut the water supply to the city. He planned to follow the El Caney attack with a frontal assault on the fortifications along the San Juan ridges.

The 1 July attack on San Juan and El Caney was as inexpert and bungling as were all of the other Army operations during the war. Shafter allowed General Lawton, commanding the 2d Division, only two hours to move to El Caney and capture that fortified village. But in two hours General Lawton could hardly begin his movement to the village, let alone succeed in capturing it. He moved across the line of departure on schedule, but he could not complete his attack within the allotted time because of poor roads; unanticipated, rugged terrain; and totally inadequate maps.

Maj. Gen. Jacob F. Kent, the commander of the 1st Division, assigned to take the San Juan forts and high ground, waited more than two hours for Lawton's attack to get under way; then he ordered his attack to begin. It was a typically uncoordinated, badly staffed, and poorly led maneuver. Within a few minutes, his troops were milling about; his headquarters had lost control of the subordinate units; and his communications were totally inadequate to the task. As if these problems were not enough to baffle and thwart General Kent, he had to suffer yet another difficulty, one almost impossible to have expected or to have planned against: a Signal Corps observer in a captive balloon being towed along above General Kent's column mistakenly took his frontline troops for the enemy and called in heavy artillery on his own troops. Another element beyond the control of General Kent that influenced the outcome of the battle was the extremely hot and humid weather. The heat nearly prostrated the 300-pound Shafter and effectively prevented him from exercising command over his attacking columns. And the troops in their winter uniforms were also extremely uncomfortable.

But in spite of these depressing and frustrating conditions, junior officers rose to the occasion and effectively pressed the attack on the San Juan ridges. Lt. John Parker, for example, commander of a Gatling gun detachment (which had traditionally been used only in the defense) got permission (or probably simply assumed it) to use the guns in support of the troops in the attack. He moved his guns onto line with the infantry and thereby established local fire superiority, which in turn restored the offensive spirit and rallied the troops trying to take the heights. Kettle Hill was a knob separated from the main San Juan ridge and was the actual area on which Lt. Col. Theodore Roosevelt and his dismounted "Rough Riders" distinguished themselves. It was one of the very few high points of the Cuban ground campaign and made Roosevelt a nationally known figure.

At El Caney, the attacking force faced the usual difficulties of lack of command and control. About five hundred Spanish troops defended the town in strong positions behind barbed wire–protected defensive positions. One of Lawton's regiments in the attack was a volunteer outfit that was still firing obsolete ammunition with black-powder cartridges. The black smoke so clearly revealed the lines and location of the regiment that Lawton was forced to withdraw it. Initially, Lawton had placed his artillery in positions from which it could not support the attack. Finally, however, he moved it forward. From its new positions the artillery could, albeit belatedly, effectively shell the enemy positions. When the village eventually fell to the Americans on 2 July, Shafter then controlled all of the outer defenses of Santiago and was faced with the dilemma of what to do next. His first inclination was to withdraw to high ground four miles to the east of the city, but the War Department vetoed that plan and ordered him to hold what he had seized. (Apparently, communications with Washington were better than from Shafter to Lawton and Kent.)

Shafter next tried to convince the Navy to run the gauntlet past Morro Castle and attack the Spanish fleet in Santiago Harbor. Sampson and the Navy Department quite wisely refused that option. They saw no advantage in running past strong batteries which they had asked the Army to knock out and which it had failed to do. In the command-and-control arrangements of 1898, only President McKinley had command authority over both the Army and the Navy forces in the war zone, and he was not inclined to exercise that option. Inevitably, the Army and the Navy spokesmen began to debate the controversy in public. For the moment, it appeared that the opposing forces and the U.S. Army and Navy were stalemated.

But once again the Spanish came to the rescue, solved the interservice squabble, and saved the battle for the deadlocked and inactive Navy and Army forces. The Spanish were running low on food, water, and ammunition in Santiago and, because of the blockade at sea and the circle of American troops around the city, had no hope of resupply. There was a near famine in the city. Madrid felt that the fall of the city was inevitable and decided that Cervera's fleet should try to run the blockade and get to open water rather than have the Americans capture the fleet intact.

Madrid, therefore, ordered Cervera to make a run for it. On the morning of 3 July, while Sampson and Shafter were ashore discussing their differences, the Spanish fleet sailed down the narrows of the harbor, past Morro Castle, and into the open sea. But the U.S. Navy was ready and waiting. In a running battle, the Navy completely destroyed the entire Spanish fleet either by sinking the ships, running them ashore, or completely disabling them. The Spanish lost 323 men killed and 151 wounded; the Americans lost 1 sailor on the *Brooklyn*.

A few days later, General Shafter met with Gen. Jose Toral, the Spanish commander of the defenders of Santiago, between the lines. After some urging by Shafter, Toral agreed that his only recourse was to surrender honorably under Shafter's terms: Shafter would have permitted the Spanish to withdraw, unarmed, from the city. Washington, however, countered Shafter's offer and demanded that the Spanish surrender unconditionally. At first, Toral balked at unconditional surrender. But then the Navy shelled Santiago from long range and thoroughly frightened but scarcely damaged the defenders. The shelling convinced Toral; he agreed forthwith to the terms of unconditional surrender.

On 16 July, the Spanish and American commanders signed terms that provided for the surrender of 11,500 Spanish troops in the city of Santiago; 12,000 troops in other locations in Cuba, including those still around Guantánamo; and other troops in various towns and locales twenty-five to sixty miles away from Santiago. The next day, during a formal surrender ceremony, the former enemies saluted one another and shook hands all around.

In Puerto Rico, the campaign was a simple, almost bloodless operation with few casualties and was carried out in a decidedly relaxed, almost amiable atmosphere. General Miles, the Army's commanding general, had arrived in Cuba to assume personal command of the U.S. Army forces there. With the fall of Santiago, he took it upon himself to lead the assault on Puerto Rico. He left Cuba with three thousand men and landed at Guánica on the southeastern coast, although his original plan was to land at Cape Fajardo, on the northeastern side. His change of plans negated Navy help in an attack on San Juan. This may have been his parochialism in action. At any rate, he deceived the enemy and landed against light opposition. He called for additional landings, and a force under Maj. Gen. John R. Brooke landed at Guayama, also on the south. Shortly, the island was overrun, and the Puerto Ricans, overjoyed at the prospect of being annexed by the United States, welcomed the troops with open arms. The Puerto Ricans' biggest problem was finding enough U.S. flags to decorate the government buildings and celebrate the arrival of the Yankees in San Juan. The Spanish-American War in the Caribbean was over.

In the Philippines, Manila was still not in American hands. Dewey had asked Washington for five thousand men to help him capture the city. As a result of that request, the War Department geared up to organize a force under the command of Maj. Gen. Wesley Merritt. By 1 July, some two months after Dewey's request, the first echelon of Army troops of twenty-five hundred men had arrived off Manila under escort of the USS *Charleston*. The two-month delay seems excessive; two factors, however, help to explain the delay: one, the "not-combat-ready" state of the U.S. Army, and, two, en route the *Charleston* stopped at Guam to accept its surrender.

During the three weeks following the arrival of Merritt's troops, the U.S. Army engaged in no ground action around Manila. The

War Department continued to build up troop strength until, by 25 July, there were eleven thousand men on the scene, and General Merritt, himself, arrived to take command.

These forces put Manila under siege. As the American strength built up around Manila, U.S. dependence on the guerrillas decreased. Aguinaldo, a proud and determined man, had hoped that with the defeat and withdrawal of the Spanish the United States would recognize the Philippine Republic with him as its head. But when it became clear to Aguinaldo that the United States was determined to take Manila without his and his guerrillas' help, relations between the two so-called allies worsened.

One reason for U.S. determination to take Manila unaided was that, early in the siege, the Spanish had given tacit agreement to surrendering the city if the city were not to be subject to insurgent control after the surrender. Probably the main reason, however, that the United States decided to fight without the Filipinos was that the United States was still trying to decide the future status and administrative control of the Philippines after the departure of the Spanish. The United States clearly wanted to avoid making commitments and being obligated to a Filipino government after the war.

Dewey and Merritt were thus caught in a bind. They had, on the one hand, to resist the aspirations and hopes of the guerrillas without, on the other hand, inciting them to rebellion against U.S. forces. To make the tactical situation even more difficult, the guerrillas held an inside line around Manila between the city and the American forces deployed in a larger, encircling arc.

The American commanders exercised all of their tact and skill with Aguinaldo and his staff and, by the end of July, were able to persuade Aguinaldo to lead his forces out of the area. The rebels left peacefully but reluctantly. The United States, however, had not heard the last of Aguinaldo and his fiercely independence-minded insurgents.

Brig. Gen. Arthur MacArthur (Gen. Douglas MacArthur's father) was a commander of forty-eight hundred volunteers who landed with Merritt's force at Cavite sometime in late July. His role in the siege is somewhat difficult to evaluate. Manchester, in *American Caesar* says, for example: "When the Spanish . . . capitulated nine days later—U.S. casualties had been thirteen killed and fifty-seven wounded—Merritt praised the 'outstanding' work of the striking force [under MacArthur] and the 'gallant and excellent judgment' of its brigadier." Given the number of casualties for the size of the operation and the fact that the surrender had already been negotiated with the Spanish, one wonders about the extent of the work of the strike force.

Gen. Douglas MacArthur, in his *Reminiscences,* describes the siege of Manila and the part played by his father, in somewhat more graphic and complimentary phrases. He writes:

> On 1 June 1898, my father was appointed a brigadier general of Volunteers and ordered to the Philippines. . . .
>
> On July 31st, my father arrived in the Philippines and was assigned to command the Second Brigade of the 1st Division, then, in conjunction with the Filipino Army, besieging Manila.
>
> The resistance in front of the Second Brigade was tenacious and the fighting along the Singalong Road, with its strong blockhouses, was severe. The city, however, shortly capitulated and a treaty with Spain was negotiated.
>
> My father was at once promoted to be a major general of Volunteers and assigned to the command of the 2d Division of the VIIth Army Corps.

Even though General MacArthur writes that "the city shortly capitulated," there were more difficulties with the insurgents than with the Spanish. The American commander arranged with the Spanish to allow his forces to occupy Manila after a token assault on the city. The attack began with the Americans moving slowly, carefully, and without firing toward the city. But then something happened to cause an eruption of firing on both sides. In the rice paddies outside the city, the rebels, who had been on the flanks and behind the Americans, became intermingled with them. As the forces moved forward, sporadic firing broke out. The Americans held their fire when they received no answering volleys from the Spanish, but the rebel fire continued. For some time the situation appeared to be deteriorating; but, shortly, the American commanders were able to stop the unauthorized firing, and the Spanish were able to carry out their part of the bargain and capitulate.

The surrender of the city was somewhat an anticlimax because the war had ended two days earlier, on 12 August. Nonetheless, the Filipino units, which had entered the city in spite of the agreement with Aguinaldo and the Spanish, were persuaded to leave, and the Spanish formally surrendered Manila to the Americans on 14 August.

The protocol that ended hostilities on 12 August had the following provisions: Spain would cede to the United States Puerto Rico, relinquish Cuba and one of the Mariana Islands (later Guam was the island selected), and agree to have the United States occupy the Philippines until its fate could be decided at a later date.

The war had cost the United States about a quarter of a billion dollars and about five thousand soldiers, only four hundred of whom, however, were combat casualties. The rest died of various diseases. The War Department justifiably came under criticism for its lack of combat readiness at the start of the hostilities and for delays in delivering medical supplies and military equipment to the troops in the combat zones. A presidential board of inquiry determined that the War Department had indeed been unprepared for the war but cleared it of a more serious charge of permitting contaminated beef to reach the troops in Cuba.

On 10 December 1898, the United States and Spain signed the Treaty of Paris, which, on 6 February 1899, was approved by the U.S. Senate. The treaty confirmed the provisions of the protocol and, in addition, required the United States to pay Spain $20 million for its various real estate, buildings, ports, and installations in the Philippines. Spain retained liability for the Cuban debt. But because of the Platt amendment to the treaty, Cuba remained under the protection of the United States, which then established a temporary military administration in Cuba.

The Treaty of Paris had two far-reaching consequences for the United States and Spain: Spain's overseas empire was virtually dissolved, and the United States conversely became a world power, thrust almost casually and unwittingly into the affairs of Latin America and tied closely to events in the Far East, a situation that would finally explode in 1941.

As far as the Philippines was concerned, the Treaty of Paris simply meant that U.S. forces in the islands stopped fighting one enemy and were forced to take on another, for with the Spanish

surrender, the relationship between the Americans and their erst-
while ally, the Filipinos, rapidly deteriorated. Aguinaldo and his
rebels were as determined as ever that the Philippines would be
a free nation governed by Filipinos. Two days before the Senate
ratified the Treaty of Paris, serious fighting broke out around
Manila between the U.S. Army and the rebels. The cause of the
outbreak is not known, but the U.S. Army once again found itself
at war. Thus began the Philippine Insurrection.

Maj. Gen. Elwell S. Otis succeeded General Merritt in command of the U.S. Army forces in the Philippines; he had about
twenty-one thousand men on hand. Unfortunately, many of these
men were volunteers and were due shortly to rotate to the United
States. Therefore, he could count on only about twelve thousand
effectives. With that small force, General Otis was able to control
only the immediate Manila area. The rebels, with a force estimated
to be as strong as forty thousand Filipinos, held a semicircle of
blockhouses around the city.

It became perfectly obvious to the War Department that a
much larger force would be necessary in the Philippines if the
United States were to exercise control over the islands. The alterna-
tive was to turn the territory over to the Filipinos. The administration, sensing that possession of the Philippines gave it tremendous
power in the far Pacific and vast new markets for its burgeoning
economy, was determined to put down the insurrection and solidify
its control throughout the islands. Consequently, the War Department raised ten volunteer regiments, and within seven months
nearly thirty-five thousand reinforcements were on the way to
the Philippines. The United States was now engaged in a battle
that rapidly degenerated into guerrilla warfare. The enemy was
terrain-wise, determined, and organized.

As in most guerrilla wars fought in mountainous and jungled
areas, the Philippine Insurrection was characterized by rugged
terrain, hot and humid climate, and a native enemy who was ill
equipped but able to blend in perfectly with the local population.
The Filipino insurgent knew the area, had a vast intelligence
network of friendly people, could live easily off the land, and
had the burning passion of freedom and nationalism to sustain
him.

On the other hand was the American fighting man, better

equipped, trained, and armed but subject to the anomalies of the guerrilla warfare situation—ambushes and surprise hit-and-run guerrilla attacks—and himself robbed of surprise by the countrywide Filipino intelligence network, invisible but effective. The American was also hampered in his unit movements by the lack of roads and the difficulty of the jungle, which limited the use of artillery and prevented the frontline deployment of the Gatling gun, which had proven so effective against the Spanish in Cuba.

In spite of the difficulties, General Otis did not sit idle behind his defenses around Manila. His forces captured a few locations in March 1899, including Malolos, the capital of the rebels, and the islands of Cebu, Panay, and Negros. Even with a shortage of manpower, Otis launched a two-pronged attack against the strength of the insurgent power in central Luzon: he sent General Lawson on to Santa Cruz and General MacArthur up the center of the island from Malolos toward San Fernando. By mid-May, organized resistance in central Luzon was crumbling, but manpower shortages and the coming rainy season temporarily halted Otis's drive until October.

In October, General Otis continued his drive up the central plain of Luzon with two smaller forces flanking the main attack. The attack failed to capture the elusive Aguinaldo, but it did succeed in scattering and weakening much of the rebel force that Aguinaldo commanded.

Nonetheless, the insurrection was far from crushed. In the thirteen months between May 1900 and June 1901, more than one thousand separate battles were fought between the Americans and the insurgents. The fights were brutal and vicious, with neither side giving any quarter. But by March, Aguinaldo had been captured, and by June, the fighting and the insurrection were, for the most part, over. For years, however, remnants of the rebels continued to harass the American occupying forces that were now in control of most of the larger, inhabited islands.

In April 1901, Aguinaldo took an oath of allegiance to the United States and retired to private life. (He again surfaced in March 1945 when the American forces took him into custody on suspicion of collaboration with the Japanese during their occupation of the islands. Subsequently, however, he was exonerated and released.)

Thus, the United States gained control of the Philippine Islands the first time. And with them, Corregidor entered the history books. Because of its location, configuration, and potential for the defenses of Manila, the tiny island of Corregidor would be thrust into an emotional forefront in World War II. During the war, Corregidor would become a bastion of hope for the United States in the dark, early days of the war when U.S. troops defended it against brutal aerial attacks by the Japanese; it would be the seat of command power in the Philippines when General MacArthur and President Manuel Quezon moved their respective headquarters there on Christmas Eve 1941; it would become a short-lived haven for some of the troops forced off Bataan in early 1942. Corregidor would loom large, but depressingly and ominously, in the U.S. people's minds when MacArthur and entourage left there on 11 March with Lieut. Bulkeley on PT-41 and three other PT boats, and it would represent the probable low point of U.S. morale in World War II when General Wainwright surrendered it and his forces to the Japanese on 6 May 1942; but it would represent U.S. optimism, confidence, and high expectation when General MacArthur returned to it on 2 March 1945 the same way he had left it three years earlier: with most of the people who had left with him in 1942 aboard the four Navy PT boats. Its shattered barracks on Topside would form the backdrop for General MacArthur's emotional remarks to Col. George Jones and his Rock Force troops who had retaken the island in twelve bloody days of fighting: "I see that the old flagpole still stands. Have your troops hoist the colors to its peak, and let no enemy ever haul them down."

But before General MacArthur would find himself in a position to make those remarks, Corregidor would witness the sights, sounds, and sensations of brutal combat; degradation of American troops and their commanders; incredible, Japanese mass suicides; and a battle like none other in military history. Corregidor would live up to its matchless personality.

CHAPTER II
Corregidor: Geography and U.S. Buildup

On 6 May 1942, President Roosevelt in Washington and General MacArthur in Australia received a message that marked for them and for the United States another in a series of abysmal low points in the early months of World War II. The 7 December 1941 messages from Pearl Harbor were stupefying and cataclysmic; but the 6 May 1942 message they received from Lt. Gen. Jonathan M. "Skinny" Wainwright, commander of all the U.S. forces in the Philippines, was spirit breaking and despairing and served to highlight the cycle of disasters that the U.S. forces had been suffering since "the day that will live in infamy."

General Wainwright's message read:

> With broken heart and head bowed in sadness but not in shame, I report that today I must arrange terms for the surrender of the fortified islands of Manila Bay. Please say to the Nation that my troops and I have accomplished all that is humanly possible and that we have upheld the best tradition of the United States and its Army. With profound regret and with continued pride in my gallant troops, I go to meet the Japanese Commander.

At about the same time, General Wainwright sent another separate message to General MacArthur in Australia. "I have fought for you to the best of my ability from Lingayen Gulf to

The Island Fortress

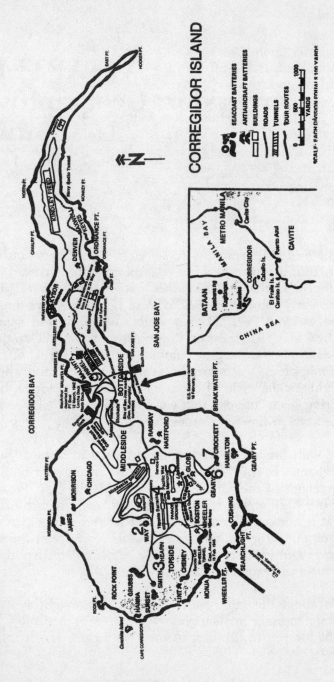

CORREGIDOR ISLAND

SEACOAST BATTERIES
ANTIAIRCRAFT BATTERIES
BUILDINGS
ROADS
TUNNELS
TOUR ROUTES

0   500   1000
YARDS
SCALE: EACH DIVISION EQUALS 100 YARDS

MANILA BAY

METRO MANILA
Cavite City
Puerto Azul
CAVITE
BATAAN
Dumanes Id.
Kaphagin
Mariveles
CORREGIDOR
Caballo Is.
El Fraile Is.
Carabao Is.
CHINA SEA

EAST PT.
HOOKER PT.
N
KINDLEY FIELD
NORTH PT.
Navy Radio Tunnel
MONKEY PT.
CAVALRY PT.
DENVER
KEYES
ORDNANCE PT.
ORDNANCE PT.
CAMP ST.
INFANTRY PT.
KYSOR
ARTILLERY PT.
SAN JOSE BAY
ENGINEER PT.
MALINTA
MAINT.
SAN JOSE PT.
South Dock
MacArthur
PT Boat
Lorcha Dock
North Dock
BOTTOMSIDE
U.S. Seaborne landings
16 February, 1945
BREAK WATER PT.
CORREGIDOR BAY
BATTERY PT.
RAMSAY
HARTFORD
MIDDLESIDE
CROCKETT
CHICAGO
HAMILTON
MORRISON
GEARY PT.
JAMES
GLOBE
GEARY
BOSTON
CUSHING
MORRISON PT.
WAY
SEARCHLIGHT PT.
HEARN
ROCK POINT
TOPSIDE
WHEELER PT.
GRUBBS
SMITH
CHENEY
HANNA
FLINT
MONJA
SUNSET
Caballo Island
ROCK PT.
CAPE CORREGIDOR

Bataan to Corregidor. Goodbye, General." That was Wainwright's last message from Corregidor.

But to Sgt. Irving Strobling, a U.S. Army radio operator from Brooklyn, goes the somewhat dubious distinction of being the man who sent the last message from the beleaguered island fortress. From one of the dusty, hot, humid, and stench-filled tunnels of Malinta Hill, Sergeant Strobling tapped out in Morse code this final message, which in a few words reflected the hopes and despair, the agony and frustration of the more than four thousand men and women jammed into laterals and passageways of Malinta Tunnel. His message, picked up by ham operators along the West Coast of the United States:

> We've got about fifty-five minutes left and I feel sick at my stomach. I am really low down. They are around smashing rifles. They bring in the wounded every minute. We will be waiting for you guys to help. This is the only thing I guess that can be done. General Wainwright is a right guy, and we are willing to go on for him. But shells were dropping all night, faster than hell. Damage terrific. Too much for guys to take. Everyone is bawling like a baby. They are piling dead and wounded in our tunnel. . . . The jig is up.

The island from which General Wainwright was about to depart was twenty-five miles southwest of Manila Harbor and was one of four island fortresses in Manila Bay. The other three were Caballo, El Fraile, and Carabao. The islands, through a fortunate quirk of nature, formed the basis for an interlocking defensive barrier that stretched along a twelve-mile line from the southern tip of the Bataan Peninsula to Ternate, on the southern shore of Manila Bay. This line was the narrowest portion of Manila Bay and formed a choke point between Manila Bay and the South China Sea. The islands were thus ideally located for the defense of Manila and its harbor.

When the Spaniards possessed the Philippines, they used Corregidor at first simply as an outpost from which lookouts, using semaphore signal lights, alerted Manila's defensive forts to any enemy force that might approach. Enemy ships might include

Chinese junks, Moro vintas, British three-deckers, or Dewey's White Squadron.

The Spanish built a lighthouse and a signal station. The island also housed a small fishing village, the barrio San José, complete with a Catholic church and a one-room schoolhouse run by the clergy.

All ships entering or leaving the bay were required to stop at Corregidor to have their papers checked. Hence, the name Corregidor, which means "corrector," or "magistrate," in Spanish.

The Spanish also built minor fortifications on the island to form an outer line of defense and as protection for the larger guns they had installed at Cavite on the southern shore of Manila Bay. In 1898, when Admiral Dewey sailed into Manila Bay, the Spaniards had emplaced three large cannons on Corregidor, each with a range of about a mile and a half.

Later, in 1913, in his autobiography, Admiral Dewey described the Spanish defenses of Manila Bay:

> Corregidor and Caballo are high and rocky, effectually commanding both entrances [to the bay], while El Fraile, though smaller, is large enough to be well fortified and to aid in the defense of the broader channel.
>
> No doubt the position is a strong one for defensive batteries, but the Spaniards, in keeping with their weakness for procrastination, had delayed fortifying the three islands until war appeared inevitable. Then they succeeded in mounting sufficient guns to have given our squadron a very unpleasant quarter of an hour before it met the Spanish squadron, provided the gunners had been enterprising and watchful.
>
> Examination of these batteries after their surrender on May 2 showed that there were three 5.9-inch breech-loading rifles on Caballo Island, three 4.7-inch breech-loading rifles on El Fraile rock, and three 6.3-inch muzzle-loading rifles at Punta Restinga, commanding the Boca Grande entrance, which our squadron was to use; three 8-inch muzzle-loading rifles on Corregidor, three 7-inch muzzle-loading rifles at Punta Lasisi, commanding the Boca Chica entrance. The complement manning these batteries, as given by the official papers found in the commandant's office at Cavite Arsenal,

was thirteen officers and two hundred and forty-six men. While the muzzle-loaders were relatively unimportant, the six modern rifles commanding the Boca Grande, at a range of a mile and a half, if accurately served, could deliver a telling fire.

General MacArthur, in his somewhat old-fashioned style of expression, describes Bataan and Corregidor this way:

It was early in October 1922 when the transport *Thomas* docked at Pier Five in Manila, and once again the massive bluffs of Bataan, the lean gray grimness of Corregidor were there before my eyes in their unchanging cocoon of tropical heat.

After acquiring the Philippines from the Spanish in 1898, the United States began an enormous engineering effort to fortify the four islands across the mouth of Manila Bay. By 1914, the immense work was virtually completed and the four islands, Corregidor, Caballo, El Fraile, and Carabao, had been transformed respectively into Forts Mills, Hughes, Drum, and Frank. The fortifications were so formidable that they were justifiably called "The Gibraltar of the East." Given the status of the Philippines, the general world situation, U.S. foreign policy, and the existing state of the weapons of war in 1914, the United States had designed the defenses of the four islands primarily to withstand an attack from the sea and, conversely, to assault enemy ships of war attempting to run the gauntlet into Manila Bay. So by 1914 standards the United States had accomplished its mission: the fortifications of the four islands, particularly Corregidor and El Fraile, were so massively constructed with steel and reinforced concrete that they could withstand attacks from the heaviest guns then known to be afloat, and they could deliver accurate, devastating fire from the biggest coast artillery weapons then in existence on any warships whose skippers were foolish enough to put them to the test.

But in the early 1920s, General Billy Mitchell began to make his mark on air warfare doctrine with what was then radical air-superiority strategy. The subsequent rapid and revolutionary development of military aviation by the world powers made the defenses of Manila Bay's islands, so carefully and expensively built over the preceding two decades, almost obsolete. But by then it was too late to alter or modernize the defenses: the Washington Naval Treaty of 1922 prohibited any major modifications. After 1922, the only authorized improvements to Corregidor were the installation of antiaircraft artillery batteries and, in 1932, the construction of the major tunnel network under Malinta Hill.

Corregidor, more familiarly known as The Rock to the troops stationed there, is an island of volcanic rock that in some prehistoric time had been belched from the floor of the bay. It is shaped like a massive apostrophe lying on its side or like a huge tadpole swimming west to the openness of the South China Sea. Its long axis runs east and west, and its narrow, curved tail arches around to the southeast and points to Caballo Island, about two miles south of the eastern tip of Corregidor. Corregidor separates the bay into a narrow, three-mile-wide channel to the north and a wider, nine-mile-wide channel to the south. Corregidor itself contains only 1,735 acres.

The primeval upheaval that formed Corregidor very nearly split it into two islands. Thus, the middle of the island between the head and the tail narrows to six hundred yards and is only a few feet above sea level. This low area was called Bottomside and, by the beginning of World War II, contained two docks (one on the north and one on the south side); the barrio of San José, which housed about six hundred Filipinos who worked for the U.S. Army on Corregidor; shops; warehouses; water-storage tanks; a power plant; a coal basin; and cold-storage units. To the east of Bottomside was Malinta Hill, with its subterranean tunnel complex resembling a void left after the spine and the ribs of the hill had been extracted by the forceps of some ancient orthopedic, colossal god.

Beyond Malinta to the east stretched the tail of the tadpole, which was only about six hundred yards at its widest point. Kindley Field, a short, grassy strip that could handle only light aircraft and a Navy radio intercept station on Monkey Point were two important features on the curved tail. There was also a gun battery halfway down the tail and near the western end of Kindley Field. Monkey Point was a small hill on the south side of the tail and would prove to be the site of an unexpected and calamitous disaster when the paratroopers of the 503d eventually cleared that part of the island.

To the west of Bottomside was a small plateau called Middleside. This was a fairly well built up area resembling the residential area of a small Army post back in the States. On Middleside were located the main hospital, barracks, a service club, quarters for the noncommissioned officers and commissioned officers, an officers' club, the post exchange, and two schools for the dependent children of the garrison. This area was one of the best-kept parts of the island, with well-groomed lawns, shrubs, and hedges. Another small Filipino barrio, San Isidoro, was also located on Middleside.

Topside, as the name implies, was the highest part of the island, rising to heights of more than six hundred feet in some places. The steep and rocky cliffs forming the sides of the tadpole's bulbous head, Topside, were etched with bare-rock ravines with jagged outcroppings. The flanks of Topside rose up on three sides to form a plateau on which was located the main living quarters for the enlisted men of the island's contingent: the three-story, concrete-and-steel-reinforced, "longest barracks in the world," sometimes referred to as the "mile-long barracks." In actuality, the barracks were about fifteen hundred feet long. Also on Topside were the headquarters for the island, a theater, a small parade ground in front of the western side of the barracks, a small nine-hole golf course with additional officer and NCO quarters arched around its northern side. The parade ground and the golf course would be important spots in the 503d's parachute jump on the island. Other supply, administrative, and maintenance buildings, some of wood, some of concrete, others of corrugated iron, studded Topside.

Three ravines cut deeply into the almost-perpendicular sides of Topside and provided access from the beaches to the congested area on top. The ravines would also prove of significance in the fighting that took place when the island was recaptured from the Japanese. Ramsay Ravine cut into the east side of the head of The Rock and reached almost to the southern corner of the barracks; Cheney Ravine sliced into the western side of the head; and James Ravine came in from the north. Defenders of the island had to guard these three ravines because they were critical points below which a seaborne attacker might land for a direct amphibious assault on the island.

One of the most important installations on the island, critical to sustaining the lives of the defenders, was the power plant located on Bottomside near the wharves of the North Dock. Corregidor was totally dependent on this power plant: fresh water had to be pumped from twenty-one deep wells on the island or barged across the north channel from Mariveles on Batáan; fresh food could be preserved in the tropical climate of the Philippines only if held in cold storage; the large seacoast batteries, even though equipped with their own auxiliary power plants, relied heavily on the main power plant as the primary source of power; the Malinta tunnels were uninhabitable if they were not ventilated by power-driven blowers; and all of the important military emplacements on the island were connected not only with sixty-five miles of roads but also with thirteen miles of track over which ran electrically driven trolleys.

The labyrinth of tunnels that the Army engineers had gouged and blasted out of Malinta Hill was a marvel of construction and an attraction for all of the officers and men stationed on the island. The engineers started the tunnel excavation in the late 1920s and continued even until Pearl Harbor. The main tunnel, completed in 1932, was 1,450 feet long and 30 feet wide at its base. The walls arched up to a domed ceiling at a height of 20 feet. The island's electrical railroad ran down through the center of the main tunnel. Branching off on both sides of the main passage were some twenty-five laterals, each about 200 feet long. All of the laterals were deadheaded, with no outside exits, except one, which led to and through the emergency, standby hospital on the north side of the complex. The twelve laterals of the hospital contained a fully equipped 300-bed hospital and had its own entrance and exit on the north side of Malinta Hill. One of the laterals on the south side of the tunnel led to an eleven-lateral quartermaster storage area; its main passage continued to the Navy tunnel on the south side. The walls, floors, and overhead arches of all tunnels were of reinforced concrete.

Originally, the tunnels were designed primarily for the storage of supplies, equipment, and ammunition for the Harbor Defense

MALINTA TUNNEL

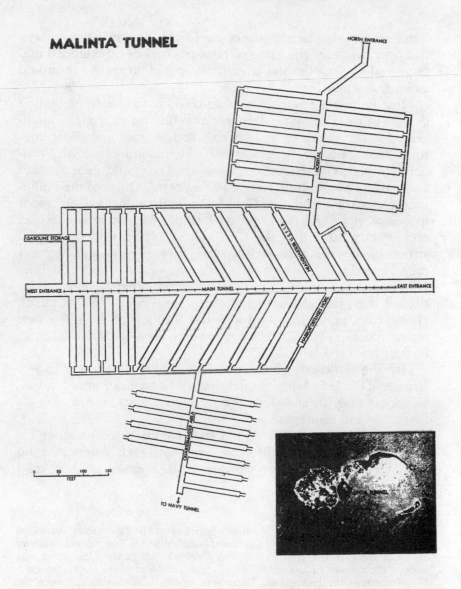

Force, the senior headquarters on Corregidor in prewar days. But over the years the maze of passages had been extended and improved to include one lateral that could store ten thousand gallons of motor fuel.

Just before the war, it became obvious to the commanding general of the Philippines Department[1] that he must make provisions for the safety of and furnish secure operational facilities for Military Advisor General MacArthur; Commonwealth President Quezon; U.S. High Commissioner Sayre; and their families and staffs. Thus, in June 1941, the Engineer's Office of the Philippines Department duly sent Capt.[2] Arnold Boettcher to Corregidor to design and build the required facilities for the senior civilian and military officials of the Philippines. Armed with precise instructions about his mission, Boettcher, his surveyors, and engineer crew blasted five new laterals off the main tunnel under Malinta Hill. In contrast to the grim austerity of the other facilities under the hill, these laterals were painted and furnished with cots, tables, chairs, rugs, and desks. And with the addition of these five new laterals, Malinta Hill now enclosed at least forty-five laterals under its four hundred feet of rock.

By the standards of the pre–World War II Coast Artillery Branch of the U.S. Army, the defenses of Corregidor were colossal, all-conquering (to any ships trying to run past), and seemingly invincible and impregnable.

Corregidor alone was dotted with twenty-three batteries for a total of fifty-six coast artillery weapons with each battery housing one or two huge guns or mortars. And, because of their solid

---

1. After 1913, the regular U.S. Army garrison on the Philippines was called the Philippines Department and was commanded by a U.S. Army general officer. In 1935, General MacArthur retired as chief of staff of the U.S. Army and became the military advisor to Manuel Quezon, president of the Commonwealth Government of the Philippines. There was no official connection between the military advisor and the Philippine Department commander. However, just before the war, the War Department informed M. G. Lucius R. Holbrook, the Philippine Department commander at that time, that assistance to General MacArthur was "the most important peacetime mission of your command."

2. Today it would probably require the services of at least a major general and his staff, supplemented by a bloated gang of civilian advisors, to accomplish the same mission.

permanence and absolute immobility, the various batteries had names of their own and, over the years, had fostered traditions and inspired esprit among the various coast artillery crews that served them. Most of the huge batteries were located around the perimeter of Topside. Batteries Wheeler, Crockett, Smith, and Hearn were equipped with 12-inch guns, and Batteries Geary and Way were armed with 12-inch mortars. By 1941, these weapons were more than forty years old—decidedly World War I vintage.

The main batteries of the island had been installed and completed by 1914. The sides of the huge gun pits (some circular and more than fifty feet in diameter and some rectangular with the long sides eighty or more feet long) were reinforced with layers of brick and concrete and were as much as fifteen feet thick. Through the rear of the pits were tunnels carved out of the rock of Corregidor in which was stored the ammunition for the guns and mortars and in which were austere quarters for the gun crews on standby alerts.

The huge projectiles for the 12-inch guns were some five feet long and weighed more than 900 pounds. The rounds were stacked neatly four to five rows high in the covered recesses to the rear of the gun pits and were moved out of the tunnel magazines on overhead chain hoists and tracks.

The main armaments of Corregidor were the 12-inch disappearing guns of Battery Crockett, located about four hundred yards to the southeast of the center of the barracks and across the golf course. Battery Crockett was sighted to attack ships coming into Manila Bay through the wider south channel. The 12-inch guns were the monsters of the U.S. Army's Coast Artillery. They had a 360-degree traverse and could hurl a projectile with considerable accuracy more than sixteen miles. A crew of thirty men was required to service each weapon. A well-trained crew could get off a round about every forty seconds—but that took considerable training and men in excellent physical condition.

Once the gun fired, its recoil would sink the gun tube back below the level of the surrounding parapet into its recoil position ready for another loading. The breechblock operator would then muscle open the 500-pound breechblock, and the gases from the previous round would flow out; then the swabbers would ram a water-soaked sponge on the end of a long pole into the tube to clean out the gases from the previous round and to extinguish any hot cinders that might have remained from the charred bag of the previous powder charge. Then the burly loaders would rush forward with another 900-pound round, which they either pushed on a wheeled cart or carried on a metal frame somewhat like a stretcher with long handles projecting out from the sides. The loaders placed the shell carrier just beneath the breech of the gun, and a rammer with a ramming staff would, with the help of a couple of other soldiers, force the projectile well into the tube and seat it. Then another crew would run forward with a 270-pound bag of powder and shove that into the breech. Finally, the breechblock operator would close the breech and lock it firmly, the gunner would adjust the sights, the disappearing carriage of the gun would then raise it above the parapet, and a bell would sound to alert the crew to the fact that the gun was once again ready to fire. At the bell, the crewmen would put their fingers into their ears to deaden at least some of the thunderous concussion of the firing gun.

By the beginning of World War II, events in the development of warfare had almost overtaken guns of this sort, and by the end of the war, they would prove to be the mastodons of military weapons, ready to take their places in the museums of history alongside the catapults and battering rams. But when the Japanese invaded the Philippines, they were aware of the potency of Corregidor's guns and fully understood their strategic significance in the overall scheme of defense. And before Corregidor fell, the batteries of Corregidor would, with their last-ditch effort, write chapters of gallantry in military history books.

Antiaircraft artillery on the island consisted of six batteries, each with four 3-inch guns that could fire to a height of thirty-two thousand feet, and four batteries, each with twelve .50-caliber machine guns. The island's AA equipment also included one battery of five SL Sperry 60-inch searchlights. These weapons belonged to the 59th Coast Artillery, the branch of the service that in the World War II Army was responsible for air defense.

The Bay's defenses were supplemented by even larger guns on the three other fortified islands in the bay, one of which was Fort Drum, "The Concrete Battleship," seven miles southeast of

Corregidor. Fort Drum must be unprecedented in the history of military fortifications. The American engineers had flattened to sea level the top of the small island El Fraile, only about an acre in area, and then reconstructed it to resemble the forepart of a battleship. The sides of the new island were vertical and were 25 to 36 feet thick; the top was 40 feet thick. The new structure was shaped like a ship, with one end flat and the other shaped like a prow. It was 350 feet long and 144 feet wide and rose about 40 feet above sea level. On top of the "battleship" were two gun turrets, each mounting two 14-inch Model 1909 guns. Drum also had four 6-inch Broadbent guns. Tunneled into the interior of the concrete structure were living quarters for three hundred men. The crew of the guns on Fort Drum not only had to be well trained in the mathematical precision of the Coast Artillery firing calculations, but in good physical condition as well: a 14-inch shell weighed 1,560 pounds, and its powder bag weighed 440 pounds.

Five miles to the north of Drum and two miles south of Corregidor was Fort Hughes, built on Caballo Island. Hughes was not the fortified blockhouse that Drum was; nonetheless, its half-mile length and 300-yard width was fortified heavily. Its western side rose to a height of 380 feet. It housed 250 men in its fighting complement, and before the war, amazingly enough, it boasted one of the best gymnasiums in the Philippines Island Coast Artillery.

Just before the beginning of the war, the combined strengths of the four islands in Manila Bay totaled about six thousand men and women (there were Army nurses on Corregidor), the bulk of whom were stationed on Corregidor, whose garrison was composed mostly of a headquarters, the artillerymen, and various service and administrative troops.

At the beginning of the war, these soldiers were proud, defiant, well trained, and confident of their invincibility. The early months of 1942 would test their mettle to an extreme; only an overwhelming and protracted assault by the Japanese and the apparent abandonment of them by their government caused their bitter defeat and subsequent shame and humiliation.

CHAPTER III
The Fall of Bataan

The first month of the war with Japan in the Philippines was marked by retreat after retreat for the American and Filipino Army forces defending Luzon and the virtual elimination of the Luzon-based Air Corps as an effective fighting force. There were some localized victories, individual displays of exceptional gallantry by the defenders (both on the ground and in the air), and an occasional demonstration of tactical superiority by some units, but the overall picture was generally grim and foreboding.

From the very first, however, and even many weeks into the battle, the American troops and their commanders had a glimmer of hope and were genuinely optimistic that relief was on the way from the United States. The beleaguered troops could not believe that they were to be abandoned; they could not comprehend that the Japanese navy was capable of blocking any reinforcements to the Philippines if the United States were willing to give it an all-out try. But as the weeks wore on, their hopes turned to despair amid the ominous realities of the Philippine battles.

At the outset of the war, to oppose an invasion of Luzon, General MacArthur had at his disposal the combined American and Philippine troops, who numbered about 125,000 men, of whom some 100,000 were recently mobilized Filipino reservists— ill trained, poorly armed, and incompetently led. When the fighting got tough, many thousands of the reservists shed their weapons and uniforms and faded back into the general populace. General MacArthur did have some well-trained and well-equipped forces, notably the Philippine Division—of which the 31st Infantry Regiment was totally American—about 12,000 Philippine Scouts, one division of the regular Philippine Army, and the 4th Regiment of the U.S. Marine Corps, which had arrived in November from Shanghai. Culling the ill-equipped and hastily called up reserves, General MacArthur could actually depend on only about 25,000 to 30,000 combat-ready, regular U.S. and Philippine Army soldiers.

The Japanese plan of attack to subjugate Luzon was a pincer's movement: the strongest arm, Lt. Gen. Masaharu Homma's 14th Army would land at Lingayen; the weaker arm, Lt. Gen. Susumu Morioka's half-strength 16th Division of seven thousand men, would land on the east coast of Luzon at Lamon Bay about eighty miles southeast of Manila and two hundred road miles southeast of Lingayen. But General Homma, the overall commander of the Luzon invasion force, held General Morioka's troops in low regard and concluded from the 16th's record of action in China that it "did not have a very good reputation for its fighting qualities." Nonetheless, General Homma, under heavy pressure from Japanese Imperial Headquarters to complete the conquest of Luzon in fifty days, had to take and use what he could get.

22 December 1941, dawn. General Homma's 43,000-man 14th Japanese Army begins an amphibious landing on the palm-lined beaches on the northern shores of Lingayen Gulf, 120 miles north of Manila. Homma's troops are battle tested and hardened to combat by their victorious battles in China; Homma himself is a veteran of the China campaigns. Homma's landings are opposed by General Wainwright's North Luzon Force, which consists of four Philippine army divisions, the 26th Cavalry Regiment (horse mounted) of the Philippine Scouts, and three batteries of Philippine Scouts field artillery. While Wainwright's forces are in the general area south of Lingayen Gulf, only a few troop units are actually dug in in defensive positions on the beach itself.

22 December, afternoon. Three Japanese infantry regiments plus supporting artillery and tanks are ashore. General Wainwright attempts to commit a company of his tanks against an enemy force mounted on bicycles or light motorcycles; because of a shortage of gasoline, the 192d Tank Battalion can furnish only a platoon of five tanks. Near Agoo, they meet Japanese light tanks. The platoon leader's tank shortly receives a direct hit; the other four are also hit by 47-mm antitank fire and are taken out of action by enemy planes later in the day.

22 December, nightfall. Japanese forces have secured most of their D-day objectives, and the North Luzon Force is in full retreat. Only the Scouts of the 26th Cavalry have fought with any distinction. The Filipino nonregulars have fled at the first sight of the enemy and have scrambled to the rear in a disorganized mob.

23 December. General Wainwright asks USAFFE (General MacArthur's headquarters—United States Army Forces, Far East) for permission to set up a defensive line behind the Agno River. Wainwright's request, plus the general retreat in the north, apparently convinces MacArthur that he must implement War Plan Orange (WPO-3), the previously distributed, reconnoitered, and rehearsed plan for concentrating all of his Luzon forces on the peninsula of Bataan after falling back through five specific delaying positions along the central Luzon plain. Any U.S. officer who has been in the Philippines for six months knows about WPO-3 and his unit's part in it—including the five successive fallback positions.

General MacArthur notifies President Manuel Quezon that he has directed the implementation of WPO-3 and that he intends to declare Manila an open city; USAFFE notifies all unit commanders that "WPO-3 is in effect."

General MacArthur reasons that, with the concentration of his forces on Bataan and with the formidable array of guns on the four islands in Manila Bay, particularly Corregidor, he has effectively denied Manila Bay to the enemy even though he might have captured Manila. "He [Homma] may have the bottle," muses General MacArthur to his staff, "but I have the cork."

23 December. To execute WPO-3 with any degree of efficiency and speed, the various units on the islands need much transportation. But there are insufficient Army trucks to transport all the soldiers, rations, supplies, fuel, weapons, and ammunition from the military bases on Luzon to Bataan. The U.S. and Filipino commanders who are not on the line fighting commandeer all of the gaudily painted Filipino trucks, cabs, and cars they can find and move to Bataan. The streets of Manila are alive with people hustling about their emergency tasks and with the roar of trucks. Convoys with trucks of all descriptions clog the roads leading out of Manila. Unfortunately, most commanders do not return vehicles for additional runs. Thus, supplies at Forts McKinley and Stotesenburg and prepositioned equipment and supplies at Tarlac and Los Baños must be abandoned.

24 December, 0700. North and west of Binalonan, the 26th Cavalry blunts the first attack of the Japanese in their drive toward the Agno River. The cavalry unit stops the enemy's tanks even though it has no anti-tank guns. The Japanese tanks then swing to the west to bypass the 26th, who next meet the follow-up infantry attack and inflict many casualties. The Scouts counterattack and are stopped only when the Japanese reinforce the area with more tanks. During the morning, the Japanese 2d Formosa joins the attack against the 26th. By now the 26th is too heavily committed to withdraw, so it continues the fight. Wainwright arrives on the scene and orders the 26th commander, Brig. Gen. Clinton A. Pierce, whose force is now down to 450 men, to get his wounded to the rear, to move out his supply trains, and to fight a delaying action southeast across the Agno River. Until 1530, the cavalrymen hold their positions against overwhelming odds and then begin to withdraw. After the action, General Wainwright, also a cavalryman, said: "Here was true cavalry delaying action, fit to make a man's heart sing. Pierce that day upheld the best traditions of the cavalry service." The 26th's gallant stand this day is one of the few commendable actions in the North Luzon Force's withdrawal to Bataan. A few more, however, are yet to come.

24 December. General Morioka's understrength 16th Division, less two regiments, lands at three points along the southern shore of Lamon Bay on the east side of Luzon, about eighty miles southeast of Manila. Mission: Land, move to the northwest, bypass U.S. and Filipino units, move along the east shore of Laguna de Bay, and get to Manila as rapidly as possible.

Maj. Gen. George M. Parker's South Luzon Force of three Filipino divisions has the mission of defending southern Luzon, but his forces are badly scattered and dispersed. The Lamon landings are a surprise to the American high command—USAFFE. Part of Parker's force is on the west coast in anticipation of a landing near Batangas, which offers a straight shot to Manila; other elements of the force are in the process of moving. Even those few units in position to oppose the landings are without artillery because of the threat to Batangas.

By evening, Morioka's forces are ashore, well established in strength and are moving rapidly to the northwest and Manila, thus carrying out the Japanese high command's pincers strategy.

24 December, afternoon. President Quezon, High Commissioner Sayre, with their families and staffs, sail to Corregidor aboard the interisland steamer *Mayan*. WPO-3 in effect. Huge explosions mark the destruction of ammunition that the troops are unable to take out of Manila and the surrounding military installations such as Fort McKinley and Nichols and Nielson fields. At Cavite Naval Yard, one million barrels of oil are put to the torch. Manila is a city in shock and turmoil. Shop windows are covered with tape, entrances barricaded with sandbags, and improvised air-raid shelters are dug where possible.

Christmas Eve. General MacArthur; his wife, Jean; his four-year-old son, Arthur; his Cantonese nursemaid, Ah Cheu; and members of his staff board another interisland steamer, *Don Esteban*, on the dock below the Manila Hotel, where they can hear the band playing for the dinner guests in the main dining room. It will be the last such affair at the Manila Hotel for four years.

24 December, 2130. The *Don Esteban* delivers General MacArthur and party to Corregidor.

25 December. General Wainwright tries to establish a defensive line behind the Agno River; General MacArthur establishes his USAFFE headquarters on Corregidor.

26 December. Japanese 48th Division breaks through the Agno line with tanks and infantry supported by heavy artillery; General Wainwright's forces are once again in full retreat.

26 December. General MacArthur declares Manila an open city.

25 December–1 January. North and South Luzon forces fight delaying actions toward and into Bataan, carrying out the dictates of WPO-3. Small boats and barges move enough supplies to Corregidor and Bataan to support a six-month campaign.

31 December. USAFFE Rear Headquarters in Manila, under Brig. Gen. Richard J. Marshall, completes its work and prepares to move to Corregidor. The capital is subdued, but a few cabarets, night clubs, and hotels are holding New Year's Eve parties in a brave and defiant "last meal" mood. There are no sirens or fireworks; the explosions from the nearby military installations and the burning fuel and supplies remind the revelers that the war is on and is not going successfully.

1 January 1942. Before leaving Manila, Brig. Gen. Charles C. Drake, the USAFFE quartermaster, throws open all military storage in the port area to the public. The mobs of Filipinos load their vehicles and arms with assorted booty and frozen foods from the ice plant. Uncollected garbage of many days litters the streets of Manila.

1 January. Wainwright's and Parker's forces begin to close in on Bataan, having fought delaying actions back toward Manila from the north and the southeast. General Wainwright has only sixteen thousand men out of his original twenty-eight thousand, reduced largely by the desertion of Filipino reservists; General Parker's South Force fares better: he has fourteen thousand out of his original fifteen thousand.

2 January. Japanese occupy Manila.

6 January. Most of the North and South Luzon forces are across the Pampanga River into Bataan and have blown the bridges behind them.

7 January. The Battle of Bataan begins. Wainwright's North Luzon Force, now I Corps, with three divisions, is on the left; Parker's South Luzon Force, now II Corps, with four divisions, is on the right. Their front lines cross the peninsula and intersect Mount Natib, which is so densely vegetated as to be virtually impassable; their mutual boundary runs down the mountain chain from Natib to Mariveles in the south. Wainwright's I Corps is deployed in an uninhabited, densely wooded area. Between them, Wainwright and Parker have fifteen thousand U.S. troops and sixty-five thousand Filipino soldiers with varying degrees of equipment, clothing, training and discipline; some Filipinos are reservists who have not fled. The situation on Bataan is grim. There is enough food for only one hundred thousand people for a month, and in addition to the military forces, there are also twenty-six thousand civilian refugees straggling along, clogging the roads of the peninsula. Medicine is in short supply, and malaria, hook-

worm, and other diseases are prevalent amid the dense jungles, high humidity, and tangled vegetation of Bataan.

Prior planning and the implementation of WPO-3 do bring some favorable results: two general hospitals are established on Bataan; petroleum products are sufficient for several months if properly rationed; the engineers have managed to ship one hundred thousand tons of explosives, barbed wire, sandbags, lumber, and construction material to Bataan and Corregidor.

9 January. Already, lack of quinine and improper diet cause many thousands of soldiers to come down with fever and chills, which render them, for the most part, ineffective fighting men.

9 January, 1500. The Japanese open their attack on Bataan with a concentrated artillery barrage on II Corps positions. II Corps Artillery replies "particularly ferociously" to the opening barrage.

10 January. MacArthur arrives at Mariveles, then drives up the East Road to Parker's headquarters and inspects positions in that sector. Later he crosses to Wainwright's area and checks out his positions. Wainwright offers to show MacArthur his 155-mm guns. MacArthur replies, "I don't want to see them; I want to hear them."

10 January. Japanese first demand for the Bataan forces to surrender by dropping a message from Homma to MacArthur behind the lines. In response, II Corps artillery steps up its volume of fire.

9–23 January. Hard fighting takes place along the entire front.

23 January. MacArthur orders I and II Corps to fall back to a new defensive line halfway down the peninsula, approximately five miles behind the initial positions along the east-west Pilar-Bagac Road.

26 January. The new line is established. Homma orders a general offensive against I and II Corps. The attack fails miserably.

23 January–1 February. Japanese 20th Infantry Regiment lands amphibiously at three points along the southwestern shore of Bataan in an attempt to outflank I Corps. Thus begins the "Battle of the Points."

24 January. Three hundred Japanese reach the slopes of Mount Pucot, a 617-foot-high hill that is only about two thousand yards from the port of Mariveles. Comdr. Francis J. Bridget (USN)

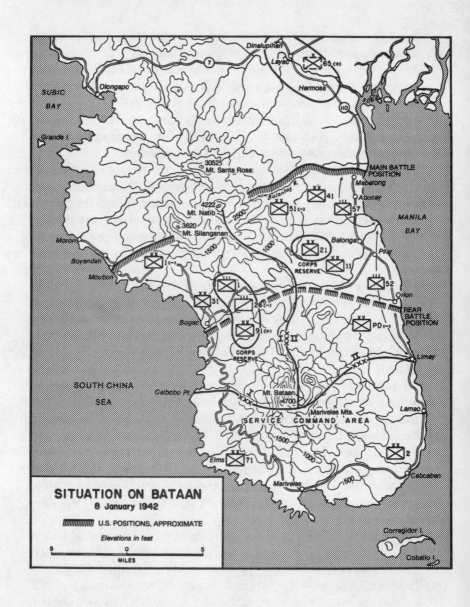

SITUATION ON BATAAN
8 January 1942

//////////// U.S. POSITIONS, APPROXIMATE

Elevations in feet

5   0   5
MILES

is the commander of a 600-man naval battalion in Mariveles. When a naval lookout reports that the Japanese are in the vicinity of Mount Pucot, Bridget commits a portion of his naval command to repel the invaders. In their first encounter, the bluejackets of the naval battalion, untrained in infantry methods, react to close combat with some nervousness and poor tactics. The sailors' conduct actually confuses the Japanese. One Japanese soldier recorded in his diary that he had seen among the Americans a "new type of suicide squad," who were dressed in brightly colored uniforms. "Whenever these apparitions reached an open space," the Japanese soldier noted, "they would attempt to draw Japanese fire by sitting down, talking loudly, and lighting cigarettes." The "brightly colored uniforms" observed by the incredulous Japanese soldier were the result of the sailors' attempt to dye their whites a khaki color. What they got was a "sickly mustard yellow."

1–15 February. Lt. Col. Edmund J. Lilly, Jr., commander of the 57th Infantry Regiment (his S-3 was Maj. Harold K. Johnson, later to become the chief of staff of the Army), in conjunction with the 2d Battalion, 45th Infantry, plus some tanks, counterattack along the Mount Pucot line on 12 February and succeed in driving the enemy back into the sea. The cost to the Americans of the three-week fight was seventy killed and one hundred wounded. The Japanese losses were huge: in one sector alone, the Americans and the Filipinos wiped out one battalion of nine hundred men; another battalion was nearly eliminated.

Maj. Gen. Naoki Kimura, the Japanese commander of the amphibious force that tried to overrun I Corps, sees the futility of continuing to reinforce the landings and to attempt to rescue those who had already landed. Consequently, only about eighty of the enemy who had landed are able to escape. By 15 February, the immediate threat to the west coast and to Mariveles is over; the Americans can savor temporarily a decisive victory. In spite of their constant retreat, they will enjoy a few more before their final defeat.

8 February. Homma confers with his staff to decide what action to take to salvage what he can of the abortive 26 January general offensive. He decides to move his troops out of contact and to call on Imperial General Headquarters in Tokyo for reinforcements. But to extricate some of his units, Homma orders an attack against II Corps on the 15th to permit the withdrawal of the 16th Division on the east flank.

15 February. The Japanese attack following an artillery preparation and aerial bombardment. The attack on the 15th is a diversion, a heavy patrol action, and the Americans are not fooled. Thus, the Japanese 14th Army, which on the 15th consisted of the 16th Infantry Division, the 65th Brigade, the 7th Tank Regiment, and some seventy fighter and bomber aircraft, is halted. Homma's forces have suffered seven thousand casualties, and between ten thousand and twelve thousand men are out of action with malaria, beriberi, dysentery, and other tropical diseases. For all intents and purposes, the 14th Army has ceased to exist as a viable fighting force. Homma goes on the defensive and asks Tokyo for more troops.

(At his war crimes trial in Manila four years later, Homma acknowledged that in mid-February 1942 his 14th Army was "in very bad shape." He estimated that he had in his army at that time only three battalions capable of effective action and that had MacArthur chosen at that time to launch a counteroffensive, he could have walked to Manila "without encountering much resistance on our part.")

Homma had been ordered by Imperial General Headquarters to complete the conquest of Luzon in fifty days; he is now at least two weeks past that deadline and is bogged down in a defensive position on Bataan with a virtually ineffective army.

Homma's situation prompted some officers, particularly Brig. Gen. Clifford Bluemel, commander of the 31st Division of the Philippine army (PA), to suggest a counterattack and the restoration of the original defensive line on Bataan. More aggressive officers opted for even more ambitious objectives—some even suggested returning to Manila.

But Bluemel's suggestion is rejected at II Corps Headquarters. MacArthur's staff would also have undoubtedly rejected the idea for a sound tactical reason: the Japanese controlled both the sea around the Philippines and the skies above. Therefore, the Japanese could reinforce at will, and the Americans would be forced ultimately to fall back once again to the Bataan Peninsula.

The Japanese and the Americans remain dug in in their defensive positions along the Orion-Bagac line. There are skirmishes, patrol actions, and artillery exchanges, but there is insignificant action.

Mid-February. Morale of the U.S. and Filipino forces is high. One officer on Bataan wrote to his superior on MacArthur's staff: "The morale of our frontline troops appears very high and they want to take the offensive. At the moment there appears to be nothing on our right except dead Japs and tons of abandoned equipment, which is being collected. . . . Prisoners give the impression that Jap morale is away down."

At this point, General Wainwright also goes on record stating that the morale of his troops has reached its highest point after the defeat of the Japanese along the Orion-Bagac line.

15 February–3 April. Lull in the battle for Bataan. Quinine and food begin to run out for the U.S. and Filipino forces. The "Battling Bastards of Bataan" become "walking skeletons," first on one-half, then on one-third rations. In spite of their own emaciated condition, the Japanese infiltrate the American lines and terrorize the rear areas, stabbing men in their sleep, burning supplies, stealing weapons, and ambushing patrols. U.S. morale, so high only recently, begins to plummet. Hunger, disease, and air raids begin to take their toll.

23 February. Roosevelt speaks to the nation; he offers no hope for the Philippines; he presents his overall strategy for the conduct of World War II: Hitler's defeat takes top priority.

(In spite of that strategy, however, the United States did, in fact, in early 1942, attempt to relieve the beleaguered forces fighting for the Philippines. General MacArthur, and later General Wainwright, constantly badgered their superiors in Washington in the strongest of terms to make every effort to break the Japanese stranglehold and to breach, by whatever means, the blockade around the Philippines. Quite surprisingly, in early 1942 the U.S. sent the bulk of war supplies and men to the Pacific theater. In addition, the U.S. organized blockade-running programs to the Philippines from Australia and the Netherlands Indies, with surface vessels, submarines, and aircraft. The U.S. effort to relieve the embattled garrison was a strong, concerted, conscientious effort.

But with the Japanese mastery of the Southwest Pacific and their domination of the seas around the entire Philippine archipelago, almost every attempt by the United States to run the

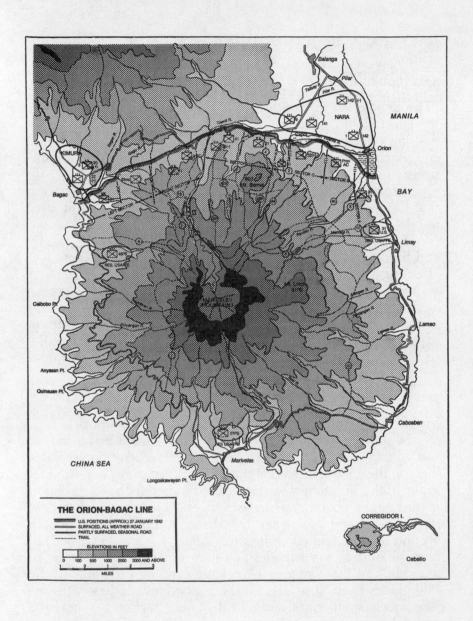

THE ORION-BAGAC LINE

U.S. POSITIONS (APPROX.) 27 JANUARY 1942
SURFACED, ALL WEATHER ROAD
PARTLY SURFACED, SEASONAL ROAD
TRAIL

ELEVATIONS IN FEET

0   100   500   1000   2000   3000 AND ABOVE

0   1   2   3
MILES

blockade was met with ultimate failure. Thus, the starving, diseased, despondent troops on Bataan felt isolated and abandoned—even though the United States had made considerable efforts to help them.)

10 March. MacArthur summons Wainwright to Corregidor and tells him that he, MacArthur, has been ordered by Roosevelt to make his way to Australia, there to begin the fight eventually to retake the Philippines. He tells Wainwright that he is now in control of all forces on Luzon, but that he, MacArthur, will retain control of all forces in the Philippines from his new headquarters in Australia. "If I get through to Australia," he tells Wainwright, "I'll come back as soon as I can."

The new command arrangement called for four commands in the Philippines: the Luzon Force, the Harbor Defenses, the Visayas Force, and the Mindanao Force. General MacArthur leaves Brig. Gen. Lewis C. Beebe as chief of staff of USAFFE. Through him and the USAFFE staff, General MacArthur intends to continue to command all of the forces in the Philippines. This arrangement will prove most troublesome to General Wainwright in the very near future.

12 March, 1915 hours. General MacArthur, his wife, son, nursemaid, and seventeen staff officers embark on four PT boats from South Dock, Corregidor. MacArthur pauses at the dock and looks back at Corregidor. He wrote later:

On the dock I could see the men staring at me. I had lost 25 pounds living on the same diet as the soldiers, and I must have looked gaunt and ghastly standing there in my old war-stained clothes—no bemedaled commander of inspiring presence. What a change had taken place in that once-beautiful spot! My eyes roamed that warped and twisted face of scorched rock. Gone was the vivid green foliage, with the trees, shrubs, and flowers. Gone were the buildings, the sheds, every growing thing. The hail of relentless bombardment had devastated, buried, and blasted. Ugly dark scars marked smouldering paths where the fire had raged from one end of the island to the other. Great gaps and forbidding crevices belched their tongues of flame. The desperate scene showed only a black mass of destruction. Through the shattered ruins, my eyes sought "Topside" where the deep roar of the heavy guns still growled defiance, with their red blasts tearing the growing darkness asunder. . . .

Darkness had now fallen, and the waters were beginning to ripple from the faint night breeze. The enemy firing had ceased and a muttering silence had fallen. It was as though the dead were passing by the stench of destruction. The smell of filth thickened the night air. I raised my cap in farewell salute, and I could feel my face go white, feel a sudden, convulsive twitch in the muscles of my face. I heard someone ask, "What's his chance, Sarge, of getting through?" and the gruff reply, "Dunno. He's lucky. Maybe one in five."

I stepped aboard PT-41. "You may cast off, Buck," I said, "when you are ready."[3]

18–19 March. Commanding general, USAFFE, receives two messages from Washington, one from General Marshall, the Army chief of staff, and one from Roosevelt. Each message makes it clear that the sender of the message believes that Wainwright, not MacArthur, is the commanding general of USAFFE.

19 March. Two messages from Marshall make it clear that Wainwright is in command in the Philippines. The first notifies Wainwright of his promotion to lieutenant general; the second tells him clearly: "Upon the departure of General MacArthur you became the commander of the U.S. forces in the Philippines. You are to communicate directly with the War Department in rendering daily reports."

20 March. General Beebe notifies Wainwright of his promotion and designation as commander of U.S. forces in the Philippines.

21 March. Wainwright moves to Corregidor.

Late March. Only a fourth of the eighty thousand U.S. and Filipino soldiers on Bataan are combat effective. Malaria, dengue, scurvy, beriberi, dysentery, and nerve fatigue more than decimate their ranks. Daily ration is cut to a fourth of the normal. Men receive eight to ten ounces of rice per day. They try to extend the ration with carabao, locally caught fish, mule, dog, monkey,

---

3. MacArthur, *Reminiscences,* pp. 142–43.

pony, and iguana. The Filipino soldiers can procure food locally, including chicken, pig, camotes, bamboo shoots, mangoes, bananas, and snakes. Morale is sinking fast. Most Americans realize that the end—defeat and prison camp—is near. The Filipino, on the other hand, thinks he can return to his home.

February–March. Homma receives large reinforcements. The 4th Division arrives from Shanghai with eleven thousand men; the Nagano Detachment of four thousand men arrives on 25 February; sixty twin-engine bombers arrive at Clark Field on 16 March; and thirty-five hundred men replace the losses in the 16th Division and the 65th Brigade.

23 March. Homma issues orders for the coming Bataan offensive to all major commanders.

26 March–3 April. Japanese air and artillery bombardment of the defenders increase daily; enemy planes are virtually unopposed by American anti-aircraft fire; Japanese air and artillery concentrate on the front lines and on artillery observation posts and larger artillery pieces.

3 April. D-day for the Japanese attack. It is also Good Friday and the anniversary of the legendary Emperor Jimmu, the first ruler to sit on the imperial throne.

3 April, 0900. Japanese artillery barrage opens with fire from 150 artillery guns, howitzers, and mortars and continues with only one half-hour pause until 1500, a "devastating barrage" in the words of the survivors. Japanese bombers also fly 150 sorties over the defenders, by now shell-shocked and combat fatigued in the worst sense.

3 April, 1500. The 4th Japanese Division and the 65th Brigade, heavily reinforced with artillery, mortars, and tanks, assault the left wing of II Corps in the area of the 41st Division (PA), which is the weakest point in the entire line. The 41st receives the heaviest part of the five-hour artillery and air assault. The 41st soldiers are dazed, demoralized, and blinded by the dust and the fires started by incendiary bombs. Fires spring up everywhere along the front. The Filipinos flee south; their commanders and American MPs cannot stop them. Even before the Japanese tank-infantry attack moves out to follow up the artillery barrage, the 41st Division has fallen apart.

4 April, A.M. Japanese resume their attack with another heavy artillery and aerial barrage in front of the salient that they had breached the day before. They penetrate more than two miles into the boundary between I and II Corps.

5 April, Easter Sunday. The Japanese resume their thunderous artillery and air bombardment. At 1000 hours, they move out on the ground.

Easter evening. The Japanese have broken through the American lines, have virtually destroyed two Filipino divisions, and have seized Mount Samat.

6 April, A.M. Americans and Filipinos launch a counterattack to restore part of the line penetrated by the Japanese. The counterattack fails. The Japanese seize the initiative and resume their march south. By nightfall of 6 April, the troops in II Corps are in full retreat.

6–9 April. Two thousand men and 104 nurses escape to Corregidor from Bataan.

8 April. MacArthur in Australia orders Wainwright to counterattack. Wainwright passes the order to General King, who has replaced Wainwright as the commander of the Luzon Force. Wainwright also tells King that "under no circumstances would the Luzon Force surrender." General King, acutely aware of the situation on Bataan, decides against the order.

7–9 April.

The story of the last two days of the defense of Bataan [by U.S. and Filipino forces] is one of progressive disintegration and final collapse. Lines were formed and abandoned before they could be fully occupied. Communications broke down and higher headquarters often did not know the situation on the front lines. Orders were issued and revoked because they were impossible of execution. Stragglers poured to the rear in increasingly large numbers until they clogged all roads and disrupted all movement forward. Units disappeared into the jungle never to be heard from again. In two days an army evaporated into thin air.[4]

---

4. Morton, *The Fall of the Philippines*, p. 442.

8 April, midnight. North Luzon Force headquarters is on the road between Mariveles and Cabcaben. General King calls his staff to his tent and tells them that he has decided to surrender the Luzon Force. He makes it clear that "the ignominous decision is entirely his own" and that he "doesn't want anyone else saddled with any part of the responsibility." He has not communicated with General Wainwright, he tells his staff, because "he doesn't want him to be compelled to assume any part of the responsibility. Already our hospital, which is filled to capacity and directly in the line of hostile approach, is within range of enemy light artillery. We have no further means of organized resistance."[5]

9 April. General King issues the order to all units to surrender and, beforehand, to destroy all equipment, supplies, ammunition, and fuel. At 0330, General King's staff officers, Colonel Williams and Major Hurt, move out as ordered by General King to meet the Japanese commander. They go through the front lines with a bed sheet billowing from their jeep. They move through the Japanese lines and past already-captured American prisoners with their hands tied behind their backs. A Japanese soldier takes them to the command post of General Kameichiro Nagano, whose troops are moving steadily and without opposition down the East Road. General Nagano tells the two American officers that he will meet General King near Lamao.

9 April. On Corregidor, General Wainwright is unaware that General King has surrendered the Luzon Force. He is well aware, however, that the Luzon Force has disintegrated. On 8 April, he had dispatched messages to Marshall and MacArthur telling them "with deep regret" that the forces on Bataan were "fast folding up."

9 April, 0300. General Wainwright speaks to General King on the phone, but General King does not mention that he has sent two officers forward to arrange the surrender of his seventy-eight thousand men.

9 April, 0600. General Wainwright learns from Lt. Col. Jesse T. Traywick, Jr., his assistant operations officer, that General King

---

5. Ibid., p. 458.

is negotiating a surrender. Gen. Wainwright is stupefied and shouts
to Traywick, "Go back and tell him not to do it." It is too late.
General King's liaison officers are already on the way to the Japanese front lines.

9 April. General Wainwright writes to General MacArthur:

At 6 o'clock this morning General King . . . without my
knowledge or approval sent a flag of truce to the Japanese
commander. The minute I heard of it I disapproved of his
action and directed that there would be no surrender. I was
informed it was too late to make any change, that the action
had already been taken. . . . Physical exhaustion and sick-
ness due to a long period of insufficient food is the real
cause of this terrible disaster. When I get word what terms
have been arranged I will advise you.

9 April, 0900. Major Hurt, who had gone forward earlier in
the day with Colonel Williams to General Nagano's command
post and had returned, now leads General King and party—two
aides and his operations officer, Col. James V. Collier—to the
meeting place with General Nagano. The party leaves General
King's command post and proceeds in two jeeps up the East Road.
On the way, in spite of the white flags prominently displayed on
both jeeps, they are strafed by low-flying Japanese aircraft every
two hundred yards or so and are forced into the ditches or into
the jungle along the road. General King's uniform, which was
his last clean and starched one, is now dirty and sweat stained.
Finally, the party proceeds over the Lamao River Bridge, where
they pass Japanese soldiers armed with fixed bayonets; the soldiers
do not interfere with the party. Finally, a Japanese soldier meets
them and escorts them to a house in front of which General
Nagano is seated with Colonel Williams.

9 April, 1100. General King meets with General Nagano and
attempts to surrender all of his Luzon Force. General Nagano
says that he is not authorized to deal with him but that shortly
an officer from General Homma's headquarters will arrive. A
few minutes later, Colonel Motoo Nakayama, the 14th Army's
senior operations officer, arrives in a shiny Cadillac. He asks King,
"You are General Wainwright?" Somewhat shocked, King identi-

fies himself. Then Nakayama tells him that he will have to get Wainwright and that the Japanese will not accept any surrender from anyone but Wainwright. King repeats that he can surrender only the Bataan forces and that they are no longer fit to fight. He requests an armistice, a twelve-hour period in which to collect his wounded, permission for his troops to walk out of Bataan under their own officers and noncommissioned officers, and authority for his sick and wounded soldiers to ride out in vehicles that he has salvaged and gathered for this purpose. He promises to deliver his men to any point designated by General Homma.

"It is absolutely impossible for me," says Nakayama, "to consider negotiations in any limited area. If the forces on Bataan wish to surrender, they will have to do so by unit, voluntarily and unconditionally."[6] General King incorrectly concludes that Nakayama is thus accepting his unconditional surrender. In any event, he knows that he has no options left. Nonetheless, he asks repeatedly for assurance that his soldiers will be treated as POWs under the provisions of the Geneva Convention. At one point in the discussions, General King asks Nakayama, "Will our troops be well treated?" Nakayama replies stiffly, "We are not barbarians." The next few weeks will prove the callousness and duplicity of that statement.

9 April, 1230. General King surrenders unconditionally his seventy-six thousand soldiers. It is the largest capitulation of a U.S. military force in history. Then Nakayama asks for General King's saber. General King tells him that he has left it in Manila along with his other noncombat possessions. Nakayama is visibly upset with this revelation but, after some discussion and brief excitement, agrees to accept General King's pistol as the symbolic surrender weapon. The other officers in General King's party also put their pistols on the table.

The events that followed General King's surrender present a confused and chaotic story of the disintegration and dissolution of a starved, diseased, and beaten army. This

---

6. Nakayama, Negotiations with King, 26 August 49, ATIS Document 50246 in Morton, *The Fall of the Philippines*, p. 466.

story reached its tragic climax with the horrors and atrocities of the 65-mile "death march" from Mariveles to San Fernando. Denied food and water, robbed of their personal possessions and equipment, forced to march under the hot sun and halt in areas where even the most primitive sanitary facilities were lacking, clubbed, beaten, and bayoneted by their Japanese conquerors, General King's men made their way into captivity. Gallant foes and brave soldiers, the "battling bastards" had earned the right to be treated with consideration and decency, but their enemies had reserved for them even greater privations and deeper humiliation than any they had yet suffered on Bataan. How hard their lot was to be none knew but already many faced the future with heavy hearts and "feelings of doubt, foreboding, and dark uncertainty."[7]

The fight for Bataan was over. The "battling bastards" had held off the Japanese temporarily and, at one point, forced them to retreat; the Bataan soldiers were overcome not only by the enemy, but by the disease, starvation, and abject physical weakness brought on by the debilitating conditions in the Bataan jungles, a lack of medicine, and a dearth of food. They deserved far, far better than the Bataan death march.

Bataan's ordeal was over; Corregidor's was about to begin.

---

7. Morton, *The Fall of the Philippines*, p. 467.

CHAPTER IV
Corregidor Lost

Six May 1942 can only be described as what must have been the most traumatic, painful, and totally depressing day in the life of 59-year-old Lt. Gen. Jonathan M. "Skinny" Wainwright, the defeated, humiliated, and, in his mind, failed commander of the eleven thousand U.S. and Filipino forces on Corregidor. That he was also the de facto commander of all U.S. and Filipino forces throughout the Philippines had made negotiations with the Japanese confusing and frustrating.

At midnight on the sixth, Japanese guards escorted General Wainwright from a meeting he had just had with Colonel Sato, the commander of the Japanese 61st Infantry, in the market place of the bombed-out Filipino barrio of San José on Corregidor. Under extreme pressure, and because he feared for the safety of his men on Corregidor, General Wainwright had just surrendered unconditionally to Sato all of the U.S. and Filipino forces in all of the Philippine Islands. From San José, the Japanese guards walked General Wainwright past dejected groups of dirty, bearded, disheveled, captured American and Filipino soldiers to Malinta Tunnel, which was now in the hands of and full of Japanese troops. In the tunnel, there were, besides the Japanese, Wainwright's staff officers and some injured and sick soldiers who had not yet been moved out of the laterals.

Once inside the main tunnel, General Wainwright walked into one of his headquarters laterals and then into a small, whitewashed room he had inherited from General MacArthur. With him was his aide; outside the room stood a Japanese sentry. General Wainwright fell wearily on his narrow GI cot. Even though he was physically exhausted and mentally battered from the climactic events of the previous two days, he could not sleep; alone, he carried the onus of the surrender of all the troops in the Philippines. Going through his mind were the events of the past few weeks that had led him inexorably to the terrible and unenviable position in which he now found himself.

Until 9 April, General Wainwright's orders had been delimiting and restrictive: to "fight as long as there remains any possibility of resistance." On the day of the Bataan surrender, Roosevelt wired Wainwright that he was "free to make any decision affecting the future of the Bataan garrison. I have every confidence that whatever decision you may sooner or later be forced to make will be dictated only by the best interests of your country and your magnificent troops." But that message, intended for Wainwright, went directly to General MacArthur in Australia with instructions to forward it to General Wainwright if MacArthur concurred "both as to substance and timing." General MacArthur had just received the news that Bataan had surrendered; he reasoned, therefore, that there was no need to forward the message with the new, more liberal orders to Wainwright. Therefore, he tabled the cable and thus in effect, "nonconcurred" with the President.

Then, shortly thereafter, the President received word of the surrender of Bataan. He sent another message to Wainwright, this time directly, informing him: "Whatever decision you have made has been dictated by the best interests of your troops and of the country." Roosevelt told Wainwright that he hoped Wainwright could hold Corregidor but assured him "of complete freedom of action and full confidence" in any decision he might ultimately be compelled to make. After a few days of cables back and forth between his headquarters and MacArthur's, Wainwright finally received a message from MacArthur which agreed that the President had given Wainwright "complete authority to use your own judgment."

From 9 April until 6 May, Corregidor was subjected to an

air and artillery barrage that was so intense and so constant that the men on the island likened the bombardment to that of "giant machine guns." After the fall of Bataan, the Japanese had moved one hundred artillery pieces ranging in size from 75-mm guns to 240-mm howitzers to Mariveles and Cabcaben on the southern tip of Bataan. Coupled with the artillery barrage were prolonged and concentrated Japanese air attacks.

These were not the first aerial attacks of the war on Corregidor. On 28 December, Homma had ordered his 5th Air Group to commence aerial operations against the island. He augmented the air group with navy planes from the 11th Air Fleet. On 29 December, the Japanese attacked Corregidor with a total of eighty-one medium and ten dive-bombers and dropped about sixty tons of bombs in just two hours. No American aircraft took off from Bataan to dispute the Japanese air supremacy over Corregidor. But on 29 December, the AA units on the island were active and reasonably accurate: they shot down three bombers and four aircraft that were strafing the island. These losses discouraged the Japanese from dive-bombing or strafing until the end of April.

For the next eight days, 29 December to 6 January, the Japanese continued to attack Corregidor from the air from about twenty thousand feet for two hours each day. The results were extensive damage to the aboveground installations on Corregidor. The bombers blasted the concrete headquarters and barracks buildings on Topside and Middleside, leveled the officers' club, destroyed the vacated hospital, smashed the PX, destroyed two of the island's water tanks, hit the wharves' shops and warehouses on Bottomside, and covered the islands with bomb craters almost every twenty-five yards. Fires burned out of control; the bombings destroyed all of the wooden buildings and the supplies they contained and, for the duration, completely knocked out the electrically driven train on the island. Communications suffered because the telephone lines were aboveground, and there was no time to dig them in.

Fortunately, the various well-protected batteries and armament of the island suffered relatively slight damage. The large guns and ammo supplies had been bombproofed before the war, and the gunners assigned to each battery had continued to dig tunnels into the sides of the parapets and gun emplacements for personal protection since once the war began they were constantly on alert at their battery positions. The gun pits became their barracks.

After the bombing of 29 December, the attitude of the men on Corregidor changed drastically. Before they had gone through the attacks of the 29th, the men appeared nonchalant and raced to the nearest windows and doors to watch the bombs and the resultant destruction. After living through the bombing of the twenty-ninth, however, the troops sought any shelter they could at the sound of the air-raid sirens or the distant rumble of the approaching bombers.

Some men, in fact, became "tunnel rats" and holed up even when there were no planes overhead. As the siege wore on, the tunnels of Malinta became crowded with men who took up residence there more or less permanently. Malinta thus became jammed not only with the interlopers but also with the legitimate occupiers of the laterals: the government of the Commonwealth, a 1,000-bed hospital, the staffs of various headquarters, and enormous quantities of fuel, supplies, machinery, and power plants. With every bombing, the crowding became more and more crushing.

The gun crews who manned their weapons day and night "on the outside" were plainly contemptuous of the pale and sallow-complected men who holed up in the tunnels and rarely saw the sun. The outsiders referred to the "tunnel rats" as moles. "We say of them," one reported, "that they will lose tunnel credit if they are seen outside the tunnel. And we josh them about the DTSM (Distinguished Tunnel Service Medal) they will receive if they gather plenty of tunnel credits. As opposed to shell-shocked, we say of confirmed 'tunneleers' that they are shelter-shocked."

The first period of intensive aerial bombardment of Corregidor ended on 6 January, when the Japanese 5th Air Group was ordered to Thailand and Homma was left with only a few planes. For the interim, he did not commit them against Corregidor or the other harbor islands.

By late March, however, Homma had received two heavy bombardment regiments of sixty aircraft, the 60th and the 62d, from Malaya. With these bombers, plus the assistance of four squadrons from the navy, Homma was able to employ substantial air power in late March and early April, both for the final assault on Bataan and for the siege of Corregidor.

On 24 March, for example, forty-five bombers and two squadrons of naval land-based aircraft hit Corregidor with seventy-one tons of bombs. The routine, heavy aerial assault against Corregidor continued until the first of April when Homma concentrated all of his air power against Bataan.

The air assault in late March, heavy though it was, found the men on Corregidor well prepared. They had profited from their previous experiences and had learned to dig in, to fortify every open position, and to fill and use sandbags to cover all openings to tunnels and caves in which they holed up. Until the last, they continued to dig tunnels near weapons pits and to cover and block every conceivable vulnerable spot with hundreds of sandbags. Even though the island had been fortified with concrete and steel during its occupation, the early months of 1942 saw the strengthening of old defenses and the barricading of new ones pursued with a dedication borne of necessity, practicality, and self-preservation.

9 April. With the surrender of Bataan, Homma now concentrates his forces for the final assault of Corregidor. The Japanese artillery in Mariveles and Cabcaben blast the island with incessant, heavy fire. One officer on the island said, "One day's shelling did more damage than all the bombing put together." Wooded areas are denuded. All buildings aboveground are damaged or demolished. The ground is covered with shell holes; even concrete buildings are shattered, and the pieces of their walls and roofs litter the island. Ninety-nine bombers and navy twin-engine bombers join the attack. High-flying bombers make their first appearance since the end of March.

12 April, 0600. The Japanese begin their artillery attack on Corregidor in earnest. A battery from Cavite joins the barrage. Japanese aircraft make nine separate attacks. Col. Paul D. Bunker, commander of the seaward defenses on Corregidor, writes in his diary: "It was a rough day all day."

12–19 April. The 150-mm howitzers from Bataan join in the assault, and the rhythm of the bombardment increases perceptively. Even the fortified guns on Corregidor now feel the effect of the constant artillery attacks. By 14 April, three 155-mm gun batteries, each with two guns and one 3-inch battery of four guns, are destroyed. Ancillary fire direction equipment is also rendered out of action.

General Kishio Kitajima, 14th Army artillery officer, sees to it that all the rounds fired at Corregidor are effective. By this time, he has eighteen batteries of all calibers under his command. He divides the target area into three zones and assigns a specific zone to each battery. He insures that the battery commanders bracket each target before firing for effect. He moves a balloon company to Mariveles so its observers can adjust artillery fire and assess the effects from their tethered, aerial observation posts. The Americans, who still have not completely lost their sense of humor in spite of the bombing and the short rations, promptly christen the balloon observer "Peeping Tom." In addition, General Kitajima uses sound and flash equipment to monitor the accuracy of the artillery fire on Corregidor. He is obviously a well-trained artillery man, using the latest equipment and techniques then available.

20–30 April. The crescendo of the shelling increases with heightened shelling intensity. On the twenty-fourth, a 240-mm howitzer, which had been moved from Cavite, scores a direct hit on Battery Crockett and knocks out its two 12-inch guns. On 25 April, another 240-mm shell lands outside the west entrance of Malinta Tunnel, kills thirteen men and wounds more than fifty soldiers who had been breathing the fresh air outside the tunnel.

By now, the tunnels are hot, dusty, and filled with the stench of bodies, vermin, and great blue flies. During air raids, with the power off, the tunnels are foul and almost unbearably hot.

During the latter part of April, the artillery bombardment almost never stops. More than one hundred weapons, ranging in size from 75-mm to 240-mm howitzers, pound all sectors of the island. Because the 240s have a high angle of fire and powerful shells, they are able to drop devastating fire directly into the gun pits. They also wreck shelters, beach defenses, and almost everything else on the surface of the island. Air attacks accompany the artillery barrages, and from 9 April to the end of the month, there are 108 air-raid alarms—a total of eighty hours of air attacks.

29 April, Emperor Hirohito's birthday. The Japanese raise the level of intensity of the aerial and artillery attacks a few notches. At 0730, the attack opens with the 260th air alarm of the campaign. "Peeping Tom" rides his balloon over Cabcaben. The air raids and the artillery fire continue without letup all day. By nightfall, Corregidor is a shambles, a pulverized, blasted chunk of rock lying under a blanket of chocolate dust and smoke. Fires rage out of control over the entire island. Two ammunition dumps start to explode. The huge warehouses along the waterfront are rubble, tortured wrecks of twisted girders, fire-blackened walls, and crumbled roofs. Installations on Malinta Hill, observation posts, and fire-direction centers across the island are wiped out.

Morale on the island plunges. Not only was there a division between the men manning the batteries and the "tunnel rats," but also between the refugees from Bataan and the men and women on Corregidor.

Leon Guerrero[8] expressed the plight of the Bataan refugees in these words:

These men, whether Filipinos or Americans, were frankly tired of war. Gaunt, unshaven, dirty, wrapped in a sullen despair, they squatted silently on the tunnel curbs by day. By night, they stretched out on their scraps of blankets or on the bare cement, across the path of trucks and cars. They cluttered up the neat tunnels with their heterogeneous possessions, with the garbage and wreckage of war.

Yet it was impossible to clear them out for they had a certain tired stubbornness that defied command or insult. And it was equally impossible to allow them to remain, not only because they made normal traffic in the tunnels difficult, but principally because their shame and despair was contagious—it was a sinister and insidious disease that daily

---

8. Leon MA. Guerrero was the author of an article, "The Last Days of Corregidor," published in the May 1943 issue of *Philippine Review*, a Japanese-controlled magazine printed and distributed in Manila.

infected and drew closer to them the garrison of Corregidor.[9]

Across the island, men are on half rations, which under ordinary circumstances the quartermaster would declare inedible. Life in the tunnel grows grimmer. Between raids, the men inside try to get to the tunnel entrance to breathe some fresh air, but even that air is filled with gasoline fumes, dust, and smoke from the fires. In their off-duty hours, men gamble away their pay—they have nothing else to do with it. Lights flicker on and off, adding to the misery of tunnel life. A good night's sleep in the open air is a night to remember. Tempers flare, and men grow tense and irritable. Men who gather outside to eat are certain to attract a barrage from the Japanese guns on Bataan. The wounded pile up in the hospital laterals; the dead lie covered at one entrance to the lateral, awaiting a truck to haul them away.

By the end of April, the physical resistance of the men is so low that scurvy and beriberi become epidemic. Because of a lack of needed vitamins, men suffer eyesight problems. The number of wounded increases; the narrow hospital corridors are filled with the wounded, the sick, and the dying. Each new bombardment inflicts new casualties and adds to the problems of the overworked, understaffed, and undersupplied hospital crews. Ambulances cannot get to the casualties at the various locations around the island because of the constant shelling; anything that moves is instantly taken under fire. The roads on the island, which had formerly been camouflaged with trees and shrubs, are now naked; all of the foliage has been blasted and burned away.

Amazingly enough, very few men suffer from battle fatigue. One man, who saw "his friend's shell-torn head fly past his face" reputedly did go out of his mind. But the number of mental cases is low—six to eight during the entire campaign. The Corregidor surgeon surmised that, since there was no place for the men to go, they made an adjustment to the conditions and learned to live with them.

Coupled with the shortage of rations was the shortage of water.

---

9. Guerrero, "The Last Days of Corregidor," p. 10.

The constant shelling knocks out the power supply by which water is pumped into the reservoirs on the island. During the month of April, the pumps operate for only one day, and the water situation is critical. Soldiers are reduced to one canteen of water per day—a grave privation to men who do hard physical labor in 100 degrees of heat during midday. The troops use ingenious ways to save water. Showers were the rarest of luxuries. In his diary, Capt. John McM. Gulick writes: "Many a night I washed myself with a cup of water and by standing in a basin saved the water to use over again on, first, my underwear, and then my socks. Order of laundering was very important. The dirtiest item always came last."

1 May. Homma concentrates his artillery fire on the narrow tail of the island and on James Ravine, which provides a narrow pathway to Topside. General Wainwright's staff reasons correctly that Homma is preparing those two areas for amphibious attacks: because there is virtually nothing left worth shooting at, the Americans conclude that those areas are being softened up for landings. The men on the receiving end of the bombardments think that the shelling of 29 April reaches some sort of a record; but the shelling of 1 May breaks that short-lived record. Bombers concentrate their attack on the entrance to Malinta Tunnel.

2 May. 1 May's record for shelling intensity is broken; today's is even worse. The Japanese guns on Bataan begin their barrage at 0730; shortly thereafter, the bombers appear. For three hours, the steady rain of fire continues. Then at 1030, the all clear sounds but lasts for only thirty minutes. At 1100, the shelling begins again and continues, with only two short breaks, until 1945. During one five-hour period, in addition to thousands of other artillery rounds, thirty-six hundred 240-mm shells blast the island with concentrations specifically singling out Batteries Geary and Crockett, the north shore areas where the landings are to be made, and Malinta Hill itself. The tail of the island lies under a cloud of smoke and dust. Battery Geary takes a direct hit from a 240-mm shell; the entire battery is demolished with a "shock like that of an earthquake." The men who counted the rounds landing on the island estimated that the rate of fire of the 240-mm's alone was twelve shells per minute. General Wainwright and General Moore estimated that "the Japs had hit The Rock with 1.8 million

pounds of shells" in addition to the bombs delivered by the Japanese bombers in thirteen separate air raids. On 2 May, the battered men and women of Corregidor are subject to the highest concentration of Japanese fire during the 27-day siege that began on 9 April.

3 May, Sunday. The heavy assault continues. Five air raids concentrate on James Ravine and Kindley Field. The antiaircraft batteries on Corregidor are by now blasted into twisted pieces of steel junk.

General Wainwright, however, can still communicate with General MacArthur in Australia. He cables: "Situation here is fast becoming desperate. With artillery that outranges anything we have except two guns, he [the enemy] keeps up a terrific bombardment as well as aerial bombing."

This day marks the last day of physical contact between the troops on Corregidor and the outside world. On the night of 3 May, an American submarine stops outside the mined channel and takes on twenty-five passengers from Corregidor. Col. Constant Irwin leaves with a complete roster of all men and women still alive on the battered island; Col. Royal G. Jenks takes out the finance records; ten other Army and Navy officers and about thirteen nurses crowd into the jammed hull of the submarine. Several bags of mail also make that last trip from the island. General Wainwright also sends out files of records and orders.

Mrs. Maude R. Williams was a hospital assistant who had been evacuated from Bataan to Corregidor just before Bataan fell. She writes emotionally and eloquently of her feelings about life in the Malinta tunnels in the closing days of the siege of Corregidor:

Under the deepening shadow of death, life on Corregidor took on a faster, more intense tempo. The smallest and most simple pleasure became sought after and treasured as they became increasingly rare and dangerous—an uninterrupted cigarette, a cold shower, a stolen biscuit, a good night's sleep in the open air.

There was a heightened feeling that life was to be lived from day to day, without illusions of an ultimate victory. Many sought forgetfulness in gambling. There was no other way to spend the accumulated pay that bulged in their pockets and they rattled the dice or played endless bridge, rummy and poker.

Jam sessions attracted great crowds which gathered in the dark and hummed softly or tapped feet to the nostalgic swing of the organ, a haunting guitar, or a low moaning trombone. Sometimes a nurse and her boy friend of the evening would melt into a dance. . . . The eyes of the on-lookers would grow soft and thoughtful, while other couples would steal out into the perilous night. . . .

Still others sought the consolations of religion and the symbols of another world, a better world of sweet and eternal peace. The Catholics gathered at dawn in the officers' mess of Malinta Tunnel where one of the tables was converted into a simple altar, and kneeling on the bare cement under the high white-washed vault they listened devoutly and a little desperately to the same hushed phrases that had been whispered in the Catacomb.[10]

4 May. In spite of General Wainwright's feeling that "the tempo of the Jap shelling could not possibly be increased," it is. In twenty-four hours, the Japanese guns on Bataan fire more than sixteen thousand shells of all calibers, focusing on the beach defenses along the north shore and James Ravine and the east end of the island near Kindley Field.

During the day, observers on Corregidor spot fifteen Japanese landing barges sailing north off the southeast coast of Bataan, probably headed to Lamao to pick up the soldiers of the landing force. This maneuver leaves the commanders on Corregidor with no doubt that a Japanese landing on Corregidor is now imminent.

General George Marshall in Washington cables General Wainwright for his frank appraisal of the situation. General Wainwright replies, "Considering the present level of morale, I estimate that we have something less than an even chance to beat off an assault." Events would soon prove that General Wainwright's estimate was overly optimistic. Since 9 April, when the siege began, the troops on Corregidor have suffered six hundred casualties, most coastal

---

10. Quoted in Guerrero, "The Last Days of Corregidor," pp. 11–12.

guns and searchlights have been destroyed, the beach defenses have become a jumbled mass of caved-in machine gun bunkers and crumpled, sandbagged personnel holes.

5 May. All previous records for the volume and intensity of the Japanese shelling are broken. The batteries on Cavite shell the southern shore of the island, and the guns on Bataan blast targets on the north side with an unprecedented volume of fire. "There was a steady roar from Bataan," wrote Captain Gulick, "and a mightier volume on Corregidor. A continuous pall of dust and debris hung over everything. There was a feeling of doom mingled with wonder. . . ."

In the past few days, the Japanese have virtually accomplished their mission of knocking out the guns of Corregidor. The only survivors are three 155-mm guns. The famous batteries of Corregidor—the 12-inch guns and mortars, the 6-, 8-, and 10-inch disappearing guns—have been blasted into twisted junk. The beach defenses along the north shore are tangles of barbed wire, crumbled dugouts, and wrecked bunkers. Telephone lines are constantly out. General Moore said, "Command could be exercised and intelligence obtained only by use of foot messengers which was uncertain under the heavy and continuous artillery and air action."[11]

When the bombardment let up momentarily late in the afternoon the dust lay so heavy over the island that the men on Topside could hardly make out the features of Bottomside below them. Beyond that they could not see. Even the topography of the island had changed. Where there had been thick woods and dense vegetation only charred stumps remained. The rocky ground had been pulverized into a fine dust and the road along the shore had been literally blown into the bay. Portions of the cliff had fallen in and debris covered the entire island. The Corregidor of peacetime, with its broad lawns and luxuriant vegetation, impressive parade

---

11. Harbor Defense Report of Operations, p. 72. (Annex VIII of "Report of Operations of USAFFE and USFIF in the Philippine Islands, 1941–1942" by Maj. Gen. George F. Moore)

ground, spacious barracks, pleasant shaded clubs and bunga-
lows, its large warehouses, and concrete repair shops, was
gone.

Men were living on nerve alone, and morale was dropping
rapidly. All hope of reinforcement had long since disappeared. There was only enough water to last no more than
a few weeks. There was a limit to human endurance and
that limit, General Wainwright told the President, "has long
since been passed."[12]

General Wainwright is well aware that the siege of Corregidor
is reaching a climax. "It took no mental giant," he wrote later,
"to figure out, by May 5, 1942, that the enemy was ready to
come against Corregidor." Agents in Manila had reported to Wainwright that the Japanese 4th Division had been practicing landing
maneuvers and that laborers had built thousands of bamboo lad-
ders, obviously for the landing force to use in scaling the cliffs
of Corregidor.

5 May, 2100. One of the still-operational sound locators of
an antiaircraft unit on Corregidor picks up the noises of a large
number of landing craft in the vicinity of Limay. General Moore
immediately notifies and alerts the beach defenses and orders
all beach defense troops to man their stations.

5 May, 2200. Men in the beach defenses on the tail of the
island observe Japanese barges offshore.

5 May, 2230. General Moore sends out the command: "Prepare
for probable landing attack."

5 May, 2345. Japanese artillery fire suddenly ceases. Captain
Gulick remembers that "the artillery base roar was replaced by
the treble chattering of many small arms."

5 May, midnight. A messenger from the Beach Defense Command Post arrives at H Station, General Moore's command post
in Malinta Tunnel, with the expected but dreaded news: "The
Japanese have landed at North Point."

Col. Gempachi Sato, commander of the Japanese 61st Infantry,
is dumbfounded when his two leading battalions land one thou-

---

12. Morton, *The Fall of the Philippines*, p. 550.

sand yards to the east of their targeted landing area between Infantry and Cavalry points and come ashore well separated, at the wrong times, and on the wrong sides of one another.

In spite of the intense preparation for the attack—training in amphibious operations, close-in fighting, removal of beach obstacles, use of smoke screens—the landing of the 61st Infantry, reinforced with tanks from the 7th Tank Regiment, is just short of a disaster. Two conditions contributed to the inept and disorderly landings: first, the tide at the time of embarkation of the landing craft at Bataan was running to the west; the Japanese planners thought it would also run west along the north shore of Corregidor. It did not; it ran east. Second, the 4th Division staff felt that part of the amphibious landing difficulty could be laid on the 1st Sea Operation Unit, the boat handlers who brought the 61st ashore. "The unit later discovered," wrote Colonel Yoshida, "that it had paid dearly for this lack."

The Japanese find, to their dismay, that there are still U.S. and Filipino soldiers on Corregidor's tail who still have weapons and who still can fight. These soldiers meet the Japanese with all the firepower they can muster. Just east of North Point, a two-gun 75-mm battery, fortuitously not knocked out by the prelanding bombardment because it had never before revealed its position, opens fire at a range of about three hundred yards on the landing craft while they are still just off the beach. There are also some 37-mm guns still operational. These guns take the Japanese under fire at point-blank range, sinking a number of the boats and inflicting heavy casualties. One observer at the scene wrote that "the slaughter of the Japanese in their barges was sickening."

The killing of the Japanese in the landing craft continues. By shortly after midnight, the moon has risen and there is sufficient light for the defenders to put continuous, devastating artillery fire on the landing craft. One remaining 12-inch mortar from Battery Way fires a number of rounds that whistle through the air and blast the landing craft. The mortars from Fort Hughes join in the attack. A Japanese, observing the fire from Cabcaben, wrote that it was "a spectacle that confounded the imagination, surpassing in grim horror anything we had ever seen before." One Japanese officer estimated that only 800 of the original 2,000-

man landing party managed to reach shore. General Homma later testified that "the disastrous state of his troops and the loss of landing craft threw him into an agony of mind."

Part of the reason for the difficulty the Japanese found on trying to land on Corregidor was men like Platoon Sgt. "Tex" Haynes of the 4th Marines. He simply met the Japanese invaders "head on." He carried two pistols and emptied both of them into the Japanese. Then he grabbed the rifle of a dead Marine—as more and more of the enemy rushed toward him—and fired as fast as he could pull the trigger. Then he picked up a .30-caliber machine gun, cradled it against his hip, and fired, spraying the rounds into the oncoming Japanese. "Despite the red-hot barrel," wrote Hanson Baldwin, "he sprayed two belts of ammo into the enemy's midst, until the high tide of little brown men engulfed him and a grenade left him half-blinded and terribly wounded."

6 May, 0130. The situation onshore is better for the Japanese than General Homma imagines. The 1st Battalion, 61st Infantry, had come ashore shortly before midnight and, after a brief fire-fight with a platoon of Company A, 4th Marines, the only U.S. force defending the landing area, gains a foothold on the island near North Point. By 0130, this outfit establishes a line across the narrow neck of the island between Infantry and Cavalry points. Tanks and artillery come ashore behind them.

6 May, 0200. Only two platoons of the 4th Marines stand between the enemy and Malinta Hill. General Moore strips the seacoast batteries of all available artillerymen and commits them as infantry to the east of Malinta Tunnel. The men form up, move out in the darkness from their batteries on Topside, across Bottomside, which is under enemy artillery shelling, enter Malinta Tunnel from the west entrance, move through the tunnel, and go out the east exit to confront the Japanese along a line to the east of the tunnel. The Japanese line runs north and south across the island, through the old Battery Denver position. For two hours the Japanese hurl back the counterattacks of the artillerymen now turned infantrymen. The 2d Battalion of the 61st Japanese Regiment, now ashore and in some semblance of order, joins the 1st Battalion.

6 May, 0430. General Moore commits the last of his reserves. This group is a 500-man provisional battalion led by Maj. Francis

Williams (USMC). It is an ill-equipped, hastily organized assortment of sailors armed with rifles very unfamiliar to them. They wait at the east entrance of the Malinta Tunnel for a few hours before being committed. From their positions in the tunnel, they had seen many wounded Marines brought in through that entrance and can hear the Japanese shelling the area just outside the entrance. Bottled up in the dank tunnel, they suffer its heat and the dust, stench, and confusion. But, when so ordered, they move out in a column of companies and immediately are pounded by artillery fire all along the blacked-out march to the front, about one thousand yards from the east exit.

6 May, 0615. The U.S. forces counterattack. On the left is the provisional battalion of sailors commanded by Major Williams; on the right is the Headquarters and Service Company of the 4th Marines, plus a mixed bag of miscellaneous Army and Navy troops. The Japanese are surprised by the attack and fall back on the flanks, but the center, anchored on a machine gun in Battery Denver's gun pit, holds. Lt. Bethel B. Otter (USN), commander of Company T, 4th Provisional Battalion, and five volunteers armed with hand grenades attack the machine gun "with the strong determination to get the gun that dealt so much misery to Company T and the rest of the battalion." Otter and his men crawl to the edge of the gun pit, hurl their grenades into the pit, and knock out the machine gun. Unfortunately, Japanese on the flank attack and kill Otter and four of his stalwart, heroic volunteers.

On the north end of the U.S. line of attack, men of Company Q, Provisional Battalion, discover two Japanese landing craft loaded with Japanese soldiers hung up on the rocks off the north shore. Thirty minutes later, and after the expenditure of a considerable amount of small arms ammo, the untrained sailors have eliminated this part of the enemy landing force.

By now, General Homma is deeply concerned about the progress of the attack. According to his plan and reckoning, his men should have been in Malinta Tunnel by dawn; in fact, they are held up about a thousand yards away. The attackers' ammunition is running low because many of the landing craft that carried ammo threw their loads overboard and departed the area when the Americans shelled the landing beach. The dwindling supply of ammunition is of deep concern to Homma's staff. And the American counterattack caused General Homma to say, "My God, I have failed miserably on the assault." General Homma's concern is misplaced. Shortly after 0800, the Japanese on the left of the American line infiltrate around the American flank and attack the Americans from the rear. Japanese light artillery is now ashore, and it blasts the American line with deadly accuracy.

6 May, 1000. Three Japanese tanks join the assault and cause panic among the U.S. troops on the front lines. The troops are now pinned down by Japanese tanks, heavy machine guns, and additional assault troops. Any mass movement to the rear brings in artillery fire from the Japanese guns on Bataan. The situation is critical. All reserves are committed; most large weapons are destroyed. The Japanese can reach Malinta Tunnel with its one thousand wounded men in a few hours. Result: possible slaughter. U.S. casualties are mounting; there are no litter bearers; the walking wounded are re-wounded or killed as they try to get to the hospital in Malinta Tunnel. In the defense of the tunnel's east entrance, between six hundred and eight hundred men have been killed and one thousand more wounded.

General Wainwright decides to surrender Corregidor, in effect trading the one day he might still be able to hold out for several thousand lives.

Some time early in the morning of 6 May, Wainwright orders Beebe to broadcast a surrender message to Homma; he orders Moore to put into effect the plan to destroy all weapons larger than .45 caliber, to lower and burn the American flag, and to raise the white flag; and he sends his "with broken heart and head bowed" message to President Roosevelt and General MacArthur.

During the next fourteen hours, Wainwright finds that surrendering his force is not only humiliating but difficult.

6 May, 1030. General Beebe broadcasts a message over the "Voice of Freedom" from his lateral in Malinta Tunnel to General Homma "or the present commander in chief of the Imperial Japanese Forces on Luzon" that contains the details of General Wainwright's offer to surrender. Immediately after General Beebe broadcasts his message, a Japanese interpreter with him reads the message in Japanese. At about the same time, General Wainwright sends a coded message to General Sharp on Mindanao

releasing to him all of the forces on the Philippines except those on the four fortified islands in Manila Bay. Wainwright hopes that this ruse will permit him to surrender to Homma only those forces under his command, that is, the forces on the four islands in Manila Bay.

The Japanese continue to shell Corregidor from Bataan, and the Japanese troops to the east of Malinta continue their attack.

6 May, 1100. Surrender message rebroadcast in English and Japanese.

6 May, 1145. Message again rebroadcast in English and Japanese. Moore implements Wainwright's order. All small arms larger than .45 caliber are smashed, classified documents burned, codes and radio equipment destroyed, and two million Philippine pesos shredded with scissors by the finance officer, Col. John R. Vance, and his assistants.

6 May, noon. Colonel William C. Braly remembers that Malinta Tunnel was a scene of "unbelievable disorder, congestion, and confusion." The soldiers were at the end of their ropes. They were grimy, hungry, and exhausted. Their once heavily starched uniforms were sweat stained and encrusted with dirt. The quartermaster finally opens the food storage laterals, and the men take what they want. They eat a last full meal before the Japanese take over the tunnels.

6 May, 1230. No reply yet from the Japanese. Wainwright makes one last effort to reach the Japanese by radio. No answer.

6 May, 1300. As a last resort to contact the Japanese, Wainwright sends Marine Capt. Golland L. Clark, Jr., with a flag bearer, a musician, and an interpreter, to find the Japanese commander on Corregidor. Clark's party moves out through the east exit of the tunnel, through the American lines, which are still holding east of the tunnel. In no-man's-land, the musician, perhaps incongruously, but effectively, sounds his trumpet, and the flag bearer waves his flag. The Japanese in the front lines allow them to move through to their rear. Clark reaches a Japanese colonel who he thinks is the commander of the forces on Corregidor. After a brief conversation, the Japanese officer radios Bataan for instructions. Then he tells Clark to bring General Wainwright to him, and he will make arrangements for Wainwright to meet with General Homma.

6 May, 1400. General Wainwright and Captain Clark leave Malinta Tunnel by sedan, ride to Denver Hill, dismount, and walk to the top of the hill. They are met by an English-speaking, Japanese lieutenant and Colonel Nakayama, the officer to whom Clark spoke. Nakayama is not the commander of the forces on Corregidor but is the same staff officer of 14th Army who took General King's surrender on Bataan. Homma had sent Nakayama to Corregidor the night before with orders to bring Wainwright to him only if Wainwright were ready to surrender all of the forces in the Philippines. When Wainwright explains to Nakayama that he will surrender only those forces under his command, that is, the forces on the four islands in Manila Bay, Nakayama explodes in an "angry torrent of Japanese"—which when translated means that any surrender must include all of the forces in the islands. "In that case," replies General Wainwright, "I will deal only with General Homma and with no one of less rank." With that exchange, Nakayama, following previous orders from Homma, agrees to take Wainwright to Bataan. As it turns out, Homma didn't hear Beebe's broadcast and learned of Wainwright's willingness to surrender only when he received reports that a white flag was flying over Malinta.

6 May, 1430. General Wainwright sends his senior aide, Lt. Col. John R. Pugh, to South Dock to bring his boat around to the north for the trip to Bataan. He sends General Moore back to Malinta "to look after things in his absence." Another aide and Captain Clark go with General Moore. Then General Wainwright, Colonel Nakayama, an interpreter, and Wainwright's remaining aide, Maj. Thomas Dooley, start out for North Dock to board the boat that Colonel Pugh had gone to get. Shortly, they come under Japanese artillery fire, and Nakayama refuses to go any farther. Nakayama takes the group to Cavalry Point, where Japanese troops are still unloading. Nakayama sends for a boat; an armored barge arrives shortly to take the party to Bataan. Meanwhile, Colonel Pugh; General Beebe; Maj. William Lawrence, Wainwright's administrative assistant; and Sgt. Hubert Carroll, Wainwright's orderly, reach Bataan in the boat originally scheduled to carry Wainwright and his party. Major Lawrence meets Wainwright and Nakayama on the dock in Cabcaben at about 1600. The rest of Beebe's party has gone forward to find

Wainwright. Nakayama leads the party to a house about three-quarters of a mile to the north of Cabcaben. Here they are met by Beebe, Pugh, and Carroll.

6 May, 1700. After waiting for at least half an hour, during which they are ordered to line up for photos, General Homma drives up in a Cadillac, salutes the group offhandedly, and strides up to the porch. The Americans follow in grim silence. Homma is large for a Japanese—five feet ten, barrel chested, heavy, about two hundred pounds. He is dressed as if for an inspection—olive drab uniform with several rows of ribbons. General Wainwright, on the other hand, according to one of the Japanese photographers, was "thin as a crane and made a pathetic figure against the massive form of General Homma." Wainwright's face reflects his anguish and the trials of the preceding five months—from Lingayen, to Bataan, to Corregidor. His khakis are rumpled and ribbonless. Homma takes the seat in the middle of a long table on the porch. He is flanked by General Wachi, his chief of staff, and Colonel Nakayama. Across the table sit the five Americans, with Wainwright in the center. On the lawn behind them stand Japanese newsmen, photographers, and correspondents.

General Wainwright makes the first move. He produces his surrender document and turns it over to Homma, who, although he can read and speak English, turns the document over to an interpreter.[13] After hearing Wainwright's terms read, Homma refuses to accept them unless the surrender includes all of the American and Philippine troops in the entire island chain. Wainwright says to the interpreter: "Tell him that the troops in the Visayan Islands and on Mindanao are no longer under my command. They are commanded by General Sharp, who in turn is under General MacArthur's high command."

Homma is not taken in by Wainwright's transparent effort to reduce his losses. He tells Wainwright that he knows the Ameri-

---

13. At his trial in Manila in 1946, Homma, supported by his chief of staff, denied that Wainwright handed him a surrender document. Wainwright's version is in *General Wainwright's Story*, pp. 130–32, published in 1946.

can radio has named him as the overall commander in the Philippines and that he, Homma, demands the surrender of all troops in the Philippines before he will order a cease-fire. Wainwright stubbornly continues to deny that he commands the troops in the Visayan-Mindanao area. Homma then asks him, rather perceptively, when he turned over the forces to Sharp. Rather weakly, Wainwright replies, "Several days ago." He adds that even if he did command them he has no way of communicating with them. Homma is ready for that reply. "Send a staff officer to Sharp," he says. "I will furnish a plane."

Stubbornly, Wainwright refuses to give in. Homma, dealing from strength, stands up, looks down at Wainwright and says: "At the time of General King's surrender in Bataan, I did not see him. Neither have I any reason to see you if you are only the commander of a unit. . . . I wish only to negotiate with my equal. . . . Since you are not in command, I see no further necessity for my presence here."

Wainwright recognizes his hapless and cornered position. After conferring with Beebe and Pugh, he decides to accept the inevitable. He then tells Homma that he will surrender the entire U.S. and Philippine force in the islands. But now Homma decides to play tough. He has the last words.

"You have denied your authority," he says to Wainwright. "I advise you to return to Corregidor and think the matter over. If you see fit to surrender, then surrender to the commanding officer of the division on Corregidor. He in turn will bring you to me in Manila. I call this meeting over." With that, Homma abruptly leaves the porch.[14]

---

14. As reported by Morton in *The Fall of the Philippines*, pp. 567–69. Morton uses as sources *General Wainwright's Story*, the transcripts of General Homma's trial, and a book by Uno, *Corregidor: Isle of Delusion*. Uno, a bilingual observer at the meeting, does not agree with General Wainwright's version in all details. But Uno is supported by Lt. Col. Yoshio Nakajima, an operations officer on the Japanese 14th Army staff, during Homma's trial. Morton accepts some of Uno's interpretation because "he was a bilingual observer and was not under the same constraints as the participants. His account is not unsympathetic to the American cause."

Futility and hopelessness overwhelm Wainwright. He then tries to surrender his forces to Colonel Nakayama and agrees to send one of his staff officers to General Sharp on Mindanao in a Japanese plane. But Nakayama refuses to accept the surrender and tells Wainwright that he will have to return to Cabcaben by auto and then to Corregidor by boat.

While General Wainwright has been negotiating with Homma and Nakayama, the Japanese on Corregidor have isolated Malinta by completely encircling it, cutting it off from the rest of the island. The Japanese have entered the tunnel by way of the east entrance and by 1600 have cleared the tunnel of all Americans and Filipinos except the patients and staff officers. The Japanese are in complete control of the tunnel.

6 May, 1615. Near the entrance to the navy tunnel, Col. Sam Howard (USMC) puts his face in his hands and weeps. "My God," he says to his executive officer, Col. Don Curtis, "I had to be the first Marine officer ever to surrender a regiment."

When Wainwright lands on the North Dock after dark, he can see that the Japanese dominate the island. He realizes that there is no point in going first to Malinta Tunnel. Therefore, he asks Nakayama to take him directly to the commander of the forces on the island. Nakayama leads the party around Malinta to the barrio of San José, on the southern side of Bottomside. There, Colonel Sato, the commander of the 61st Infantry, meets them. Sato tells Wainwright that the terms of the surrender must be unconditional and must include all of Homma's original demands. He also demands that the troops in the Visayan and Mindanao islands surrender within four days. Sato produces a surrender document that he had obviously prepared ahead of time. The closing paragraph of the document rings with finality and resolution.

The Japanese Army and Navy will not cease their operations until they recognize faithfulness in executing the above-mentioned orders. If and when such faithfulness is recognized, the commander in chief of Japanese forces in the Philippines will order "cease fire" after taking all circumstances into consideration.

6 May, 2400. General Wainwright and Colonel Sato sign the surrender document. General Wainwright returns to his office in Malinta Tunnel.

The Japanese conquest of Corregidor is complete. It was not until 9 June, however, that the one hundred and forty thousand men of the combined U.S. and Philippine army in the other parts of the Philippines were brought to terms and surrendered. Thus, Homma had missed his target date for subjugating the Philippines by four months. Each day's delay meant a loss of face for the Japanese. As a result, as soon as the campaign was over, Imperial Japanese Headquarters, flushed as it was in the early days of the war with an unbroken string of successes, relieved Homma of command in the Philippines and brought him back to Tokyo, where he served the rest of the war as a reserve officer in unimportant roles.

Some good did come out of the American obstinacy and stubborn resistance on Corregidor. To the American people back home, Corregidor became the symbol of defiance and endurance. Shortly before the surrender, President Roosevelt expressed his sentiments to General Wainwright this way:

> In every camp and on every naval vessel, soldiers, sailors, and Marines are inspired by the gallant struggle of their comrades in the Philippines. The workmen in our shipyards and munitions plants redouble their efforts because of your example. You and your devoted followers have become the living symbols of our war aims and the guarantee of victory.

Thus, the loss of Corregidor was not totally in vain. And partly because of its symbolism, its reconquest became a compulsion for the United States—but particularly for General MacArthur for whom Corregidor now became a personal symbol, its recapture an all-consuming goal.

CHAPTER V
Invasion of the Philippines and the Recapture of Manila

By early February 1945, General MacArthur and his forces were reasonably well established on the island of Luzon. MacArthur had thus fulfilled his 1942 pledge to the Filipino people—"I shall return." But it had not been without serious and prolonged debate among the chief planners of the United States and its allies.

In the two and a half years since the fall of the Philippines, the U.S. forces in the Pacific had fought their way back from Australia, up the Pacific chain of islands along two great, roughly parallel arcs. On the southern flank was MacArthur and his Southwest Pacific Command, invading, fighting, winning, and then leaping forward in great bounds along the northern coast of New Guinea, leaving behind large pockets of Japanese to "wither on the vine," cut off from their supplies and reinforcements. On the northern flank was Adm. Chester W. Nimitz and his Pacific Ocean Area Command, island hopping through the Japanese-held bastions of the Solomons, the Gilberts, the Marshalls, and the Marianas. In addition to seizing the islands held by the Japanese and establishing bases for projecting his forces ever farther and farther west, Nimitz and his command, fighting at sea, had crippled the air arm of the Japanese navy.

By September 1944, both elements of the U.S. Pacific forces were nearing the southernmost island of the Philippines—Mindanao. MacArthur's advanced echelons had reached Morotai Island, three hundred miles south of Mindanao; Nimitz's forces were in the Palau Islands, five hundred miles east of Mindanao.

At this stage of the operations, the two competitive commanders, Nimitz and MacArthur, agreed that they should take Mindanao next, as a base for further operations; but they could not agree on their basic strategy after Mindanao for the final thrust to the Japanese homeland. MacArthur, with a strong emotional tie to the Philippines, argued that the United States was honorbound next to liberate all of the Philippines, including the main island of Luzon. Admiral Nimitz, however, was interested in the Philippines only as a steppingstone to Formosa. He felt that Formosa should be the next major objective after Mindanao because with U.S. bases on Formosa the United States could sever Japan's sea lanes, thus blocking her source of raw materials from the south. Holding Formosa would also permit the Allies to jump to the China coast, there to build air bases from which to launch the final air attacks against the Japanese main islands and to support the ground invasion of Japan, which all strategists at this point believed would be necessary.

President Roosevelt decided to hear personally each commander's arguments. He flew to Hawaii in July 1944 specifically to settle the strategic dispute. MacArthur, with his usual eloquence, presented his case: Luzon, he said, would serve roughly the same strategic purpose as Formosa and could be taken more easily because of the vast network of Filipino guerrillas already in place and because of the friendly, cooperative population eagerly awaiting liberation. He added that the prestige of the United States was at stake and that the United States should free its own territory first. Nimitz presented his arguments in favor of the seizure of Formosa and a follow-up landing on the China coast. Some observers at the conference felt that MacArthur won his case. Roosevelt, however, did not announce a final decision; in truth, he probably did not make one.

In September 1944, the issue was still not settled. In that month, the Joint Chiefs of Staff ordered MacArthur to invade Mindanao with a D-day of 15 November and to land on Leyte with a D-day of 20 December. But the Joint Chiefs had still not really decided the question of Luzon versus Formosa; they felt that Mindanao was a convenient base for the invasion of Leyte, and Leyte was a steppingstone for the next phase of the operation, whether against Formosa or Luzon.

In actuality, the debate within the Joint Chiefs continued even longer. By the end of September 1944, most members of the Joint Chiefs were wavering on the necessity for attacking Formosa at all. All of the military considerations began to point forcibly toward a strategy in favor of securing Luzon, bypassing Formosa, scratching the invasion of the China coast, and heading straight for Okinawa. However, Admiral King, the Navy representative on the Joint Chiefs, still held out stubbornly; he would ignore Luzon and take Formosa instead. King's argument was that Mac-Arthur's plan for the invasion of Luzon would tie up all of the Pacific Fleet's fast carriers for at least six weeks; to pin down the carriers for so long would be unsound, he reasoned. Therefore, he deemed MacArthur's plan unacceptable to the U.S. Navy.

MacArthur's deputy chief of staff, Maj. Gen. R. J. Marshall, was in Washington at the time on official business. Marshall alerted MacArthur by cable to King's last-ditch arguments. MacArthur quickly countered King's position by radioing the Joint Chiefs of Staff that he needed carriers for only a few days—during the initial assault on Luzon to provide close air support for ground operations; thereafter, his engineers would build fields behind the invasion forces for land-based, close air support.[15] He also pointed out that his requirement for the fast carrier forces would be for a far shorter length of time than would be needed for an invasion of Formosa, particularly if Luzon were still in Japanese hands. Based on these considerations, Admiral Nimitz then withdrew his objections; he recommended to the Joint Chiefs that MacArthur initiate the invasion of Luzon on 20 December and that his (Nimitz's) Central Pacific Forces attack Iwo Jima in late January 1945 and then Okinawa on 1 March.

Admiral King finally accepted Nimitz's plan of operations. With his acquiescence, the Joint Chiefs had the unanimity they needed. On 3 October, the Joint Chiefs directed General MacArthur to invade Luzon on or about 20 December and ordered Admiral Nimitz to attack Iwo Jima and Okinawa according to his recommended timetable.

---

15. MacArthur's faith in his engineers was not misplaced. On one occasion, his airfield engineers carved out and laid a 2,500-foot pierced steel planking runway in two days.

The 3 October directive of the Joint Chiefs settled the strategic debate that had been argued within the Joint Chiefs for a number of months—the next major objective would be Luzon; Formosa would be skipped. The directive also endorsed General MacArthur's overall plan—one that he had advocated from the day he left Corregidor in 1942. His plan was called "Reno."

General MacArthur wrote in *Reminiscences:*

My plan, called "Reno," was based on the premise that the Philippine archipelago, lying directly in the main sea routes from Japan to the source of her vital raw materials and oil in the Netherlands, Indies, Malaya, and Indo-China, was the most important strategic objective in the Southwest Pacific Area. Whoever controlled the air and naval bases in the Philippine Islands, logically controlled the main artery of supply to Japan's factories. If this artery were severed, Japan's resources would soon disappear, and her ability to maintain her war potential against the advancing Allies would deteriorate to the point where her main bases would become vulnerable to capture. Mindanao was selected as the tactical objective in the Philippines. . . .

Even though MacArthur, Nimitz, and the Joint Chiefs had agreed that Mindanao would be the initial point of attack in the Philippines and the base from which the U.S. forces could launch their assault against the remainder of the Philippines, particularly Luzon, Admiral Halsey and his Third Fleet aircraft caused the strategists to revoke their plans for an invasion of Mindanao and to move up the schedule to hit Leyte.

Halsey's influence on the strategic decision makers came about this way. To soften up Mindanao in preparation for the proposed landings there, Admiral Halsey's Third Fleet carrier-based aircraft launched attacks against Mindanao on 9 and 10 September. Halsey and his pilots found a surprisingly weak response to the attacks. They met few Japanese airborne aircraft and impotent air defenses on the ground. General MacArthur, never one to miss taking credit where he felt it due, wrote that "further probing disclosed that Southwest Pacific land-based bombers, operating out of New

Guinea fields, had caused severe damage to enemy air installations."

On 12 and 13 September, Halsey's aircraft attacked Japanese installations in the Visayans. Again they ran into unexpectedly weak opposition, and the U.S. Navy aircraft heavily damaged grounded Japanese planes and air bases. General MacArthur wrote, again somewhat parochially, "It became more and more apparent that the bulk of the once mighty Japanese air force had been destroyed in the costly war of attrition incidental to the New Guinea operations."

Vice Adm. Marc Mitscher was the commander of the Third Fleet's Task Force 38, whose planes raided Mindanao and the Visayans air installations. After the raids, his pilots reported that they had destroyed 478 planes, most of them on the ground, and had sunk 59 ships. They reported little opposition.

Admiral Halsey's reaction to the report was that it was "unbelievable and fantastic." He concluded that the Japanese strength in the Philippines was "a hollow shell with weak defenses and skimpy facilities." He reasoned that the schedule for the invasion of the Philippines could therefore be speeded up. "Such a recommendation," he wrote later, "in addition to being none of my business, would upset a great many applecarts, possibly all the way up to Mr. Roosevelt and Mr. Churchill. On the other hand, it looked sound, it ought to save thousands of lives, and it might cut months off the war. . . . I sent for my aides and told them, 'I'm going to stick my neck out.'" He then wired Nimitz and recommended that the invasion of Mindanao be canceled in favor of an immediate landing on Leyte, which, according to Halsey's view, was "wide open."

Nimitz agreed with Halsey's recommendation and passed it on to Washington and coincidentally to Quebec, where the Joint Chiefs were about to meet with Roosevelt and Churchill.

MacArthur wrote later:

At the time he [Halsey] radioed this suggestion, virtually the whole strategic apparatus of the United States government had moved to Quebec in attendance at the conference then being held between Mr. Roosevelt and Mr. Churchill.

My views were requested on the proposed change of the invasion date for Leyte, and I cabled my assent to Halsey's proposal. Thus, within ninety minutes after Quebec had been queried as to the change in plans, we had permission to advance the date of our invasion of Leyte by two months.

On 20 October 1944, MacArthur invaded Leyte's east coast. Unfortunately, it was the rainy season, and the typhoons and monsoons laced the island with thirty-five inches of rain and turned ordinary trails and roads into slippery, soggy, paths, quagmires that even the carabao, Filipino beasts of burden, would not negotiate. Crossing the almost-uncharted mountains to the west coast was an exercise for which no amount of training in Louisiana or New Guinea prepared the troops. It was simply on-the-job training under miserable conditions. Ponchos were little protection from the rains and the jungle dampness, and boots rotted off the feet of the slogging infantrymen, who had to carry on their backs virtually all of the equipment and gear they needed for the fight in the mountains against the dug-in, resolute Japanese defenders.

But by Christmas of 1944, Leyte was in American hands from the east to the west coast. The Japanese had decided that they would fight the decisive battle of the Philippines on Leyte and lost approximately sixty thousand men in the defeat; the U.S. losses were thirty-five hundred soldiers killed and twelve thousand wounded. The fall of Leyte was a disastrous debacle for the forces of General Yamashita; General MacArthur called it "perhaps the greatest defeat in the military annals of the Japanese Army." Leyte was ours, but Yamashita still had a formidable army on Luzon. The fight for the Philippines was by no means over.

On 15 December, MacArthur launched his attack against Mindoro with the Western Visayan Task Force, under the command of Brig. Gen. William C. Dunkel. His command was composed of the 19th Regimental Combat Team of the 24th Division and the separate 503d Parachute Infantry Regimental Combat Team. Initially, the 503d was scheduled to parachute onto Mindoro, but planners for the operation could not find sufficient airfields on Leyte to accommodate all of the troop-carrying aircraft needed to drop the 503d. So the paratroopers landed amphibiously, abreast of the 19th Regimental Combat Team (RCT) on the west

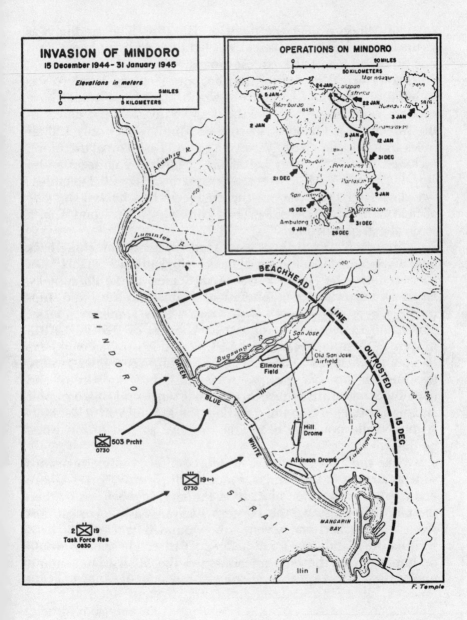

INVASION OF MINDORO
15 December 1944 – 31 January 1945

Elevations in meters

OPERATIONS ON MINDORO

F. Temple

coast of Mindoro near the town of San José. The landing was virtually unopposed; the island was lightly held by no more than one thousand assorted Japanese troops.

The principal reason for invading and securing Mindoro was to build airfields and bases from which MacArthur would have ground-based air support for the decisive invasion and defeat of the Japanese on Luzon. (San José on Mindoro was only 150 air miles from Manila.) The Western Visayan Task Force, therefore, included four U.S. Army battalions of airfield engineers and a Royal Australian Air Force works squadron. By 20 December, five days after the invasion, the engineers had hacked out one airfield and by 23 December had constructed a second one, a week ahead of schedule.

Fortunately, the airfields were ready to assist in turning back a relatively new Japanese aerial tactic—the kamikaze attack.[16] On 21 December, the Japanese Naval Air Service in the Philippines, based on Luzon, renewed operations against the Navy and ships in the waters off Mindoro with some twenty kamikaze attacks. The kamikaze assaults continued for the rest of December. But in spite of them, by 9 January, the U.S. and Australian engineers had built sufficient air bases on Mindoro for three fighter groups, two medium bomber groups, two night-fighter squadrons, and five other squadrons of tactical reconnaissance and photographic and air-sea rescue. Certainly, without the Mindoro airfields, MacArthur would not have been able to move against Luzon when he did.

While the Third Fleet off Mindoro suffered numerous ships sunk as a result of the kamikaze attacks, the ground forces ashore had a much easier time of it. By 4 January, in what was by then the mopping-up stage, the Western Visayan Task Force had lost sixteen men killed and seventy-one wounded and had virtually secured the island, now a full-fledged air base. These bases would be important in the days ahead, when the 503d would mount up for their attack on Corregidor.

---

16. In 1281, a kamikaze, or "divine wind," typhoon destroyed Kublai Khan's fleet, foiling his invasion of Japan. Toward the end of World War II, Vice Adm. Takejiro Onishi formed a "suicide" squadron of navy planes and pilots to crash into American warships; 1,228 kamikazes sank thirty-four U.S. ships.

On 3 January 1945, the Luzon invasion force and the Navy forces to protect and support it sailed from Leyte Gulf. In this vast armada were 850 ships of various sizes and classes led by Vice Adm. Jesse B. Oldendorf's fleet of battleships, cruisers, escort carriers, and destroyers. The transports carrying the invasion force, Sixth Army, were about three days' sailing time behind the Navy's fighting ships.

During the trip to Luzon from Leyte, through Surigao Strait, past Mindanao and Mindoro, Admiral Oldendorf's ships took the brunt of the desperate Japanese last-ditch kamikaze attacks. On 4 January, a twin-engine Japanese bomber plunged into the escort carrier, *Ommaney Bay*, killing ninety-seven men and scuttling the ship; on 5 January, sixteen kamikazes hit Oldendorf's fleet one hundred miles off Corregidor, blasting nine U.S. and Australian ships, including two heavy cruisers and an escort carrier. One carrier, the *Savo Island*, thwarted a diving kamikaze pilot by blinding him with her searchlight as the kamikaze plunged seaward in his final, suicidal dive.

The fleet, nonetheless, sailed on to Lingayen Gulf. On 6 January, the Japanese, in frustration and rashness, ordered the last big kamikaze attack of the Philippines campaign. One kamikaze flew into the bridge of the battleship *New Mexico*, killing twenty-nine men, including the ship's captain and British Lt. Gen. Herbert Lumsden, who was Winston Churchill's personal liaison officer to General MacArthur. Another kamikaze knocked the cruiser *Louisville* out of action; another hit Oldendorf's flagship, the battleship, *California*, but its bomb was a dud; another rammed the light cruiser *Columbia*. After all the reports were in, it became tragically clear that 6 January 1945 had been the worst day for the U.S. Navy in more than two years.

In the month between 13 December 1944 and 13 January 1945, the kamikaze attacks against the U.S. ships in Philippine waters had sunk twenty-four ships, including an escort carrier and a destroyer; heavily damaged thirty ships, including three battleships, two heavy cruisers, and seven carriers; and lightly damaged another thirty-seven ships. Approximately 1,230 sailors of the U.S. and Australian navies were killed and 1,800 wounded. Some 150 U.S. Army men were killed and 200 wounded on transports hit by the kamikazes. One beneficial result and one that measured the intensity and fury of the kamikaze attacks was that by the evening of 13 January, the Japanese had only about twelve operational aircraft left in the Philippines.

At 0930 on the morning of 9 January, 68,000 men of Gen. Walter Krueger's Sixth Army began the invasion of Luzon at Lingayen. During the initial days of the invasion, Lt. Gen. Oscar W. Griswold's XIV Corps moved rapidly and with hardly any opposition through the coastal towns and down the dusty roads toward Manila. But, to the east, along the foothills of a mountain stronghold where Yamashita had regrouped and dug in the bulk of his forces, two divisions of General Swift's I Corps met heavy resistance. The Japanese had dug their forces into a maze of tunnels, caves, and pillboxes and had buried tanks up to their turrets, a tactic that made the tanks formidable, defensive redoubts. One such position held thirty dug-in tanks, fifteen mobile ones, and a thousand determined defenders, who held up the 25th Division for a week.

On the coast, the going was still much easier. XIV Corps moved forward somewhat ploddingly, against virtually little resistance. The delighted Filipinos welcomed them along their route of march with chicken, bananas, and rice cakes. But MacArthur was not satisfied with the progress of XIV Corps—twenty-five miles in a week. He urged General Krueger—then, out of frustration, ordered him—to get his troops moving. MacArthur wanted to get to Manila as rapidly as possible to secure the city and to utilize its port facilities; additionally and humanely, he wanted to free as soon as possible the Allied prisoners, civilian and military, who were starving in wretched camps in the city and in the countryside. He knew that they were in danger of dying from disease and starvation and of being massacred by the thwarted and cornered Japanese. The longer it took to liberate the prisoners, the more of them would die.

Griswold stepped up the pace of his advance, prodded on by General MacArthur's formal order of 17 January. But on 23 January, Griswold ran into the forward defenses of a 30,000-man force that General Yamashita had ordered to hold Clark Field and the Zambales Mountains to the west.

Initially, General Griswold had underestimated the strength and defenses that the Japanese had strung along the heights north of Clark Field. Thus, General Griswold sent only two battalions of the 40th Division to attack the area. When they ran into a complex system of tunnels and caves, protected by mortars and machine guns, the troop commanders called for tanks, flamethrowers, and artillery and demolition men to breach the defenses. Finally, as the advance ground slowly, nearly to a halt, General Griswold assigned almost two divisions to capture Clark Field. It still took about a week of extremely rugged combat to overwhelm the suicidal Japanese defenses around Clark. The attackers ran into mines, tanks, and antiaircraft guns that were sighted parallel

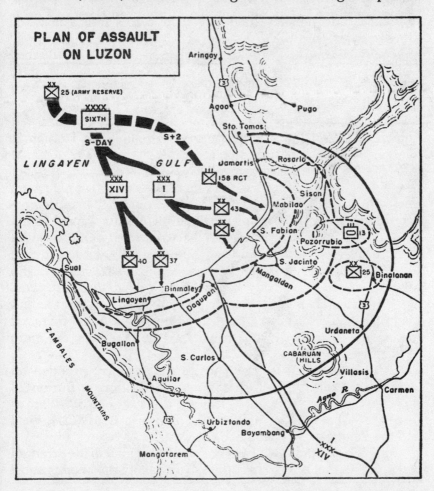

to the ground for antipersonnel use. But after losing two thousand men in the defense of Clark, the Japanese pulled out on 30 January.

With the fall of Clark Field, the Luzon campaign entered a new phase. Manila was now the objective, achievable in a relatively short time; and MacArthur's staff had gathered ten full divisions, plus the elements of other units—the equivalent of at least four more divisions—for the final push on the Philippine capital.

On 29 January, another invasion of Luzon took place, this one by forty thousand troops of Maj. Gen. Charles P. Hall's XI Corps, which landed at San Antonio on the west coast of Luzon

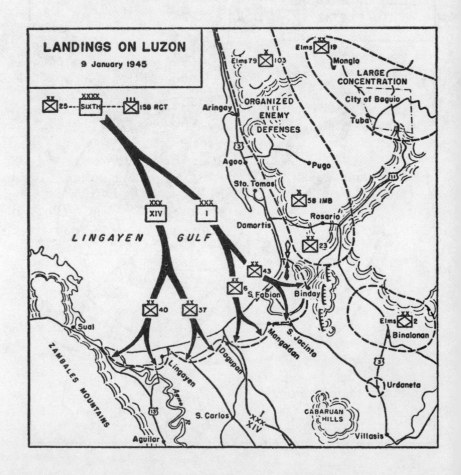

just to the north of the Bataan Peninsula. General Hall's mission was to seize the airfield at San Marcelino, capture the naval base at Subic Bay, and cut off the Bataan Peninsula so that the Japanese soldiers there could not hold out as the Americans had done so stubbornly in 1942.

As they so often failed to do, the Japanese did not oppose the landings of XI Corps on the beaches. Instead, they pulled out from the beach areas and holed up in hilly terrain some three miles to the east. With this defensive move, they abandoned valuable naval and air bases. But as was their usual tactic in defense, the Japanese had dug in along a twisting road in the mountainous terrain, which the American soldiers promptly dubbed "ZigZag Pass." As the Americans tried to force their way up the pass, the Japanese blasted them with a lethal shower of artillery and mortar fire. During the first week of February, the Americans made little progress against the stubborn Japanese defenders.

By 7 February, U.S. engineers had completed the rehabilitation of the San Marcelino airfield, and U.S. Air Corps planes were then available to strafe, bomb, and napalm the defenders of ZigZag Pass. American artillery zeroed in on the Japanese defensive positions, and the infantrymen finally began to make slow but steady progress up the road. By 15 February, ZigZag Pass was in American hands, and XI Corps was able to run a line from Subic Bay to Manila Bay and seal off Bataan. The tenacious defenders suffered 2,400 men killed and 25 captured; the attackers had 1,400 casualties, of which 250 were killed.

The next phase of the buildup of forces to surround and capture Manila occurred with the amphibious landing of the two glider regimental combat teams of the 11th Airborne Division, the 187th and the 188th, on 31 January at Nasugbu Bay, fifty-five miles southwest of Manila. The 11th Airborne had been bloodied in fighting across the soggy, mountainous, heavily jungled waist of Leyte from Burauen to Albuera on the west coast. The glider-riders of the 11th welcomed the clear, sunny days of Luzon, and the few Japanese (about one hundred) near Nasugbu to counter their landing.

The 11th Airborne glider units were the vanguard of Lt. Gen. Robert Eichelberger's Eighth Army. For many days, they were almost the only elements of the Eighth Army. Eichelberger's land-

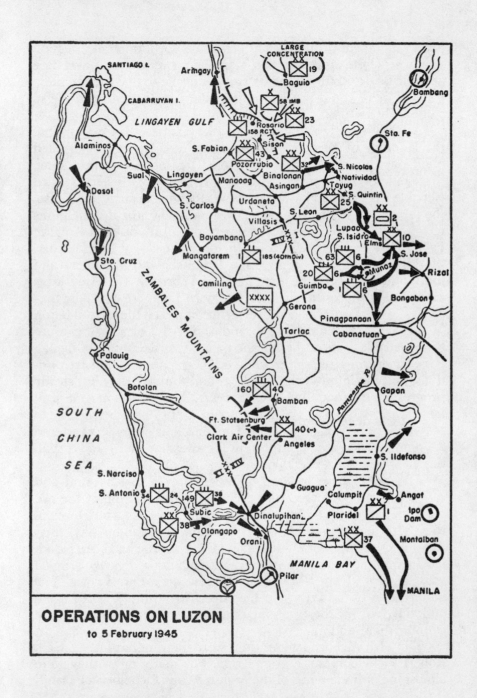

OPERATIONS ON LUZON
to 5 February 1945

ing was designated a "reconnaissance in force" by General MacArthur's planners. If he ran into little resistance, Eichelberger was authorized by MacArthur to move out as rapidly as possible to race up Route 17 and attack Manila from the south; if he ran into insurmountable opposition near Nasugbu, he was authorized to pull out. General MacArthur told Eichelberger, his former secretary of the general staff when MacArthur was the Army's chief of staff, that he wanted him to "undertake a daring expedition against Manila with a small mobile force," employing tactics "which would have delighted Jeb Stuart." The implication of the order was not lost on Eichelberger. He knew that MacArthur was anxious for General Krueger to abandon his deliberate and cautious approach to Manila from the north. Eichelberger had written to Miss Em, his wife, that "the commander in chief is very impatient" and that he has had to "speed up your palsy-walsy" and that "Krueger doesn't even radiate courage."

MacArthur was obviously playing one commander off against the other in a ruse to get to Manila as soon as possible. He was deeply worried about the status and fate of the prisoners, both civilian and military, who had been captured and incarcerated by the Japanese all across the Philippines.

He wrote later in *Reminiscences:*

I was deeply concerned about the thousands of prisoners who had been interned at the various camps on Luzon since the early days of the war. Shortly after the Japanese had taken over the islands, they gathered Americans, British, and other Allied nationals, including women and children, in concentration camps without regard to whether they were actual combatants or simply civilians. I had been receiving reports from my various underground sources long before the actual landings on Luzon, but the latest information was most alarming. With every step that our soldiers took toward Santo Tomas University, Bilibid, Cabanatuan, and Los Baños, where these prisoners were held, the Japanese soldiers guarding them had become more and more sadistic. I knew that many of these half-starved and ill-treated people would die unless we rescued them promptly. The thought of their destruction with deliverance so near was deeply repellent to me.

But MacArthur was also concerned about liberating the capital of the Philippines from which he had left in defeat three years earlier. "Get to Manila," he ordered his field commanders. "Go around the Japs, bounce off the Japs, save your men, but get to Manila. Free the internees at Santo Tomas. Take Malacanan and the legislative buildings!"

Eichelberger reacted to MacArthur's orders with verve, dash, and imagination. He recognized that if he could bluff the Japanese into thinking that he commanded a large force moving up Route 17 across Tagaytay Ridge and heading north toward Manila, he would have a tactical advantage and a possible rapid and generally uncontested race to the southern limits of Manila.

Eichelberger ordered the 187th and 188th, regiments with only two understrength infantry battalions each, about half the size (fifteen hundred men each) and half the firepower of a standard World War II infantry regiment, to charge up Route 17 toward Tagaytay Ridge, making as much dust and firing as many weapons as possible at any roadblocks, even if the weapons were only the pack 75-mm howitzers of the glider field artillery battalions that supported them.

Eichelberger later called the tactic a "monumental bluff."

Our vehicles were roaring up and down the road, raising never-ending clouds of dust. By the generous use of what artillery we had, by our heavy and confident assaults, by repeated strikes from the air, we gave the enemy the impression that a force of army proportions—complete with an armored division—was invading southern Luzon. This impression was not lessened by the fact that American radio announced the news that the "Eighth Army" had landed there.

The bluff worked. The initial amphibious assault of 1st Battalion, 188th, had been so successful that Eichelberger called for the landing of the rest of the 11th Airborne units still afloat. The 188th charged up some secondary roads toward its first important objective, the Palico River Bridge, which spanned a gorge some 85 feet deep and 250 feet wide. If the 188th could not secure that bridge before the Japanese blew it, the lightly equipped engineers with the 11th would have a time-consuming and difficult feat of engineering to rebuild it. The 188th raced up the road toward the bridge, down a small hill to the west of it, dashed across the bridge, and surprised a squad of Japanese who were about to demolish it. By midafternoon of the 31st, the day of the landings, the entire 188th and an attached battalion of the 187th were across the bridge and onto Route 17. They continued to march up Route 17 until 1800. Then the troops halted, dug in, ate their C-rations, and tried to get some sleep before moving out. By 0100, the 188th was on the move again, advancing along Route 17 to the east. With each mile, the road got steeper as it rose upward toward Tagaytay Ridge.

At daybreak, the lead units approached the Mount Cariliao–Mount Batulao defile, through which ran Route 17. As the 188th advanced elements moved into the defile, Japanese machine gun and rifle fire slowed their advance. Then artillery and mortar fire from Cariliao fell on them. The two wooded crests on either side of the defile gave the Japanese defenders innumerable caves and well-camouflaged positions from which to attack the troops on the road. From caves and tunnels close to the road, the Japanese used hand grenades to attack the by-now-deployed troops. The 188th had run into the Japanese 31st Infantry's main line of resistance, which consisted of bunkers, dugouts, and tank traps, all interconnected by zigzag trenches. The Japanese artillery on Mount Cariliao backed up the dug-in infantry with weapons that ranged from 37-mm antitank guns to 155-mm howitzers.

It took the 188th and the attached battalion of the 187th two days of tough infantry fighting, assisted by the 674th and 675th Glider Field Artillery Battalions and air strikes, to dig out the Japanese, reduce the defile position, and to continue the march up Route 17.

Unfortunately, the defense at the defile had slowed the 11th's advance up to Tagaytay Ridge and had ruined General Eichelberger's hopes that he could bring in the parachute echelon of the 11th Airborne Division, the 511th Regimental Combat Team, a day early, on 2 February instead of the originally planned 3 February. Eichelberger was under a restriction from General MacArthur:

he could not drop the 511th unless and until the other elements of the division could link up with it within twenty-four hours. With the delay of the 188th, Eichelberger went back reluctantly to the 3 February date for the jump. He knew that the 188th could be on the ridge by the third; therefore, he ordered the 511th to parachute onto the ridge on that date.

Lieutenant Plover and the pathfinders of the 511th had come ashore with the 188th and had marched forward with them along Route 17. Now it was time for them to accomplish their rather hazardous but vital mission—mark the drop zones for the 511th RCT. During the hours of darkness on the morning of the third, Plover and his men left the 188th lines and moved out along a trail north of Mount Cariliao. By daybreak, undetected by the Japanese, they were on top of the ridge at the preselected 511th drop zones. At 0815, Col. "Hard Rock" Haugen, leading his regiment in the first plane of Col. John Lackey's 317th Troop Carrier Group of C-47s, looked out the jump door of his C-47 and saw what he was looking for—the green smoke of Plover's grenades marking the go-point for the jumpers. Haugen looked back at the stick of men crowded behind him, then checked the light on the side of the jump door. John Lackey had turned on the green light. Haugen shouted, "Are you ready?" and then "Let's go," and jumped. He was quickly followed by the men from his plane.

The initial element of the 511th, 345 men in the first eighteen C-47s, hit the designated drop zones marked by Plover and his men. But the second echelon, 570 men in thirty planes, were six miles and three minutes behind the lead aircraft. A jumpmaster in one of the planes, seeing another plane inadvertently drop some equipment bundles, thought that he was over the go-point and jumped, leading his men behind him. The other planes followed suit. The pilots and crew chiefs tried to stop the early exits but could not. Fortunately, the entire plateau of Tagaytay Ridge was fairly open and gently sloping terrain, so the troopers generally landed without mishap, even though they were five miles from the proper DZ. Further, the guerrillas in the area had cleared the Japanese from the DZs, so there was no opposition on landing.

At about 1210, another battalion of the 511th in fifty-one C-47s, approached the ridge. The first five aircraft dropped in the proper area; but the jumpmasters in the succeeding planes, seeing on the ground the parachutes of the earlier, premature jump, parachuted down into that area. In all, about 425 men landed on the proper DZ; 1,325 landed between four and a half to six miles to the east and northeast.

In spite of the scattered landings, the men of the 511th were assembled into their proper units in about five hours. By 1300 that afternoon, the lead elements of the 188th had moved up the ridge and had made contact with the 511th's paratroopers. There was still some fighting to the west of the ridge, but for all intents and purposes General Swing had his division back together. He claimed later that he then had a bridgehead sixty-five miles long and a thousand yards wide.

Originally, the mission of the 11th Airborne Division, as outlined by MacArthur to Eichelberger, was to control the Japanese forces in southern Luzon and to determine Japanese dispositions and intentions in the area. But General Eichelberger very much wanted to beat General Krueger to Manila. It is also possible that General MacArthur wanted him to lead the first troops into the capital. (While General MacArthur's headquarters was still on Leyte, General Sutherland, General MacArthur's chief of staff, came to General Eichelberger's Eighth Army headquarters on Leyte and told him that MacArthur wanted him to capture Manila.) In spite of the original mission of the 11th to stay in southern Luzon, Eichelberger apparently personally contacted General MacArthur and got permission to change the mission of the 11th.

And so on the afternoon of the third, when Eichelberger saw that the 511th was assembled on the ridge and that the 188th had come up from the west, he changed the mission of the 11th and directed General Swing to move out with all possible speed to Manila. Eichelberger had hoped that the 11th could move out on the afternoon of the third; unfortunately, there were simply not enough trucks readily available on the ridge to mount sufficient paratroopers of the 511th for the dash to Manila that afternoon.

General Swing immediately ordered all makes and kinds of vehicles to move up the ridge and assemble along Route 17 just beyond the Manila Hotel Annex, a beautiful prewar vacation spot overlooking spectacular Lake Taal. He ordered Col. Shorty Soule, the hard-fighting, diminutive commander of the 188th, to guard and secure Tagaytay Ridge. Then he ordered the equally pugnacious and unbelievably intrepid Col. "Hard Rock" Haugen, commanding officer of the 511th, to prepare to move out with one of his battalions along Route 17 as rapidly as possible and as far as he could go toward and/or into Manila.

At daybreak on the fourth, the 511th started toward Manila in battalion-size shuttles. The convoys moved rapidly at first. A couple of times the columns were slowed by having to run the gauntlet of cheering Filipinos who crowded the roads and shouted at the troops. The uncontested advance halted, however, when the truck convoy ran into a roadblock at a knocked-out bridge across the Imus River, where about fifty Japanese, in an ancient stone building dating from the early days of the Spanish occupation, blocked another bridge across the Imus.

T. Sgt. Robert C. Steele of D Company, 511th, saw that the pack 75s of the 674th Glider Field Artillery Battalion were having no effect on the five-foot-thick walls of the building. He climbed up on the roof, punched a hole through it with an ax, poured gasoline down into the building, and then ignited the gasoline with a white phosphorous grenade. The Japanese poured out of the building only to be cut down by the men of D Company, who had the building surrounded. Sergeant Steele personally killed two who remained in the building in spite of the fire. He was awarded the Distinguished Service Cross for his heroism, but unfortunately he did not live to receive it. He was killed a few days later in the assault on Manila.

The 2d Battalion, 511th, drove another three and a half miles past the Imus River to the bridge over the Las Pinas River at Las Pinas. The Japanese had prepared the bridge for destruction, but the paratroopers surprised the defenders on the north bank of the river and seized the bridge after an intense firefight. The 2d Battalion stayed at Las Pinas, and the 1st Battalion, 511th, passed through at about 1800 on the fourth. The battalion ran into increasingly heavy fire from the Japanese and at the Parañaque River Bridge two miles beyond Las Pinas, found the badly damaged span defended by Japanese from the north bank and covered by mortar and artillery fire from Nichols Field, about a mile and a half to the northeast. Here, five miles south of the

Manila city limits, the spirited and cavalrylike charge of the 11th Airborne Division ground to a halt.

The 511th had run into the Genko line—a formidable defensive position that stretched from Manila Bay, through Nichols Field, east to Fort McKinley and was anchored on the high ground of Mabato Point along Laguna de Bay. The line was actually a series of concrete and steel pillboxes, mutually supporting, and extending in depth six thousand yards as far as the Manila Polo Club. Five- and 6-inch guns and 150-mm mortars were set in concrete emplacements facing south, and 20-, 40-, and 90-mm antiaircraft guns were fired horizontally to assist in the ground defense. Many of the automatic weapons had been salvaged by the Japanese from sunken ships and wrecked aircraft. The Genko line bristled with automatic weapons out of all proportion to the number of men who manned the line. Some of the fortifications were stone and had dome-shaped roofs piled high with sod and soggy dirt and were so overgrown with a tangle of weeds and growth that they could be recognized from only a few feet away. Embrasures were narrow but controlled a wide field of fire. Most of the pillboxes were defended by two men and either a .50-caliber machine gun or a 20-mm automatic weapon.

The force manning the Genko line was the Southern Unit, Manila Naval Defense Force, some six thousand men who occupied more than 1,200 pillboxes and who generally defended each one to the last man. There were 44 heavy-artillery pieces (120-mm coastal defense and dual-purpose AA guns), 164 other AA weapons, and hundreds of machine guns, 333 of which were captured by the 11th Airborne during the period from 5 to 23 February. The line was further reinforced with 245 100-pound bombs, and 35 antisubmarine depth charges, emplaced and rigged as land mines. All roads approaching the line were heavily mined with 500-pound bombs armed with low-pressure detonators. Later in the fighting to breach the Genko line, one of the 511th's company commanders, hammered too often by some 5-inch naval guns, sent the following note to General Swing: "Tell Halsey to stop looking for the Jap Fleet. It's dug in on Nichols Field."

The 188th found and destroyed one of the most elaborate pillboxes on Nichols Field. It was three stories deep and built of reinforced concrete into the side of a hill. The first level, containing a mahogany bed and cushioned chairs, presumably housed Japanese staff officers; the second level had a room for enlisted men; the third level was used as a storehouse.

The Genko line was but one of a series of defensive positions that the Japanese had fashioned during the days of their occupation of Manila and had supplemented intensely prior to the impending invasion of Luzon. The positions surrounded the approaches to the capital. Unfortunately for the city and the thousands of Filipinos and Americans who died in the assault, the house-by-house, street-by-street defense of the city was not what the overall commander of the Japanese forces in Luzon had in mind.

General Tomoyuki Yamashita, commander of 14th Area Army, was the overall commander on Luzon, and he had decided early in December to evacuate the city. In testimony at his war crimes trial after the war, he spelled out his reasoning for not defending the city. He said:

First the population of Manila is approximately one million; therefore, it is impossible to feed them. The second reason is that the buildings are very inflammable. The third reason is that because [Manila] is on flat land it requires tremendous . . . strength to defend it. For these reasons my policy or plan was to leave Manila outside the combat zone.

In effect, General Yamashita would have declared Manila an "open city" as General MacArthur had done when he left it in 1941. But General Yamashita had no clear line of authority over the naval forces in the Manila and Manila Bay area. Vice Adm. Denshichi Okochi was the senior Japanese naval officer in the Philippines. He decided, apparently on his own, to bolster the navy's defenses of Manila and assigned four thousand men to the Manila Naval Defense Force under the command of Rear Adm. Sanji Iwabuchi. But because of transportation problems, Okochi could not move the large number of other naval men out of the area, and by early January Iwabuchi had under his command more than sixteen thousand naval troops and four thousand army troops who could not be evacuated. Iwabuchi's ostensible mission was to hold Nichols Field and the Cavite Naval Base, mine Manila Bay, direct navy suicide boat operations in the bay, and assure the destruction of all Japanese naval installations and supplies in the Manila and Cavite areas. But even this mission of destruction was far more than Yamashita had envisioned for the naval forces.

In subsequent disagreements between General Yokoyama, whom Yamashita had left behind in Manila with some minor missions, and the naval staff, it became clear that the navy intended to defend Manila to a man in order to carry out their missions and also because they felt that Manila was easily defended and that its defense could cause great casualties to the Allied attackers. Yokoyama, recognizing a lost cause, turned over to the naval commander the four thousand army troops who were still in the Manila area.

Iwabuchi was a hard-core, dedicated officer who saw it as his duty to accomplish his assigned missions and to defend the city's harbor installations as long as possible. In addition to manning the Genko line, he deployed his troops around the city in houses that they converted into machine gun nests. He had them set up barricades of barbed wire and overturned trucks and cars at tactical locations, sandbag entrances to houses, and set up large naval guns, taken from ships, at strategic street intersections. He had his men blow up all of the city's military forts, raze the port area, destroy every bridge he could, and wreck the water supply and electric power system. As Iwabuchi's sailors blew bridges and fired buildings, the nearby houses of bamboo caught fire. Shortly, half of the northern part of the city was aflame.

By 7 February, the U.S. forces—the 37th Infantry Division, the 1st Cavalry Division, and the 11th Airborne Division—had the city surrounded, and MacArthur had isolated the battlefield—Manila. It would take until 3 March, almost a month of savage fighting, before Manila would be totally free. By the end of that time, much of the "Pearl of the Orient" would be destroyed—its public transportation system defunct, its electric power system knocked out, and its thousands of buildings and installations (among them the University of the Philippines and the Philippine General Hospital) largely destroyed and irreparable. Iwabuchi's Manila Naval Defense Force lost at least 16,000 men; the American losses in the attack on Manila were 1,010 killed and 5,565 wounded.

William Manchester in *American Caesar* writes eloquently of the destruction of Manila:

> The devastation of Manila was one of the great tragedies of World War II. Of allied cities in those war years, only Warsaw suffered more. Seventy percent of the utilities, 75 percent of the factories, 80 percent of the southern residential district, and 100 percent of the business district were razed. Nearly 100,000 Filipinos were murdered by the Japanese. Hospitals were set afire after their patients had been strapped to their beds. The corpses of males were mutilated, females of all ages were raped before they were slain, and babies' eyeballs were gouged out and smeared on walls like jelly. The middle class, the professionals and white-collar workers, suffered most. Ironically, the chief survivors of the prewar oligarchy were the members of Laurel's puppet government who were safe in Baguio with Yamashita.

Manila—battered, bloody, virtually destroyed, a dying if not dead city—would require intensive care in the weeks and months ahead. It was, nonetheless, back in American hands.

But even before the recapture of Manila, General MacArthur had been thinking of that other symbol of American gallantry, even though it recalled that ignominious defeat in the early days of the war—Corregidor. Whether Corregidor was of strategic importance to the Allies was unimportant; what was important was sentiment, drama, shock action, even, perhaps, revenge. He would not allow Corregidor to be disregarded and scorned; he must recapture it—and the more dramatically the better. Corregidor was much too symbolic to be treated with indifference.

CHAPTER VI
Japanese Buildup of Corregidor

On 3 February, the battle for control of Manila had just been joined. The capital of the Philippines was in the grip of a mammoth vise that squeezed the city between two attacking forces—the 37th Infantry and the 1st Cavalry Division from the north and the 11th Airborne Division from the south. But the recapture of the Pearl of the Orient was still many bloody days and many city block–by–city block and building-by-building fights away. Nonetheless, General MacArthur was, of course, totally optimistic. When a fast-moving cavalry column under Brig. Gen. William C. Chase of the 1st Cavalry Division entered Manila on 4 February, General MacArthur announced somewhat prematurely that for all strategic purposes, Manila was now in our hands.

But not for tactical purposes. The bloody battle for Intramuros, an old walled Spanish City with outer walls up to forty feet thick and as high as twenty-five feet, would consume at least another month and eight thousand rounds of artillery as the troops fought from one stone building to the next.

But on 3 February, with the battle for Manila raging, General MacArthur looked ahead to Bataan and the Manila Bay islands, particularly Corregidor. On that date, MacArthur sent a radio message to General Krueger that outlined his plan for securing Manila Bay.

MacArthur's radiogram suggested (and a suggestion from MacArthur carried with it the force of a directive) that Sixth Army

secure Manila Bay in three operations: one, seize the Bataan Peninsula so that Japanese escaping from the Manila fight would not
be able to retreat to the peninsula as the Americans had done
in 1942; two, capture Corregidor and the other fortified islands
in the Bay; three, seize the Ternate area on the southern shore
of Manila Bay. MacArthur, although not precisely telling Krueger
how to recapture The Rock, did suggest that his forces might
assault Corregidor either by a parachute landing, an amphibious
landing, or a combination of the two. The final decision, he said,
would await the results of a planned, intensive, aerial bombardment.

The operational side of the plan to neutralize the bay area
was clear; the intelligence side was fuzzy, at best. Early in the
planning for retaking Corregidor, both MacArthur's and Krueger's staff intelligence sections grossly underestimated the number
of Japanese who were on the island in early February 1945. As
late as the day of the assault, U.S. intelligence estimates held
that there were only 850 Japanese on Corregidor.

In their defense, because of the isolation of Corregidor, the
G-2 staffers had no really valid intelligence sources from which
to develop an accurate count of the Japanese strength. One source,
four U.S. soldiers who had escaped from Fort Frank (Carabao
Island) in May 1944 and who had then joined guerrillas in Cavite,
thought that there were about three hundred Japanese on The
Rock. Another source, aerial photography taken as late as January
1945, was not much help because by then most of the Japanese
on the island were underground in caves and tunnels. A third
source, guerrillas, reported an increase in the amount of shipping
going back and forth from Manila, but this source did not know
whether the supplies and men were coming or going.

Even the widely acclaimed and usually successful Sixth Army
Alamo Scouts, a highly trained, clandestine team that operated
behind the lines, ran into difficulty when trying to gather information about Corregidor before the attack. Brig. Gen. George Jones,
the commander of the 503d, remembers that "the Alamo Scouts
participated in stealth operations, usually landing at night in various target areas. I was informed that they had tried on a number
of occasions to land on Corregidor, but had never been able to

do so. I would guess that the estimate [of 850 Japanese defenders] was more of a 'guesstimate' than based on any bonafide information."

So to be on the safe side, the Sixth Army "Estimate of the Enemy Situation" noted the 300 figure supplied by the escaped soldiers and reported that "this is considered low" and guessed that "present strength may approximate 1,000 troops." The GHQ SWPA estimate of the Japanese strength was 850. These two erroneous assessments influenced the development of the Sixth Army's operational plan for the assault on The Rock. Fortunately, the inaccurate intelligence evaluations were not, in the long run, calamitous.

The need to retake Corregidor quickly, even while the battles for Manila, Intramuros, and the Genko line were in full fury, is perhaps debatable. From the Allied military standpoint, the unconquered Japanese and their guns on Corregidor obviously posed a threat to Allied shipping, now poised to enter Manila Bay. Corregidor could also serve as a haven for Japanese soldiers escaping from Bataan, Manila, and the south shore of the bay.

General Jones recalls:

I do not believe that it is generally known why General MacArthur determined that Corregidor had to be in American hands before the Bay of Manila could be opened up for shipping to support the continuance of the war.

When the U.S. Forces were on the island, the U.S. Navy had installed numerous mines in the harbor which were controlled by a panel on the Island of Corregidor. The mines, as I have been informed, were still there and subject to detonation by whatever forces controlled the panels. So it is my feeling that it was the Navy that was very eager to get control of the Island of Corregidor so that the control panel could be eliminated and the mines could be swept from the harbor of Manila. Until this was done, it would have been unsafe for American ships to enter the harbor.

Of course, on taking the island, we controlled the panels. I personally did not see this panel that controlled the mines in the harbor.

But these military reasons for retaking Corregidor, sound and compelling as they might be, undoubtedly ranked lower in the minds of General MacArthur and his staff than the emotional and sentimental reasons for recapturing the island: after all, MacArthur and many of his current senior staff officers had fled the island in defeat three years earlier. General Wainwright had surrendered the island in 1942, a stigma not usually attached to the U.S. military forces. And throughout the war the American people had looked upon The Rock as a manifestation of American heroism and Alamo-like doggedness and tenacity. The American people also connected it to the ignominious and sadistic death march of the Bataan survivors and wanted it avenged. Therefore, in the minds of General MacArthur and his staff and reflecting the views of the American high command and the American public, Corregidor must be retaken—the sooner and more excitingly the better.

The two senior Japanese commanders in the Manila and Luzon area viewed Corregidor from different defensive standpoints. When General Yamashita elected to take his forces out of the Manila area and establish strong defensive positions in the mountains in northern Luzon, he knew that Corregidor had no strategic value for him. Iwabuchi, on the other hand, considered Corregidor essential to the defense of the Manila area and was determined to hold the island, and the others in the bay, no matter what the cost in men and supplies.

After the Japanese captured Corregidor in 1942, they went about cleaning up the island and repairing the battered U.S. weapons, but at a very haphazard and leisurely pace. There was no sense of urgency because it never occurred to the victorious Japanese that they would ever have to fight again in the Philippines. By late summer of 1944, however, it began to register on the minds of the Japanese hierarchy, at least, as they plotted and considered the relentless westward movement of MacArthur and Nimitz, that the 14th Army might again have to fight for the Philippines.

Until August 1944, the 14th Army had garrisoned Corregidor with only three companies of troops, one infantry and two artillery, totaling about three hundred men. (This corroborated the escaped Americans' report.) In June 1942, because the Japanese high command would allocate no troops to repair the guns of Corregidor, the 14th Army's commanding general requisitioned U.S. labor from the POW camps to clean up the various bombed-out installations, to gather up scrap and munitions, to rebuild barracks and quarters, and to help repair some of the weapons that the same POWs had purposely destroyed in the last days of the siege of Corregidor. Five hundred U.S. soldiers—coast artillery and ordnance men—found themselves once more on the familiar contours of The Rock.

The Japanese in charge did not push them severely. In fact, they fed them quite well and treated them civilly. "The Japanese were apparently satisfied," wrote Lt. Col. George A. Sense, one of the men drafted to work on Corregidor, "to have a presentable area where the prisoners could manually retract a disappearing gun, to be tripped into firing position, while visiting VIPs could 'ooh!' and 'ah!' and take pictures."

Another American, Capt. Ronald O. Pigg, an engineer, asked a Japanese ordnance officer if the Japanese intended to reconstruct and repair the weapons and the fortifications of the island. The Japanese officer replied with the overweening confidence of the victors, "Why? In ten years Corregidor will be a beautiful Japanese park to which visitors from Manila may come on Sundays."

If the Japanese had been serious about restoring Corregidor's guns, they probably could have repaired at least half of them. The Americans, in their last days on Corregidor, attempted to destroy their weapons by firing them with the recoil cylinders drained of oil and with the barrels jammed—standard coast artillery doctrine for destroying a weapon. This procedure worked well in a few instances. "Battery Smith's gun tube, for example, snapped off when the weapon burst after being fired with a 12-inch projectile rammed nose first into the muzzle."[17] But in many other attempts to destroy the weapons, the Americans either did not have the time or their efforts rendered the pieces only partially inoperable.

Given the Japanese indifference and the American inclination to sabotage, few of Corregidor's weapons were restored prior to

---

17. Belote, *Corregidor—The Saga of a Fortress*, p. 189.

1945. By the time of the American landings on Luzon, probably only eight or nine weapons were operable. None of them had been test-fired, there was no fire-control equipment, and the Japanese never provided gun crews. And even if they had tried to fire them, there might have been disasters. Capt. Herman Hauck, a "tiger" in the fight before the surrender of Corregidor, put a link of chain in the recoil cylinder of one of Battery Crockett's operational 12-inch guns. If it were ever fired by the Japanese, it would have self-destructed immediately. Other Americans secretly sabotaged the munitions, powder, and guns.

By mid-1943, the number of Americans on Corregidor was gradually reduced until, by 12 May 1944, there were only twenty-one left. This group was headed by Maj. Robert Lothrop, the former post engineer. Rumor has it that at the time of the recapture of Corregidor by the Americans, fifteen POWs were still on the island. No trace was ever found of them.

By August 1944, even the local Japanese were beginning to realize that they would have to fight to retain their hold on the Philippines. And with that realization, the Japanese navy, responsible for Corregidor, requested the army to increase the strength of the Corregidor garrison. Fourteenth Army reluctantly shipped two infantry companies to the island. In September, the navy sent from Manila to Corregidor the 31st Naval Special Base Force, Imperial Marines. The marines brought with them eight 25-mm AA guns and ten other, presumably American, heavy guns. Corregidor's strength was now eight hundred men.

When the Americans landed on Leyte in October 1944, the Japanese knew full well that they would have to fight for Luzon. But there was still a division of command and strategy between the Japanese army and navy concerning the defenses of Manila and Manila Bay. The army simply evacuated Manila and moved to the northern mountains. But the navy, in the person of the stubborn Rear Adm. Sanji Iwabuchi, was determined to use the men of the 31st Naval Special Base Force to defend the city, a mission far in excess of the one assigned him by his navy superiors. Iwabuchi expanded his mission to include the defense of Corregidor and the other bay fortified islands.

To beef up his forces on Corregidor, in October Iwabuchi sent to Corregidor two batteries of antiaircraft guns and four fortress batteries with ten 150-mm naval guns commanded by Navy Lieutenant Endo. He also sent three Imperial Marine Construction units with the mission of repairing the American guns. Each of these construction units actually consisted of about 1,500 trained combat troops. By the end of January, the Japanese had 5,062 men on Corregidor, a far cry from the 850 or so that General MacArthur's and General Krueger's G-2s had estimated were there.

Iwabuchi undoubtedly regretted that more had not been done to restore Corregidor, but in the limited time that he knew he now had available, he did everything that he could to make Corregidor as formidable as possible offensively and as impregnable as possible defensively. The naval guns that he ordered to Corregidor, plus the efforts of the construction units to repair the old American coast artillery weapons, enhanced the offensive capability of The Rock; the tons of ammunition and food that he sent to the island and jammed into old storage tunnels gave his defenders an increased potential and durability on defense. In addition, he ordered the men on Corregidor to mine the beaches and the waters around the island; he deployed half of his troops into defensive positions blocking the vulnerable James, Cheney, and Ramsay ravines against possible amphibious landings. He positioned other troops near Malinta Hill. He held the other half of his soldiers in reserve in the tunnels beneath Malinta and in caves and other underground positions around the island. He ordered a few small units to dig in near the tail of the island.

Iwabuchi had another naval unit shipped to Corregidor. It was a unique unit, conceived out of desperation. The weapon of this bizarre naval force was the "Shinyo" boat, an oversize rowboat about twenty feet long powered by a four-cylinder gasoline engine and manned by one man, perforce a volunteer. It had no guns, no seaworthiness, a speed of about twenty knots on calm waters, and a 500-pound TNT charge in the bow, which detonated on impact with the target or when triggered by an electric key. By January 1945, Lt. Comdr. Shoichi Koyameda, the Shinyo commander and a regular fleet officer, had about one hundred of these waterborne kamikaze boats under his command.

Iwabuchi assigned all of the forces in the Manila Bay area—including 160 men at Mariveles, 373 on Fort Hughes, 400 on

Fort Frank, and 65 sailors, survivors from the sunken battleship, *Musashi*, on Fort Drum—to the Manila Bay Entrance Defense Force, under the command of Capt. Akira Itagaki, Imperial Japanese Navy, whose headquarters was on Corregidor.

By this time, Itagaki commanded a strong, fairly well armed, and reasonably combat ready force. He had them deploy in strong defensive positions at James, Cheney, and Ramsay ravines and at Malinta Hill. He had adequate reserves well dug in or living in underground caves and the tunnels of Malinta Hill. He had built up heavy reserves of food, ammunition, and other supplies in the tunnels and around the old gun positions. But he lacked one important element in the defensive posture of the island—communications. His ravine defenses could not communicate with one another even though wire lines did lead back from each ravine position to a central location on Topside. But he had "all his eggs in one basket"—the communications central at his command post. Another of Itagaki's problems was his inability to move forces from one location to one that might be threatened by amphibious attack or an airborne drop. But his one major problem was communications. And because he had the telephone central located at his command post, he would be in considerable command-and-control trouble if that communications center were knocked out.

By mid-February, the Japanese defenses of The Rock were as ready as the dogged and single-minded Iwabuchi could make them. Itagaki had deployed his forces in as tactically sound defensive positions as he could imagine. The stage was set for an attack. But Itagaki, even warned against the possibility by his higher headquarters in Tokyo (a Japanese prisoner later reported) of a parachute landing on Corregidor, disregarded the advice and planned and waited for what he considered was the inevitable amphibious landing. Itagaki had made a personal reconnaissance of the island and had concluded that there were no suitable drop zones for a parachute landing, especially on Topside. He was almost, but not quite, right. On 16 February, the 503d would prove him a false prophet.

CHAPTER VII
The 503d Comes of Age: Nadzab

Paratrooper units are, by their very nature, subject to many operational alerts over the course of a campaign. In the Pacific theater, General MacArthur had both the 11th Airborne Division and the separate 503d Parachute Regimental Combat Team at his disposal. Because an airborne unit has the inherent potential for entering combat any place in a circle whose radius is the range of the transport aircraft, for a number of reasons it is a valuable asset to a commander even while sitting uncommitted near an air base. First, the enemy commander undoubtedly knows where the airborne unit is, but he has no idea where or when the airborne unit might drop. Therefore, he must deploy his combat forces, which he might otherwise use in a current campaign, to guard his rear or his flanks against a possible parachute assault. Second, once the commander commits his airborne forces, the enemy commander must commit his forces to meet the airborne threat wherever it occurs—many times in his lightly defended rear. Third, the enemy commander never knows when another airborne attack might be launched. And even if the airborne attack scatters the paratroopers far and wide, as happened in Sicily in July 1943, the enemy, as he did in Sicily, thinks that the airborne force is far greater numerically than it actually is.

The U.S. High Command was highly critical of the parachute operations in Sicily because the troops were scattered over a wide area and the loss of U.S. aircraft and paratroopers to our own antiaircraft fire was unacceptable. Not so Field Marshal Albert

Kesselring, the commander of all the German troops in the Mediterranean area. "The paratroopers effected an extraordinary delay in the movement of our own troops and caused large losses," he said after the war. And Gen. Karl Student, founder and commander of all German airborne forces and the generally accepted developer of airborne troops and their use, said: "It is my opinion that if it had not been for the Allied airborne forces blocking the Hermann Goering Armored Division from reaching the beachhead, that division would have driven the initial seaborne forces back into the sea." Thus, a "busted" airborne operation can cause the enemy difficulties far out of proportion to the size of the airborne unit committed.

General MacArthur was apparently a great believer in the potential and value of the threat of airborne forces. He planned to use them on a number of occasions. Some of the operations never came off. For example, when the 11th Airborne was in its base camp at Dobodura on New Guinea in the summer of 1944, General MacArthur alerted the division for a possible jump farther up the island. But the alert was canceled even before the 11th Airborne troops were aware that they might be entering combat for the first time.

General MacArthur did, however, use his other airborne force, the 503d Parachute Infantry Regiment, in two airborne operations, one at Nadzab and the other at Noemfoor, before he committed them to the formidable task of jumping on Corregidor and wresting the island from the Japanese defenders.

In October 1942, the War Department ordered the 503d Regiment, still without its third battalion, to the Pacific theater. Col. Robert F. Sink had left the regiment to form the 506th Parachute Infantry Regiment at Taccoa, Georgia; and Col. Kenneth H. Kinsler, then commanding the 501st Battalion in Panama, was ordered to Fort Bragg to take over the 503d. On short order, the War Department instructed him to fly ahead to Australia to prepare for the arrival of the 503d; Lt. Col. Jack Tolson, as the executive officer of the regiment, led it overseas. Tolson had with him, in addition to the regimental staff and the two infantry battalions, Company A of the 504th Infantry Regiment from the newly formed 82d Airborne Division at Fort Bragg.

The trip to Australia began with the inevitable train ride across country, which, on a crowded, hot, troop train, crossing the vastness of the United States from Fort Bragg to San Francisco, seems endless. The troops gamble, read, commiserate, and occasionally get into trouble. The 503d was no exception. When their train stopped in Elko, Nevada, one afternoon to take on water and food, the sharp-eyed troopers saw a liquor store across the tracks. They enlisted the aid of some passersby, tossed money to them out of the train windows, and urged them to race to the liquor store for whatever libations were available. Even as the train was pulling out, the helpful civilians were still running back and forth to the liquor store. That evening on the train was far more uproarious than were the preceding, boring ones. Even a shakedown by the regimental officers failed to produce many contraband bottles. Perhaps some were even dissuaded from a thorough search with a drink or two.

The train finally arrived at Camp Stoneman, near Pittsburg, California, where the troops unloaded and made ready for the next leg of their trip to an unknown destination—unknown at least to the majority of the men in the 503d. Stoneman, situated in the more beautiful part of California, is flanked by scenic hills and lies in a fertile green valley about thirty-five miles northeast of San Francisco. It was designed for a specific purpose: readying a unit for overseas movement. Stoneman and its hundreds of administrators and logisticians, received a unit, supplied it with odd items of equipment that it might have been unable to procure previously, gave the men their pre-embarkation innoculations, fed the troops better than they had been fed in many months, entertained them with various movies, stage shows, and band concerts—all in a routine, expeditious, and gracious manner. Even some of the slow learners among the troops said that "they were being fattened for the kill."

For a few days, the out-processing soldiers were indoctrinated on such important matters as how to leave a sinking ship; how to climb up and down a rope ladder; how to find, wear, adjust, and operate individual life belts; where to find the life rafts; what was in the life-raft kit and how to operate it. Censorship of letters, with amazingly minor gripes by the troops, began at Stoneman and would continue throughout the war. Finally, the 503d troops boarded the converted Dutch freighter, the *Poelau Laut*, on the night of 19 October 1942.

The SS *Poelau Laut* was by no means a luxury liner. It was registered in Batavia, Java, and had been built in Amsterdam in 1929. She was 494 feet long and powered with an eight-cylinder oil engine. The crew was Indonesian. The men climbed up the steep gangplank, looked around for their designated holds, and pushed their way down into the cramped areas that would be their home for the next month or more. The holds, formerly for cargo, had been outfitted with tiers of bunks four and five high. Air conditioning was nonexistent. Even a nonclaustrophobic soldier began to feel a bit crushed.

At dawn on the twentieth, the *Poelau Laut* steamed down Suisun Bay, through Carquinez Strait, through San Pablo and San Francisco bays, and under the fabled Golden Gate Bridge. Even the hardened paratroopers felt pangs of nostalgia as they watched the orange bridge pass overhead and then fade from sight. They knew then that they were on their way—someplace.

The 503d's destination was still a mystery to the bulk of the paratroopers aboard. If one of them had had a compass and used it, he might have been surprised to learn that the ship was headed due south and not southwest or west, which he thought was the direction of combat.

On 1 November, the ship docked at Balboa in the Panama Canal Zone. No troops got off, but the 501st Parachute Infantry Battalion less its C Company came on board. The 503d Parachute Infantry Regiment was now complete. The 501st, under Lt. Col. George M. Jones, would become the 2d Battalion, 503d; and A Company, 504th, already aboard the *Poelau Laut*, would become D Company of the 2d Battalion, 503d.

The month-long trip on the crowded, hot, smelly troopship, wallowing across the vast stretch of the Pacific at twelve knots, could have been a disaster if the troops had not been kept busy and if discipline had not been enforced. Lieutenant Colonel Jones, now the senior officer aboard the *Poelau Laut*, because he ranked Jack Tolson, became the commander of all the 1,939 men and officers aboard the ship. He insisted on a full daily schedule of activities for all the troops. Their heterogeneous tasks, activities, and pastimes included standing the inevitable KP duty, sweating through paratrooper calisthenics, swabbing down the decks, cleaning personal equipment, standing inspections, and following the usual off-duty pursuits of reading, writing letters, and practically unavoidable gambling. Training continued. The regimental S-2 conducted classes on the size and intelligence of the Japanese soldier, which the troops discovered later was about 50 percent understated. They learned the hard way that the fighting Japanese soldier was bigger and smarter than they had been led to believe.

The medics continued their innoculations against smallpox, yellow fever, diphtheria, and tetanus. More than one paratrooper passed out when he received shots simultaneously in both arms and under his shoulder blade.

As the days aboard the *Poelau Laut* passed in seemingly endless monotony, the officers and men of the regiment were becoming a little more familiar with the man who joined them in Panama, Lt. Col. George M. Jones, West Point, class of 1935. By the time of the Corregidor jump and by virtue of the unusual death of Colonel Kinsler, who had gone ahead to Australia to make ready for the arrival of the regiment, Colonel Jones would later become the commander of the 503d.

In November 1942, George Jones was thirty-one years old. He was a well-built 5 feet 11 inches and weighed about 180 pounds. He liked to say that he graduated near the top of his class at West Point, but that was true, he added, only if you turned the graduation roster (arranged by academic rank) upside down. He also liked to say that he was in the upper 93 percent of his class.

After six years of the peacetime regular Army, he got wind of a new concept for warfare—the paratroopers, then being tested at Fort Benning, Georgia. In March 1941, he signed up, became the thirty-first officer qualified as a U.S. Army paratrooper, and joined the newly activated 501st Parachute Infantry Battalion. In September 1941, Captain Jones moved to Panama with the 501st as a company commander. In March 1942, Major Jones became the commander of the 501st and was promoted to lieutenant colonel in October 1942.

The man the 503d saw aboard the *Poelau Laut* as their commander was a slender, boyish-looking man whose looks belied his stern and no-nonsense approach to matters, particularly military and disciplinary. Aboard ship, some of the officers of the 503d had the temerity to purchase several cases of beer from the ship's steward and to drink them—contrary to the standing orders of no drinking aboard ship. Colonel Jones ordered the beer drinkers to the confines of their crowded and small quarters for a week, allowing them out only to march to meals. From that incident and because the troops had heard that somewhere in his past, presumably in Panama, he had served as a Military Police Officer, he was dubbed "The Warden."

Finally, after a 42-day trip, hardly what one would term a cruise, the troopship docked at Cairns, North Queensland, Australia, on 2 December 1942.

In Australia, the paratroopers settled down to building their camp out of pyramidal and squad tents. Once that chore was over, they trained, parachuted, and put on mass parachute jumps for visiting VIPs, including Generals MacArthur, Krueger, Eichelberger, and various Australian generals and dignitaries. Colonel Kinsler had reassumed command when the regiment docked in Australia. The high heat and humidity of their area of Australia acclimatized them for later combat in New Guinea and the Philippines.

On 7 August 1943, the regiment received general orders to move to New Guinea in preparation for combat operations. The troops left Australia by air and sea in the middle of August and moved into a large bivouac area near Port Moresby on New Guinea's southeastern tip.

The first combat test of the 503d was to be a jump on the Nadzab airfield in connection with the Lae operation. In General MacArthur's words:

My plan to advance in northeast New Guinea and to seize the Houn Peninsula was entrusted to what was called the New Guinea Force. It was largely composed of Australian troops under the command of General Blamey. My order to the Force was to seize and occupy the sector that contained Salamaua, Lae, Finschafen and Madang. Lae was to be the first main objective—its capture would breach the vital gate into the Houn Peninsula. The advance pushed the enemy back toward Salamaua with the purpose of deceiving him into the belief that it, and not Lae, was the prime objective.

General MacArthur continues:

On September 4th, the attack on Lae was launched by the Australians moving along the coast to strike from the east. At the same time, another Australian column was being prepared to fly in overland by way of the Markham Valley to strike from the west. The success of this second column depended upon the seizure of an unused prewar airfield at Nadzab. With this field in our possession, and made usable, we could land troops, close the gap, and completely envelop Lae and the enemy forces there.

It was a delicate operation involving the first major parachute jump in the Pacific War. The unit to make the jump was the United States 503d Parachute Regiment. I inspected them and found, as was only natural, a sense of nervousness among the ranks. I decided that it would be advisable for me to fly in with them.[18] I did not want them to go through their first baptism of fire without such comfort as my presence might bring to them. But they did not need me.[19]

One suspects also that the paratroopers did not know he was there.

At Port Moresby, a week before the drop, Colonel Kinsler assembled his battalion commanders and staff at his regimental headquarters and briefed them on their mission. The overall mission of the 503d, he said, was to drop on, seize, and hold the abandoned Nadzab airstrip. Australian engineers would come in and upgrade the strip to permit the landing of planes bringing in a complete Australian infantry division. That division, he continued, would attack Lae from the west, and the 503d would continue to secure the Nadzab airstrip.

---

18. Obviously, he was not going to jump in with them.
19. MacArthur, *Reminiscences,* p. 179.

He told Lt. Col. John W. Britten to jump his 1st Battalion directly onto the airfield and clear it of all enemy troops, although the intelligence available indicated that there were relatively few Japanese on the strip. He directed Lt. Col. George Jones to jump his 2d Battalion north of the field to provide flank protection for Britten's battalion. And he assigned Lt. Col. Jack Tolson and his 3d Battalion the task of jumping east of the field and securing the village of Gabmatzung.

In August 1943, the 503d had no attached or organic artillery. To make up for this deficiency, one week before the drop, General MacArthur's headquarters attached to the 503d thirty-one non-jump-qualified but jump-volunteer artillerymen of the Australian 2/4 Field Artillery Regiment and their two 25-pound artillery pieces. To Lt. Robert W. Armstrong of headquarters of the 1st Battalion fell the formidable task of training the Australians in the basic skills of jumping from an aircraft: plane-exit procedures, parachute checks, reserve-parachute operation, body positions, prelanding checks, landing falls, and chute control on the ground—especially in a wind. The Australian artillerymen learned to disassemble the 25-pounders and pack them in parachutable bundles. By 5 September, they were ready to go.

Three days before the jump, Colonel Kinsler arranged for his staff and his three battalion commanders to make a high-altitude aerial reconnaissance of the target area. When they returned to Port Moresby, Colonel Kinsler gathered his company commanders together and briefed them on the mission. The troops, however, had not yet been informed of the pending operation. But they sensed something was up: their officers went to secret meetings, and C-47s kept arriving on the airstrip outside Port Moresby. Finally, on 4 September, the day before the drop, the company commanders assembled their companies and spelled out in some detail their companies' missions.

On 4 September, the 9th Australian Division under Maj. Gen. G. F. Wooten landed amphibiously twenty miles to the east of Lae in the Bula River area against very light opposition. However, by midmorning, Japanese bombers attacked the congested beaches. The bombers returned in late afternoon and, in spite of being intercepted by U.S. P-47s, managed to damage two ships and kill more than one hundred Australian and American seamen.

That evening, the 9th Division moved out to the west against the Japanese in the Lae area.

Predawn conditions at the Port Moresby airstrips, Ward and Jackson, on 5 September, the day of the planned airborne assault, threatened to abort the mission. As the troops were getting out of their bedrolls and trying to eat the usual soggy pancakes with a sugar-and-water syrup, the weather started to turn bad. By the time they had been trucked to the departure airfields, the rains came, and the airstrips were socked in with fog. Takeoff had been scheduled for 0530, but at that time the fog and light rain completely enveloped the strips. However, by 0730 the fog began to dissipate rapidly. A weather plane over the saddle of the Owen Stanley Mountains radioed back an all clear. The mission was on. The troopers strapped themselves into their parachutes and about eighty pounds of combat gear and began to climb aboard their assigned aircraft. At 0825, the first of seventy-nine C-47s of Col. Paul H. Prentiss's 54th Troop Carrier Wing roared down the runway; in less than thirty minutes seventeen hundred men of the 503d were airborne, in the literal sense.

General Kenney, the Fifth Air Force commander, made certain that the troop carrier convoy would not be defenseless en route to the Nadzab airstrip. He assigned one hundred fighter aircraft to protect the slow-moving and necessarily bunched up transports. Ahead of the troop carrier column, General Kenney placed six squadrons of B-25s, each loaded with eight .50-caliber machine guns and 120 fragmentation bombs in the bomb bays. The mission of the B-25s was to strafe the drop zones just minutes before the jump. Six smoke-laying A-20s followed the B-25s to lay smoke alongside the DZs just before the drop to screen the descending paratroopers from snipers.

Flying high above these three hundred or so massed aircraft were three heavily armed B-17s—one carried General Kenney, another General MacArthur, and the third was protection for the first two. And above the three bombers flew six P-47s, ready to pounce on any Japanese aircraft that might have the temerity to attempt to infiltrate this armada. After all, kamikazes were not yet in vogue in the Japanese air force. This was 1943; the Japanese were not yet desperate.

The C-47s flew across the saddle of the Owen Stanley range

at an altitude of nine thousand feet and then descended to thirty-five hundred feet as they approached the U.S. airfield at Marilinan. Above Marilinan, the transports rearranged their flight into three columns, each six planes wide. There were some twenty-six C-47s in each column, and each column carried one battalion of the 503d. As the planes approached the drop zones, they descended to treetop level and hedgehopped toward the DZs. The bumpiness of the last part of the ride, the heat at the low altitude, and the traces of the soggy breakfasts did little to improve the airworthiness of the paratroopers. By the time they reached Nadzab, they were anxious for the green light.

As the columns crossed the Markham River, they ascended to their prescribed jump altitude of between four hundred and five hundred feet, a relatively low altitude for a drop but low enough to limit the time a paratrooper is in the air and a possible target for a sniper on the ground. At 1009, the red warning lights flashed on near the jump doors of the C-47s. The jumpmasters shouted, "Stand up and hook up," "Check equipment," and "Sound off for equipment check." "Close in the door" bunched the men together as closely as possible for rapid jumps and tight landing patterns. At 1021, the troopers were ready to jump. At 1022, the green light flashed on, and the first man in each of the three battalion columns swung out of the door to his left, grabbed his reserve, tucked his head into his chest, and waited for the opening shock—often a neck-snapping but welcome jolt. In rapid succession the twenty or twenty-one men in each of the sticks followed the lead jumper. In four and a half minutes, the entire regiment was on its way to the ground. The pilots of Colonel Prentiss's 54th Troop Carrier Wing had, for the first time in the war, dropped a regiment of paratroopers with pinpoint accuracy on the assigned drop zones. High above the drop, General MacArthur watched the proceedings with gleeful enthusiasm and ardent approval. "One plane after another poured out its stream of dropping men over the target field," he reminisced. "Everything went like clockwork. The vertical envelopment became a reality.

"We closed in from all sides and entered the shambles that had been Lae on September 16th.

"To my astonishment, I was awarded the Air Medal. Like all ground officers, this exceptionally pleased me, even though I felt it did me too much credit." Some of the paratroopers on the ground might have agreed.

Jack Tolson's 3d Battalion was the lead battalion in the regimental column; he was, of course, jumpmaster of the lead ship in that formation. Fortunately, he had been over the DZ a few days before in a B-25 that had been on a bombing mission over Lae. He was fortunate to have had some idea of where his DZ was because while he was standing in the door of the plane after having been given the red light by the pilot, the red light went off, but the green jump light did not come on. He immediately glanced back out the door and recognized that he was, in fact, over the proper DZ. Therefore, he decided to jump without the green "go" light. Not only did the stick in his plane follow him out, but so did the rest of the jumpers in his battalion because all jumpmasters took their cue from the lead ship. Jack Tolson had wasted a few seconds checking for the green light and, therefore, landed a bit farther down the DZ than he had intended. But, fortunately, the mass of the battalion was with him. Later, he checked with his plane's pilot and found that when the copilot switched off the red light, he left the switch in the neutral position, thinking that he had turned on the green light. Jack Tolson's quick thinking and previous trip over the DZ saved the day. In retrospect, Jack Tolson thinks that "our jump on the Markham Valley was a classic airborne operation."

General MacArthur obviously agreed with him. General Kenney later wrote to Gen. Hap Arnold that during the jump General MacArthur was "jumping up and down like a kid." When Generals Kenney and MacArthur landed at Port Moresby, MacArthur told Kenney that the drop was "the most perfect example of training and discipline he had ever witnessed."

Once on the ground and surrounding the airfield, the paratroopers were faced not so much with Japanese resistance, which was negligible, but with the suffocating heat, the enervating humidity, and the eight-foot-tall, razor-sharp kunai grass that covered the drop zones and through which the men had to hack their way with machetes to get to their assembly areas. From the air, the kunai grass had looked short and inoffensive; on the ground, it was a formidable obstacle—not unlike a field of the notoriously sharp Spanish bayonet.

But in short order, the three 503d battalions were on their assigned objectives, the Australian engineers had moved to the Nadzab strip, and by the next day the strip had been sufficiently cleared to permit the landing of C-47s carrying the lead elements of the Australian 7th Division. By the tenth, the Aussies had relieved the 503d of its mission of defending the Nadzab airfield.

Because bad weather prevented the arrival of all of the Australian 7th Division and because the aggressive Aussie 25th Brigade, attacking down the Markham River toward Lae, had its rear exposed, Gen. Sir Thomas Blamey, commander of the Australian 7th Division, asked for and got permission to use the 3d Battalion of the 503d to protect the tail of the 25th. On 14 September, Jack Tolson and his 3d Battalion moved down the Markham Valley to the Jalu village area, about halfway between Lae and Nadzab. There Jack Tolson set up a base of operations and sent out numerous patrols in all directions to prevent the Japanese from attacking the 25th from the north and west and to keep open the 25th's supply lines from the airstrip at Nadzab. The battalion ran into several small groups of the enemy who were escaping to the north from the Lae area. Under General Vasey's orders, the battalion also sought to cut off the escape of large numbers of the Japanese Imperial 51st Division.

On the fifteenth, I Company of the 3d Battalion ran into a large group of the Japanese north of Log Crossing village. The lead elements of the company, especially the platoon commanded by Lt. Lyle Murphy, had a fierce firefight with a large mass of the enemy. The firefight lasted from 1600 until almost dark; Jack Tolson sent forward additional companies from the battalion, and they dug in for the night around the village.

Even nature gave the 3d Battalion a jolt. Before dawn on the sixteenth, a severe earthquake rocked the area where the troops had dug in. The shock knocked down large trees and shook the area. The rumble and the quivering did little more, however, than alert the troops. The man-made quakes they were to feel later on Corregidor were far more formidable, deadly, and ominous. By midmorning of the sixteenth, a patrol of Australians, operating from the Lae area, moved across the stream below Company H's outposts. With this linkup, General Vasey relieved the

3d Battalion of its mission, and the battalion returned to Nadzab for aerial evacuation.

On 14 September, the Aussie engineers had completed two parallel, 6,000-foot runways at Nadzab. And by the sixteenth, Lae had fallen to the two Australian divisions converging from the northwest and the east. On the seventeenth, the 503d was relieved of its mission at Nadzab and started its flight back to Port Moresby. By the nineteenth, the regiment was closed in its base camp.

Even the Japanese admired the work of the 503d. After the war, Colonel Shinoara, intelligence officer of the Japanese Eighth Army, which was defending the Lae-Salamaua area, said: "We were retreating from the Salamaua area over the Finistere Mountains toward Reiss Point when Allied paratroopers landed at Nadzab, which was one place where we thought the enemy would never attack. The remaining elements of our 51st Division were virtually cut in half by this surprise pincer movement."[20]

The 503d in its first taste of combat had had a number of casualties. Three men were killed on the jump, two when their chutes malfunctioned, and one when he landed in a tall tree and then fell to his death after sliding part of the way down on his jump rope. Thirty-three men were injured on the jump. Eight men were killed and twelve were wounded in the actions that followed. Most of these men were with Jack Tolson and his 3d Battalion.

General MacArthur showed his pride in the 503d with a radio message to Colonel Kinsler.

Advanced Echelon
General Headquarters
By Courier

18 September 1943

COLONEL KINSLER
Now that the fall of Lae is an accomplished fact I wish to make of record the splendid and important part taken by five nought

---

20. Quoted in Devlin, *Paratrooper,* p. 266.

three parachute infantry regiment stop under your able leadership cma officers and men exhibited the highest order of combat efficiency stop please express to all ranks my gratification and deep pride

MACARTHUR

Official:
N./S./W.Allen
Lt. Col., AGD
Asst. Adjutant General

At Nadzab, the 503d had exhibited its prowess as an airborne regiment and that it could mount a parachute operation with skill, discipline, and speed. These were qualities that the 503d would need in abundance when it made its airborne assault on Corregidor—an assault that would be unique in the history of airborne warfare. But before it would be called upon to test its mettle, competence, and courage on Corregidor, it would have to undergo other tests by fire; Noemfoor was the next airborne operation on its schedule.

CHAPTER VIII
Noemfoor

After a few weeks back at Port Moresby, the troops were restless. The weather was hot, humid, and wet. Many of the paratroopers were suffering from the usual tropical diseases—jungle rot, a fungus infection of the skin, especially the feet, from wearing wet boots and socks for days at a time; malaria; scrub typhus; Japanese river fever (the ague); and dysentery. In addition, the food was barely edible—nothing fresh, bully beef often, dehydrated potatoes that the cooks managed to reduce to rocklike pebbles, dehydrated eggs that bore a resemblance to the real things only in color, and jungle butter, which was advertised not to melt in the tropics. It did not—nor did it in a trooper's stomach. But the regiment licked its wounds; trained replacements; fired weapons; trained in "the field"; and, in their off-duty hours, went to outdoor movies, played cards, talked endlessly, drank an occasional beer, usually warm, and reveled in the infrequent USO shows that made their way to the area.

Col. Ken Kinsler, the 503d regimental commander, was personable, smart, and a "staff officer type," according to one officer who knew him well. He was an introvert, a man "improperly assigned as a leader of a Parachute Regiment." He made frequent parachute jumps because apparently he was afraid of losing his nerve to jump. But before each jump, he had the regimental surgeon, Major "Jock" Gall, tape his ankles. Both of them "made a big thing about preparations" for a jump. Behind his back, the troopers referred to him as "Egg Shell." Apparently, he was not a "soldier's soldier."

The commanding general of Sixth Army sent his inspector general to the 503d base camp to investigate the condition of the regiment. The inspector general spent three days interrogating various officers and men and looking at the records of the 503d. The inspector general debriefed Colonel Kinsler and then left.

That evening, 22 October, Colonel Kinsler invited his four lieutenant colonels—the executive officer and the three battalion commanders—to his tent "for a drink." "Liquor was pretty scarce," General Jones remembers, "so we didn't turn down the invitation. We had a drink and a friendly conversation." It was, seemingly, an ordinary evening with the five officers talking and ruminating about what's next? Colonel Kinsler seemed not at all tense or under any strain. He had undoubtedly already made up his mind to take a final, drastic action.

Sometime after the four lieutenant colonels left Colonel Kinsler's tent, he walked to a nearby gravel pit and, in the dark New Guinea night, committed suicide. No one ever found a note that might have explained his extreme solution to whatever problems he thought he had. The next day his body was found in the gravel pit, which was just outside the base camp at Port Moresby.

Word of the suicide got to Lt. Col. Joe Lawrie, the regimental executive officer, during the morning of the twenty-third. He immediately sent for George Jones, the senior officer in the regiment, who was out in the field training his battalion. He arrived at the regimental command post about noon and immediately assumed command of the regiment.

General Krueger, commanding general of Sixth Army, had his headquarters on Good Enough Island. He directed Colonel Jones to report to him there. He met with Jones in his tent. After Jones had saluted and reported to General Krueger, the general said, "Jones, how old are you?" Colonel Jones answered, "Thirty-two, sir." General Krueger then said, "I had more years of service than that before you were born." Then General Krueger continued with his welcome to the new 503d commander: "Jones, I don't know anything about you. You have assumed command of the 503d Regiment because you are the senior lieutenant colonel. I am not going to recommend your promotion. Of course, if you do well at some future date, I will recommend your promotion. If you don't, I'll be forced to relieve you." Colonel Jones later made the comment, "To the point, eh?"

Shortly after Colonel Jones assumed command of the regiment, he asked for Maj. "Jock" Gall's reassignment because he felt that he was not giving the proper leadership to the other medical officers in the regiment. Three or four months later, in an unusual coincidence, Major Gall also committed suicide.

General Krueger was as good as his word and waited for Colonel Jones to prove himself. Lieutenant Colonel Jones was promoted to full colonel in July 1944.

Colonel Jones was a positive, strong-willed, firm, self-possessed commander. Recently, he expressed his leadership style in a letter:

> My philosophy of command was to put out as few orders as possible. To simplify the task of seeing that they were carried out, ascertain by roll call that everyone got the word. After forty-eight hours had passed, find an officer who was not obeying the order and promptly courtmartial him for disobedience to orders. I found after doing this a couple of times that I got excellent responses and compliance to my few orders.

For the next couple of months, the 503d carried on its training mission in and around Port Moresby. General Krueger, meanwhile, was developing plans for the capture of Rabaul, on the eastern tip of New Britain Island. "Rabaul," said General MacArthur, was his "primary goal in 1943." He wanted "to cut off the major Japanese naval staging area, the menacing airfields, and the bulging supply bases at Rabaul." In 1943, Rabaul alone was manned by more than 135,000 Japanese troops of their army, navy, and air force.

To seize New Britain and Rabaul, General MacArthur assigned to General Krueger the 1st Marine Division, the 32d Infantry Division, the 503d Parachute Infantry Regiment, and the 632d Tank Destroyer Battalion. This was the Alamo Force. On 22 September, MacArthur's headquarters directed the Alamo Force to seize the Cape Gloucester area on the western tip of New Britain,

to establish airfields on Cape Gloucester, and to prepare to participate in the reduction of the huge Japanese naval and air base at
Rabaul.

General Krueger assigned the 503d to the Backhander Task
Force under Maj. General William H. Rupertus (USMC), commander of the 1st Marine Division. Backhander Task Force's mission was to seize Cape Gloucester airfields and establish control
over the western end of New Britain. In addition to the 503d,
General Rupertus had parts of his division and the 12th Marine
Defense Battalion. General Rupertus intended to drop the 503d
near the Cape Gloucester airfields in conjunction with the amphibious landing of his Marine elements on Cape Gloucester's beaches
on the twenty-sixth of December.

Once again, however, circumstances over which the 503d had
no control canceled out their participation in an airborne operation
for which they had been alerted. General Kenney told General
Krueger that, to make room for enough transport planes at Dobodura to lift the 503d to Cape Gloucester, he would have to move
a heavy bombardment group from Dobodura to Port Moresby
on the western side of the Owen Stanley range. General Krueger
realized that "the frequent heavy-weather fronts over the Owen
Stanley range raised doubts as to effective support from Moresby;
and to assure this support, the group was kept at Dobodura and
the 503d deleted from the Backhander troop list."

General Krueger could have committed the 503d to the Cape
Gloucester area piecemeal, using a few transports that could have
squeezed onto the Dobodura airfields. But he decided against
that option, which would have had two strikes against it from
the start.

The Marines invaded Cape Gloucester, and the air forces pum-
meled the shipping in the harbor and the airfields at Rabaul. By
the end of January, the Marines had established a comfortable
perimeter around Cape Gloucester, Rabaul was isolated, and the
Japanese aircraft that ventured out from Rabaul to attack the
advancing Allied forces, some seventy to eighty at a time, were
shot down "by the dozens" by American P-38s. Rabaul, that once-
formidable bastion of the Japanese in the South Pacific, was no
longer a threat. More than 135,000 Japanese were still dug in at

Rabaul, but they were isolated and impotent. They were still there at the end of the war.

In January 1944, Colonel Jones, sensing the frustration and boredom of his regiment, requested General Krueger either to commit his regiment to combat or to send it back to Australia for R and R. For some reason, General Krueger decided to send the regiment to Australia. The 503d thus spent the next eight weeks at Camp Cable, about thirty miles outside Brisbane.

Camp Cable had been a jungle-warfare training center for Australian units and for the U.S. 32d Division. Once at Cable, Colonel Jones granted leaves for the men to the nearby larger cities and weekend passes to the nearer towns and villages. The usual training, jumping, and integration of new men into the units were the order of the day at Cable.

In the spring of 1944, General MacArthur's Allied offensive was moving rapidly up the coast of New Guinea; Admiral Nimitz's forces waded ashore and fought on the islands of the central Pacific. By early April, the 503d was on its way back to the combat zone. The regiment left Camp Cable on 8 April 1944 aboard another Dutch island ocean liner, the SS *Van Der Lijn*. The ship touched land at Milne Bay, New Guinea, but the troops did not debark. The following day, 16 April, the ship pulled into Oro Bay, and the troops unloaded in the Dobodura area. The 503d established a base camp at Cape Sudest and settled down to the usual life of troops waiting for a combat mission—they were hot, the weather was humid and rainy, and the days in the field were boring. Soon, however, they were to be back in combat in the Hollandia operation—they were still hot and wet, but they were not bored.

On 22 April, Lt. Gen. Robert Eichelberger, with two divisions— the 41st, commanded by Maj. Gen. Horace H. Fuller, and the 24th, commanded by Maj. Gen. Frederick A. Irving—launched his two-pronged attack, dubbed Operation Reckless, against Hollandia in Humboldt Bay and, to the west, against Tanahmerah Bay, about twenty-five miles west of Hollandia. There were about eleven thousand Japanese troops at Hollandia, only five hundred of whom were combat troops. The Japanese had no plans for the defense of the areas nor even enough arms for the service troops who garrisoned the towns. The Allied landings completely surprised the Japanese, and they fled into the interior when warships supporting the landings opened fire.

Between Humboldt Bay and Tanahmerah Bay were the Cyclops Mountains, to the west of which the Japanese had built three substantial airfields bordering narrow Lake Sentani. The two divisions of Eichelberger's command double-enveloped the mountains, and by 26 April, all three of the airfields were in American hands, but thousands of Japanese combat and service troops were still at large.

General MacArthur had launched the attack on Hollandia using his highly successful strategy of leap-frogging enemy strong points, setting up his own bases and airfields, and then allowing the Japanese to "wither on the vine," to be subdued later by follow-up forces—usually Australian—moving up the vast reaches of the island. He needed the Hollandia area on which to base heavy bombers in support of his drive toward the Philippines and Nimitz's operations in the Marianas and Palaus. Unfortunately, the soil near Hollandia was too soft to support heavy bombers until the engineers had done extensive work. Eventually, but behind schedule, Hollandia would become a major air and naval base.

On 2 June, the 503d boarded C-47s at the Dobodura strip and flew into Cyclops Field, one of the three airstrips captured from the Japanese in the early assault on Hollandia. After landing, the 503d moved to a bivouac area about seven miles to the south of Hollandia. The mission of the 503d was to guard the airfield on which they had landed, to protect the advanced headquarters of General Krueger's Sixth Army at Hollekang, to patrol the area to a radius of about fifteen miles, and, according to General Krueger, "to be ready for employment on Biak if that should become necessary." As events turned out, it would not be necessary.

The 503d met relatively little resistance, and the Japanese they did meet were demoralized and sickly. The 503d's greatest enemy was the jungle, with its thick canopy, enervating heat, and stifling humidity. During the month-long patrolling action, the regimental units killed some 56 Japanese, mostly stragglers, and captured 12 men, 11 of whom were Formosan laborers and one who was a crewman of a Japanese merchant ship. The regiment suffered only one casualty, a man slightly wounded in action. The entire Hollandia-Aitape operation had cost the Japanese some 12,153 killed and 819 captured. "Our own losses were disproportionately lower," was General Krueger's modest report.

General MacArthur wrote of the invasion:

> The Hollandia invasion initiated a marked change in the tempo of my advance westward. Subsequent assaults against Wakde, Biak, Noemfoor, and Sansapor were mounted in quick succession, and, in contrast to previous campaigns, I planned no attempt to complete all phases of one operation before moving on to the next objective. I was determined to reach the Philippines before December, and consequently concentrated on the immediate utilization of each seized position to spark the succeeding advance.[21]

On 27 May, the 41st Division, under Maj. Gen. Horace H. Fuller, waded ashore on the beaches of southern Biak near Bosnek against relatively light opposition. But that light initial Japanese response to the invasion gave no hint of what was to come. The Japanese used the peculiar terrain of Biak to devise a brilliant defense. Colonel Naoyuki Kuzume, the Japanese commander of the eleven thousand men on Biak, a third of whom were combat forces, positioned the bulk of his units in the rugged coral hill masses and caves of the island and waited patiently until the American forces tried to move up into the hills. Then his units poured deadly artillery and machine gun fire onto the beaches and airfields. The caves held thousands of men, amply supplied with ammunition, food, and, most important of all, water. Each advance of the Americans was met with accurate and heavy fire from the crevices and creases in the hills. On one occasion, the Japanese even surprised the attacking forces by using five-ton tanks, which, however, were no match for the Americans' Shermans. The fierce battle for Biak raged until 22 July. It was only after persistent aerial reconnaissance found the entrances to the caves that the attacking forces were able to defeat the tenacious enemy. Units

---

21. MacArthur, *Reminiscences,* p. 192.

of the 41st poured hundreds of gallons of gasoline into the entrance of the main tunnel complex and ignited it. The engineers lowered a charge of 850 pounds of TNT into the cave and blew it. Hundreds of Japanese died in the fire and explosion. This kind of warfare was a small preview of what was to come on Corregidor.

By 21 June, the defenders were desperate. Colonel Kuzume presided over a ceremony in which the Japanese flag was burned. Then he directed all men able to walk to evacuate the caves in which they were hiding for a final assault against the Biak Task Force. He distributed hand grenades to the wounded and then set the example: he committed hara-kiri. The fight for Biak was finally over.

The tenacity and strength of the Japanese on Biak surprised and puzzled the U.S. commander. Eichelberger, who had relieved General Fuller on 18 June, finally discovered that the Japanese brought in replacements at night by barge from Noemfoor.

Noemfoor became General MacArthur's next target in his relentless and determined drive toward the Philippines. Seizing Noemfoor would stop the flow of Japanese replacements and provide him with two or three more airfields along his path to vindication—a return to Manila.

Noemfoor Island, only fifteen miles long and twelve miles wide, lies about seventy-five nautical miles due west of Biak. On it, the Japanese had partially developed three airfields, Kornasoren, Kamiri, and Namber. Kamiri, with a strip about five thousand feet long and ample side taxiways for parking and dispersal areas, was the one most developed. It was on the northwest corner of the island, which was shaped like a catcher's mitt. But it was to prove to be a terrible drop zone for the 503d. Even so, it was far more forgiving than the two postage-stamp-size drop zones on Corregidor would prove to be.

Operation Tabletennis, code name for the seizure of Noemfoor, really got underway on 20 June when the Allied air forces began to bomb the small island, particularly the airdromes; By H-hour, 0730 on 2 July 1944, the Fifth Air Force had pounded the island with more than eight thousand tons of bombs. Beginning at H minus 80 on D-day, three cruisers, twenty-three destroyers and three LCIs armed with rockets opened fire on the Kamiri beach area and on enemy fortifications near Namber. At H minus 15, the naval gunfire shifted to the flanks of Kamiri beach, and thirty-three B-24s bombed enemy shore defenses while six B-25s and fifteen A-20s, on call, strafed and bombed enemy positions on the high ground south of and near the ends of Kamiri airfield. General Krueger's G-2 had estimated that the enemy had about 1,750 troops on the island but that he might be able to increase that number to 3,250 before the landing. The G-2 estimated that most of the Japanese were combat troops of Colonel Shimizu's 219th Infantry Regiment. General Krueger later wrote that "considering the presumably weak enemy forces on Noemfoor, the

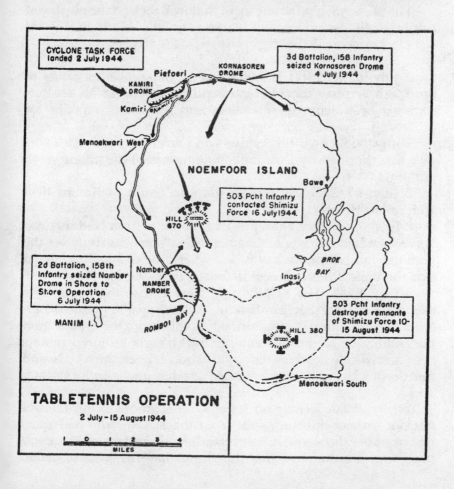

CYCLONE TASK FORCE
landed 2 July 1944

3d Battalion, 158 Infantry
seized Kornasoren Drome
4 July 1944

Piefoeri

KORNASOREN
DROME

KAMIRI
DROME

Kamiri

Menoekwari West

NOEMFOOR ISLAND

Bawe

503 Pcht Infantry
contacted Shimizu
Force 16 July 1944.

HILL
670

2d Battalion, 158th
Infantry seized Namber
Drome in Shore to
Shore Operation
6 July 1944

Namber

NAMBER
DROME

Inasi

BROE
BAY

MANIM I.

ROMBOI BAY

HILL 380

503 Pcht Infantry
destroyed remnants
of Shimizu Force 10-
15 August 1944

Menoekwari South

TABLETENNIS OPERATION

2 July – 15 August 1944

1 0 1 2 3 4
MILES

preliminary bombardment may seem unduly heavy. But I felt it was better to use gunfire and bombing liberally than expose my ground troops, in particular my infantry, to unnecessary losses."

Nor was General Krueger going in with the odds against him as far as the size of the attacking force was concerned. The Noemfoor Task Force, under the command of Brig. Gen. Edwin D. Patrick, was composed of the 158th Regimental Combat Team (Reinforced). In all, his units numbered 8,069 combat troops, 5,495 service troops, and about 10,000 Air Corps men. General Patrick also had the 503d Parachute Infantry Regiment and the 34th Infantry Regiment in reserve.

The prelanding softening up of Yellow Beach on the northwest corner of the island, and the landing of the 158th RCT went like clockwork on D-day, 2 July.

2 July, 0500. Forty LCMs carrying the combat elements of the 158th lie three thousand yards offshore. The LCMs are surrounded by twenty-one Australian and American warships for protection.

2 July, 0640. Escorting cruisers and destroyers unleash a barrage that thunders over the crouching figures of the infantrymen in their LCMs.

2 July, 0745. Naval gunfire shifts to flanks of Kamiri field and Yellow Beach.

2 July, 0746. Thirty-three B-24 Liberators from Nadzab drop 108 tons of antipersonnel fragmentation bombs directly on the high ground behind Yellow Beach where the G-2 had estimated that the bulk of the Japanese defenses were dug in.

2 July, 0747. The LCMs begin their run to the beach over the wide coral reef that lies offshore; B-24s drop 500-pound demolition bombs behind Kamiri airfield; A-20s strafe the area behind the landing beach; an LCI equipped with eight hundred rockets fires a salvo; the rockets flare and whoosh over the LCMs and rain down with pulverizing, widespread effect on the entire landing area.

2 July, 0800. Exactly on schedule, the troops begin to land but not without difficulty—not from the enemy, who had withdrawn under the devastating prelanding air and naval firepower but from the coral reef that the troops have to cross to get to

land. The coral reef is pitted with deep depressions that were totally hidden from the aerial photos and from the LCMs. Initially, shallow-draft Buffaloes and DUKWs unloaded equipment and supplies, but shortly the demolition teams blast channels through the coral, and the deeper-draft ships come ashore. Fortunately, the Japanese had not planted any underwater obstacles or mines.

The first waves of wading infantrymen find no Japanese opposition on the beaches. The Japanese do fire sporadically some mortars and artillery from the hills—some of which hits the beaches—but the few Japanese who are around the airfield are so stunned by the prelanding softening up that they are totally ineffective. Others have fled to caves in the coral terrace south of Kamiri.

2 July, 0900. The infantrymen of the 158th quickly put up a perimeter defense and send out patrols to clear out the nearby caves; immediately after they come ashore, three combat and airfield engineer battalions, equipped with bulldozers, heavy trucks, and graders, start to improve the Kamiri runway by filling in the craters and smoothing the runway. Infantrymen along the perimeter of the airfield run into a small detachment of Japanese. After a brief firefight, a few wounded Japanese are taken prisoner. One of them tells his interrogator that a week before the landing three thousand Japanese reinforcements had landed on Noemfoor.

2 July, 1115. General Patrick, concerned about the report and under orders to secure the other two airfields on the island, radios General Krueger and requests the prompt dispatch of the 503d to reinforce his troops. "Late on D-day" (General Krueger's estimate), General Krueger receives General Patrick's request for the 503d. He immediately orders the 503d to proceed by air to Noemfoor.

General Krueger's order to Colonel Jones does not take him by surprise. As soon as he had learned that his regiment was in reserve for Operation Tabletennis, Colonel Jones ordered twenty-two hundred freshly packed personnel parachutes to be sent by air from the 503d's rear base near Gordonvale, Queensland, Australia. By 1 July, the chutes had arrived at Hollandia. In addition, he had proceeded on the assumption that the regiment would drop (rather than air-land) on Noemfoor. He arranged for sand tables, maps, and briefings to inform all his men of the coming operation. He also arranged for his battalion commanders and certain of the regimental staff officers to fly over Noemfoor's Kamiri airfield in four separate reconnaissance flights.

On the afternoon of 30 June, thirty-eight planes of the 54th Troop Carrier Wing arrived at Hollandia. On 1 July, the wing commander ordered a practice flight to stress formation flying and proper airspeed and altitude for dropping troops. The jump-masters for the first day's drop flew along. Lt. Larry Browne, the regimental operations officer, supervised the preparation of the planes for the jump—removing cargo doors, taping sharp protuberances near the doors, setting up a parking plan, and arranging for thirty-eight trucks, each numbered the same as the plane that would carry the men, to assemble at the regimental command post if and when the regiment was ordered to drop.

3 July, 0300. The trucks report to the command post. The 1st Battalion, 503d, commander, Maj. Cameron Knox, supervises the truck loading of his battalion, slated to drop first on Kamiri airfield. The 3d Battalion, under Maj. John R. Erickson, will drop on 4 July, and the 2d Battalion, under Lt. Col. John W. Britten, will drop on 5 July.

3 July, 0505. The 1st Battalion arrives at Cyclops airfield, Hollandia. The men detruck, finish their final checks and inspections for the jump, and climb aboard the C-47s at 0615.

3 July, 0630. The first C-47, carrying Colonel Jones as jump-master, takes off for Noemfoor. The following planes take off and form into Vs in trail, a three-ship-wide formation. The plan is for the planes to form into a column two planes wide, echeloned to the right rear for the drop itself. The width of Kamiri is only two hundred feet, and this narrowness dictated the alignment of the planes. But even two planes wide would prove to be too much. A Canadian paratroop officer assigned to the Tabletennis staff had advised General Patrick that the troop carriers should fly in single file because of the width of the area. Unfortunately, this message did not get to the Fifth Air Force until the planes were airborne and well on their way to Noemfoor. It was too late to change the formation.

3 July, 0930. George Jones stands in the door of the lead C-47 and watches the water beneath the plane. Noemfoor is not

far ahead. Colonel Jones thinks to himself that they seem "pretty low for a drop" but attributes it to the fact that they are over smooth water and he could be deceived; his jump altitude, after all, was only four hundred feet.

3 July, 1000. Colonel Jones's pilot gives him the green light. Colonel Jones jumps. He oscillates only once and hits the runway with a bone-crushing crash. He smashes his head against the coral and is saved from a crushed skull by his steel helmet. But the headache lingers for several days.

His premonition had been correct: his pilot had failed to adjust the plane's altimeter and, as a result, dropped him and his stick from a height of 175 feet, a radically unsafe jump altitude for paratroopers.

The remainder of the formation, fortunately, was at four hundred feet—a barely safe altitude. In twenty minutes, 739 men of the 1st Battalion and the regimental staff jumped on Kamiri. There were 72 jump injuries sustained by the paratroopers who landed hard on bulldozers, parked LCMs, trucks, and other military construction equipment used by the engineers to improve the runway. The most seriously injured were the men who had jumped from the first two planes. Of the 18 men in Colonel Jones's plane, 9 were critically injured from their bone-jarring landings with chutes just barely opened. Colonel Jones's enlisted aide, who jumped just before he did, broke both legs. The battalion commander, Major Knox, suffered a broken foot and had to be evacuated a few days later. A radio operator broke his back. The high percentage of injuries might have been acceptable if some of them had been caused by the enemy. But in this case, none was.

4 July, 0955. The 3d Battalion, led by Maj. John Erickson in the first plane, begin their jumps. This time, the planes are in single file at 400 feet, and General Patrick has ordered the military vehicles pulled back off the runway into the jungle that borders it. Nonetheless, the coral runway, the DZ, is like concrete. The T-5 parachute worn by the troopers had a 28-foot canopy and lowered a man none too gently under the best of field conditions. But coral is not grass. The 3d Battalion suffered 56 jump casualties —more than 8 percent—an unacceptable injury rate. Of the 1,424 men of the 503d who jumped on Noemfoor, 128 suffered severe

injuries. The regiment lost one battalion commander, three rifle company commanders, the regimental communications officer, and several squad and platoon sergeants.

On the ground, Colonel Jones had had enough of watching his regiment shatter itself on the coral of Kamiri. He told General Patrick that the 2d Battalion, under Lt. Col. John Britten, should not jump in but should be brought in by landing craft. General Patrick agreed and notified General Krueger of his request. General Krueger approved and ordered the 2d Battalion, 503d, to fly from Hollandia to Biak and then sail by LCI to Noemfoor.

Forty-some years after this operation, one must question the wisdom of dropping paratroopers onto a heavy-equipment-lined coral runway that is completely in friendly hands, especially when a fully and heavily equipped 34th Infantry Regiment was on Biak and could have been on Noemfoor in ten hours, ready to fight before midnight of D-day. It took two full days for two very lightly equipped parachute battalions to land on the island, incurring a very high—9 percent—jump-casualty rate. Besides that, when the 158th landed on Noemfoor, Japanese strength was about twenty-five hundred; the POW who reported three thousand more either didn't know or lied.

After the 1st and 3d battalions of the 503d had closed in on the Kamiri airfield, they and the 158th extended the perimeter with vigorous patrolling, especially to the south and the southwest. On the night of 4 July, the Japanese launched their only offensive operation of the Noemfoor campaign. The 1st Battalion of the 158th had established a night perimeter around a Japanese garden area near the town of Kamiri village. The garden was overgrown with tropical fruits and bushes. The 158th called for protective fires on the incline that approached the garden area. The 641st Tank Destroyer Battalion and the 147th Field Artillery Battalion responded with mortars and artillery fire. But the Japanese in the area were undaunted. In the dark of the morning of the fifth, Colonel Shimizu ordered an attack by his 219th Infantry Regiment against the perimeter of the 158th around the garden. The forward observers for the artillery and the mortars and the machine gunners of the 158th were ready. Their concentrated fires broke the attack, and the perimeter held. The Japanese offensive cost the attackers more than four hundred casualties. Thereafter, the enemy broke contact and drifted to the south of the island.

On 6 July, based again on information from a Japanese POW that Namber airfield was virtually abandoned, General Patrick ordered the 2d Battalion of the 158th to land at Namber on the southwest corner of the island. At the same time, a detachment of the 2d Battalion, 503d Parachute Infantry, went ashore on Nanin Island, three miles west of Namber, to install a radar there.

Because the paratroopers had reinforced General Patrick's command, he was able to get ahead of schedule with the task of clearing the island of the Japanese. For three days, starting on 7 July, General Patrick expanded his perimeter around the Kamiri airfield. His patrols ran into little opposition, and General Patrick correctly concluded that the Japanese had withdrawn into the interior of the island to make their usual and expected last-ditch stand.

On 11 July, General Patrick called a meeting of his senior subordinate commanders. His G-2 briefed them on the enemy situation as best he knew it, concluding that the enemy had withdrawn into the interior of the island. Then General Patrick spelled out his plan for the clearing of the island. "The 158th Infantry," he said to its commander, Col. J. P. Herndon, "will patrol the northern half of the island. And your regiment," he said to Colonel Jones of the 503d, "will work the southern half." Colonel Jones did not know it at the time, but his lightly equipped parachute regiment had just been assigned the toughest half of the island—overgrown with thick jungle and punctuated with high peaks. The northern half of the island was flat and generally clear. Hence, the enemy had selected the southern half in which to hide.

On that same day, the 2d Battalion, 503d Parachute Infantry, was finally committed to combat on Noemfoor after its jump on the fifth had been called off. On the afternoon of the tenth, General Krueger's headquarters ordered Lt. Col. John W. Britten to move his battalion by LCI from Biak to Namber on Noemfoor. He moved his battalion to the loading area and at about midnight on the tenth loaded his men aboard the LCIs for the ten-hour trip to Noemfoor. He landed at 0930 on the eleventh and reassembled his battalion. General Patrick's headquarters then ordered Britten and his battalion to move out overland on foot to the native village of Inasi on the east side of the island and to patrol the area from that village. The battalion arrived in Inasi on the thirteenth.

On the eleventh, Colonel Jones and the 1st and 3d battalions of the 503d began their mission of patrolling and clearing the southern half of the island. General Patrick had assigned to Jones one battery of the 147th Field Artillery Battalion, a tremendous asset since the heaviest weapons the paratroopers had were 81-mm mortars.

For two days, the patrolling produced no decisive results. But on the thirteenth, the 1st Battalion, now commanded by Maj. Robert H. Woods, reached the foot of Hill 670, located in the west-central part of the island about five miles southeast of Kamiri airfield. General Patrick's G-2 believed that Colonel Shimizu and a large detachment of the 219th Infantry were dug in on top of the hill. Major Woods sent his C Company to contact the main portion of the enemy and force it toward the 2d Battalion, which had just reached Inasi. At 1400, the lead elements of C Company came under intense small arms, mortar, and machine gun fire from the slopes of Hill 670. Capt. John Rucker, C Company commander, knew that he was in trouble. Subtracting his jump casualties, his company could muster no more than about ninety men. And from the firepower the enemy was throwing at him, he guessed that he was facing a force of at least four hundred Japanese. A prisoner later reported that Rucker had grossly under-estimated the force facing him—there were more than twelve hundred Japanese on Hill 670, according to the POW, and they were commanded by Colonel Shimizu. In the next few weeks, Colonel Shimizu would prove to be a most elusive foe.

For three and a half hours, Company C fought fire with fire, but their light weapons were no match for the entrenched Japanese with numerous heavy machine guns, screened and abetted by a line of snipers. Captain Rucker ordered his company to withdraw three hundred yards to the north and radioed Major Woods of his situation. Woods ordered them to dig in for the night. But he also sent Companies A and B to join C Company in its defensive position at the foot of Hill 670. A and B companies arrived at 1845.

The next day, "Pug" Woods sent patrols onto and around

Hill 670 to try to find the dimensions and the location of the enemy's main positions. He found out shortly that the Japanese were still there. Their heavy machine gun fire and accurate snipers forced the patrols to withdraw. The artillery forward observer with the 1st Battalion called in an intensive and accurate artillery barrage against the targets so far located on the hill. For the rest of the day, Pug Woods probed the enemy's positions with patrols.

At 0700 the next morning, the artillery of Battery A, 147th Field Artillery Battalion, fired a barrage in front of B and C companies before they moved up the slope of the hill. The paratroopers ran into only light opposition; they shortly discovered that the main body of Shimizu's command had left the area. Major Woods set up a perimeter defense on the crest of Hill 670 and sent patrols on a sweep of the area around the hill to try to locate the Japanese.

The troopers of the 503d were beginning to realize the difficulties of jungle fighting—they gained expertise only through trial and error, and sometimes bitter experience. It is simply on-the-job training. Roads were nonexistent in the thick, vine-entangled jungle and had to be hacked out at times with machetes and axes. An advance of four hundred yards seemed like a mile. Medics had a difficult time getting to the wounded and an even more arduous task carrying them by litter to an area where they might be moved to an evacuation airstrip. Toting just one wounded man required four litter bearers plus a few riflemen to protect them. Field telephone wire was almost impossible to lay in the jungle, and, even when the wire was strung out along the ground, communication on the field phones was impossible beyond eight miles. Thus, operational and intelligence information was rarely available to a battalion in the field. Resupply of food, water, and ammunition was sometimes available by drops from small planes, but their capacity was limited. An occasional C-47 drop was possible, but this was rare and often not accurate. Coupled with the jungle diseases—malaria, scrub typhus, dysentery—life in the jungle, aside from clashes with the enemy, was not pleasant.

Colonel Jones tried to keep in touch with his widely scattered battalion elements by flying over them in a small Cub artillery spotter plane and calling for colored smoke grenades to mark their positions. He could thus check the accuracy of patrol location reports and inform patrol leaders of just where they were. He also used the artillery planes to drop blood plasma, ammunition, messages, and other pertinent supplies.

For a week after 15 July, neither the 1st Battalion, patrolling south and southeast of Hill 670, nor the 2d Battalion, patrolling to the north and northwest of Inasi, could pin down Shimizu and the remnants of his 219th Infantry. But on 23 July, patrols of the 2d Battalion operating four miles north of Inasi finally ran into the bulk of the Japanese. During an intense firefight, a platoon of Company D was cut off from the rest of the company. D Company's commander ordered Sgt. Roy E. Eubanks and his squad to try to relieve the pressure on the trapped platoon so that it could return to the rest of the company.

Sergeant Eubanks led his squad toward the Japanese position. Within thirty yards of the position, he came under Japanese fire. He ordered the bulk of the squad to take cover, and he and two scouts crawled through a shallow ditch that led to the enemy position. Within fifteen yards of the stronghold, Eubanks and the two scouts came under even heavier machine gun fire. Eubanks took a BAR from one of the scouts, stood up, started firing on automatic, and raced toward the Japanese position. He had almost reached the machine gun nest when he was knocked down by a burst of fire and dropped the BAR. Dazed and bleeding, Eubanks picked up the BAR and, using it as a club, succeeded in killing four of the enemy before they killed him. He was awarded the Medal of Honor posthumously.

Distracted by the one-man Rambo-like charge of Sergeant Eubanks, the Japanese temporarily halted their fire, and the isolated platoon of paratroopers managed to return to the company perimeter. Company D resumed its attack and pushed the enemy back from his dug-in position. When the company reached the Japanese position, they found forty-five dead, but the bulk of the force had once again eluded them. The 2d Battalion returned to its base for resupply. For more than two weeks, the 503d had no further contact with Shimizu even though the battalions sent out numerous patrols from their bases at Inasi, Menoekwari, and Namber.

On 10 August, a patrol from the 3d Battalion found a trail

about two miles southwest of Inasi that looked as if a large body of Japanese had recently traveled over it. Major Erickson, the 3d Battalion commander, sent G Company to try to find the enemy. G Company discovered the remnants of Shimizu's men—probably now down to two hundred effectives—poised atop Hill 380, three miles south of Inasi.

As usual, the Japanese were well dug in and armed with machine guns and mortars. G Company took them under fire in a firefight that lasted all afternoon then withdrew so that the artillery and air could attack the position the next day. The next morning, after a rolling barrage and air strikes by B-25s operating out of Kornasoren airfield, five companies of the 1st and 3d battalions moved up Hill 380 shortly after dawn. The troopers found many dead and wounded, but once again Shimizu and his main body had taken off in the darkness to escape to yet another hilltop and yet another assault by increasingly frustrated paratroopers. Colonel Jones was more than ever determined to find Colonel Shimizu and his men and destroy them.

The Japanese, elusive and wily, skilled at camouflage and stealth, were wearing down. They had been cut off from all supplies for over a month by the paratrooper patrols, the strafing fighter aircraft, and naval gunfire. The Japanese, stoic and dedicated to their no-surrender vow, were reduced to eating whatever they could find—bugs, birds, weeds, leaves. In their final desperation, they were reduced to cannibalism. In early August, patrols of the 503d found corpses from which large pieces of flesh had been sliced. At first, the unbelieving and puzzled paratroopers thought that the wounds were the result of artillery fire. But a Japanese medical officer captured later confirmed the atrocities when he admitted openly that he had used surgical instruments to slice flesh from both Japanese and American dead. Some of the patrols of the 503d found human flesh in the knapsacks of dead Japanese. When Jones's staff reported the atrocity to General Patrick's staff, they wouldn't believe it. Jones's staff finally sent photos of butchered bodies and samples of flesh in the socks of slain Japanese to convince them.

The three battalions of the 503d continued their extensive patrolling of the south half of Noemfoor. About 1730 on 14 August, A Company contacted what the company commander thought was the main body. For two days, A Company fought a battle south of Inasi. Finally, on 17 August, near the town of Pakriki on the southern shore of Noemfoor, the 1st and 3d battalions cornered what was left of Shimizu in a pocket formed when the paratroopers surrounded the Japanese on three sides; the ocean formed the fourth. Even at the end, twenty Japanese escaped the trap—the unbelievably slippery Shimizu among them. Neither Shimizu's 300-year-old samurai sword, long sought by the 503d, nor the colors of the 219th were ever found.

Just before the close of the operation, the 503d G-2 received a report that a small boatload of Japanese soldiers had slipped away in the night from the southern shore near Pakriki and seemed to be heading toward a small island about twenty-five miles away. Jones immediately took off in one of his artillery spotter planes, armed with hand grenades, a Thompson submachine gun, and many clips of ammunition. "The Warden" was determined to "get" Shimizu; he was convinced that the elusive Japanese commander was on the boat.

Jones and his pilot searched the area for a long time; the pilot finally reported that the plane was getting low on gasoline and they should head for home. Just then, Jones and his pilot spotted a small boatload of naked men about a mile and a half away. "That's when the fun began," Jones remembers. The small Cub plane flew over the boat; each time it made a pass, the Japanese in the boat dived overboard. Jones dropped grenades and strafed the bodies with his submachine gun blazing each time they made a low-level pass. Finally, a small U.S. J boat appeared on the scene. Jones had killed one of the escapees; the J boat picked up eleven. The fate of Shimizu, however, is still not known.

On 31 August, Sixth Army declared the Noemfoor operation over. The 158th Infantry had killed some 611 of the enemy, captured 169, and liberated 209 Javanese slave laborers. These laborers were all that was left of more than 3,000 Javanese captives whom the Japanese had abducted and forced to work on the three airfields on the island. The 158th had lost only 6 men killed and 41 wounded. The 503d killed more than 1,000 Japanese, captured 82 prisoners, and liberated 312 Formosans and 9 Javanese slave laborers. The 503d lost 38 men killed and 72 wounded but had almost 400 ineffectives from various jungle diseases.

On 28 August, the 503d moved to a base camp near the Kamiri airfield. While the 503d was fighting in the jungles, a dramatic transformation had taken place on the airfields of Noemfoor. By 20 July, the Kamiri airfield had been extended to 5,400 feet and had been paved with coral. But on 6 July, a squadron of Australian P-40s were operational from Kamiri. By 9 September, there were two fighter groups there. In July, Namber was dropped from the construction program. At Kornasoren, by 25 July, one fighter group of fifty P-38s was operating; by the twenty-sixth, a B-25 landed on the strip; and on the twenty-seventh, 2,000 additional feet of runway became operational. The airfields at Noemfoor moved bombers and fighters increasingly closer to the heart of the Japanese empire. From Noemfoor, bombers could support the upcoming invasion of the Vogelkop Peninsula and Moratai Island and could attack the large Japanese petroleum resources on Borneo.

Near the end of the Noemfoor campaign, the 503d was reinforced with two elements that were to become an integral part of and make the 503d a regimental combat team: the first was the 462d Parachute Field Artillery Battalion, equipped with twelve 75-mm pack howitzers and commanded by Lt. Col. Donald F. Madigan; the second was Company C of the 161st Parachute Engineer Battalion, commanded by Capt. James Byer.

During the late summer and early fall of 1944, the paratroopers of the by-now 503d Regimental Combat Team settled down in their base camp at Kamiri. General MacArthur, during that time, had pushed his New Guinea campaign to the maximum. On 30 July, the U.S. 6th Division landed amphibiously at Sansapor on the Vogelkop Peninsula supported by fighters and bombers operating out of Noemfoor's Kamiri airfield. The 6th pushed rapidly inland and cut off more than eighteen thousand Japanese on the south side of the peninsula. With this operation, the battle for New Guinea was virtually over.

Early in August, it suddenly occurred to General Marshall in Washington that little had been said about the disposition of the thousands of Japanese troops who had been bypassed by MacArthur's progress up the coast of New Guinea and as far east as the Solomons. He queried MacArthur about it. "The various processes of attrition will eventually account for their final disposition,"

MacArthur replied. "The actual time of their destruction is of little or no importance."

Fortunately, the Australians were unaware of this exchange of radio messages, for in mid-July General MacArthur had directed Sir Thomas Blamey, the supreme commander of the Australian forces, that henceforth he was responsible for the "continued neutralization" of the bypassed Japanese, a task that the Australians had already been performing. His directive to Blamey included responsibility from the northern Solomons to New Britain to Australian New Guinea and excepted only the Admiralty Islands.

By 15 September, American forces were ashore at Moratai, MacArthur's most advanced base, and only three hundred miles from the Philippines. Only two hours after the invasion, MacArthur arrived. "He gazed out to the northwest," one aide remembers, "almost as though he could already see through the mist the rugged lines of Bataan and Corregidor. 'They are waiting for me there,' he said. 'It has been a long time.'"

The 503d Regimental Combat Team did not yet know it, but it was to be an integral part of MacArthur's dream to return to Bataan and Corregidor.

So far, the combat history of the 503d had been mixed—some relatively easy and some of it hard fought. But all of it trained the regimental combat team and hardened its mettle for what the Japanese commander on Corregidor thought was an impossibility: attack Corregidor by an airborne assault.

CHAPTER IX
Mindoro

By late January 1945, the 503d Parachute Regimental Combat Team was reasonably comfortably established in a base camp near San Jose, Mindoro, along the banks of the Bugsanga River. The Bugsanga flows from the northeast to the southwest, runs through a lush, green valley fanned by a steady breeze that does little to improve the energy-sapping, humid climate. The river empties into the Mindoro Strait on the west shore of the island.

Even though rain is generally a daily occurrence through much of Mindoro even in the "dry" season, it could not compare to the rains that the 503d (and the rest of the combat forces) endured on Leyte during November and December: heavy, unexpected, and torrential monsoons engulfed the island and formed a sea of mud waist deep in some low-lying areas. The rains on Leyte were so heavy that they greatly impeded the construction of necessary airfields. The resultant shortage of aircraft forced General MacArthur, very grudgingly, to postpone the invasion of Mindoro for ten days and to cancel the planned parachute drop of the 503d, which would have preceded the amphibious assault on Mindoro. The paratroopers thus arrived on Mindoro as reluctant amphibians.

The base camp of the 503d was as luxurious as the imaginative and scrounging troopers of the 503d and their supporting engineer company, Company C of the 161st Parachute Engineer Battalion, could make it. Luxury, however, needs to be defined: sleeping in shifts in a muddy foxhole, rolled up in a poncho in soggy clothes with a couple of other rain-soaked men (the Leyte model), is not luxurious, but sleeping on a canvas cot under a pyramidal tent in dry clothes (the Mindoro model) is.

In the base camp, rows of pyramidal tents formed company streets; in back of the tents were the primitive latrines, boxes set over holes dug in the ground and protected from the elements by a makeshift canvas covering. Daily, the latrine orderlies—a task usually assigned to errant soldiers for minor misdeeds—burned out the latrines with used engine oil, which produced not only black smoke but an unforgettable odor that permeated the air of every base camp in the Philippines. The mess halls and kitchens were housed in larger tents at the ends of the company streets. The dining tables were often strips of pierced steel planking mounted on logs stuck vertically into the ground. Some companies had tents for dayrooms in which there might be a scrounged easy chair and some months-old magazines. There was often a box of paperback books supplied by Special Services. The Red Cross tent was in full operation, and Special Services showed outdoor movies every night. The really enterprising companies had appropriated used P-38 belly tanks, adapted shower heads to the bottoms, erected them on poles, and had, for them, luxurious showers. The engineers had also carved out baseball fields and volleyball courts.

Life on Mindoro, however, was not all fun and games for the 503d. Far from it. During January, the 503d integrated its new recruits into the regiment through a rigorous training schedule not only to acclimatize them to the heat and humidity of the Philippines, but also to fit them solidly into their fighting units. The staff requisitioned the necessary supplies and equipment to bring all units up to full allowances. The commander shifted officers so that there was a balance of combat experience in all his units.

The regimental staff set up schools for officers and NCOs on such subjects as the regimental standard operating procedures (SOP), jumpmaster training, leadership, and field artillery forward observer procedures. The commanding officer emphasized small unit training to include squad tactics, the use of the engineer assault teams, and, very foresightedly, the use of the artillery pack 75-mm howitzer as a direct fire weapon. (This was a tactic that would prove extremely useful in the Corregidor fighting.) All men in the regimental combat team, especially including the cooks, clerks, and other administrative types, fired all of the weapons in the regiment. Replacements went through extra jump training to teach them in exacting detail the regiment's SOP for plane loading, in-flight procedures, and jumping with all combat equipment. And as paratroopers are wont to do, hard physical training continued even in the oppressive climate of the tropical Mindoro. And Colonel Jones insisted, again with great foresight, that training stress squad and platoon leaders' initiative, leadership, and responsibilities.

Even though the Japanese on Mindoro were relatively few and generally invisible, the regiment sent out patrols each night from its perimeter on the outpost line of defense. The patrolling was not only to locate any Japanese who might be lurking nearby but also to investigate the Air Corps, Navy, and service troops' supply dumps that were located just outside the perimeter. The patrols returned with enough canned chicken, beef, vegetables, and fruit to prove what the infantry had thought was true all along—the other branches and arms of service lived and ate far better than they did.

In addition to the patrols that went out only a few hundred yards beyond the perimeter, General Dunkel's task force headquarters, the senior headquarters on the island, ordered a series of larger patrols along the southern, western, and northwestern shores of Mindoro and on some small offshore islands to flush out the Japanese who had fled to the hills, to control areas along the beaches where the Japanese might possibly land troops from Luzon, to establish and defend radar and ground force observation posts, and to free the local Filipinos from whatever Japanese remained in the areas. Local guerrilla forces played a large part in these operations by guiding the patrols and, on some occasions, furnishing the bulk of the forces on the patrols.

Generally, the patrols met little opposition. One exception was a patrol formed from a Philippine Scout company that was led by Lt. L. M. Dean of the 503d. The Task Force Headquarters had sent the company to the northwestern section of Mindoro on reconnaissance. On 1 January, the patrol found some sixty Japanese dug in around the barrio of Palauan. Dean radioed the information back to the 503d headquarters, and Colonel Jones dispatched Company B (Reinforced) to assist Dean and his guerrillas.

Company B went by LCI to Mamburao and planned then to go overland to the vicinity of Palauan. Company B arrived at Mamburao in the middle of the night on 2 January and started to unload men and gear. During the debarkation, an unidentified plane buzzed the LCI, causing the LCI skipper hastily to order the ship off the beach. Unfortunately, a number of troops of Company B, who were still unloading equipment, jumped off the boat and started swimming and wading to shore. In the black of night, several of them became disoriented. S. Sgt. Bernard O'Boyle sensed the confusion and realized that some of the men who had jumped overboard were in trouble. He quickly shed his equipment and his fatigues and jumped naked into the water. He swam to one group of flustered men and headed them to shore. Then he swam farther out to sea and pulled a nonswimmer back to the beach. For his heroism, Sergeant O'Boyle was awarded the Soldier's Medal. Unfortunately, two men drowned because of the precipitate departure of the LCI.

At dawn the next morning, Company B set out on a hard 20-mile march toward Palauan. On the way, they were forced to cross a stream loaded with crocodiles. The company commander managed to secure a small boat and ferried his men across two at a time. Around noon, on the road to Palauan, a young Filipino met them and alerted them to the fact that a 13-man Japanese patrol was advancing their way. Company B immediately pulled off the road and set up an ambush; at about 1400, the Japanese patrol walked into it and sprung the trap. The 503d troopers killed nine of the enemy with no loss to themselves.

Before dawn on the third, Company B neared the barrio of Palauan and moved into positions selected for them by their advance party. The Japanese unfortunately had been alerted to the company's progress and were well dug in. During the hours of daylight, the two sides traded sniper fire. But by dawn of the fourth, Company B had forced the Japanese to withdraw. The company overran the Japanese positions and counted twenty-six Japanese bodies. Company B lost four men killed and fourteen

Col. George M. Jones, Commander of the Rock Force, on Corregidor in late February 1945.

Malinta Hill and tunnel entrance.

Ruins of the Topside officers' quarters.

Golf Course Drop Zone at the top of the photo; officers' quarters and water tanks at the bottom. View looks north.

Gun crew of a pack 75mm howitzer of the 462d Parachute Field Artillery Battalion firing direct fire at a cave on Topside.

Black Beach near San Jose and South Dock. Site of the amphibious landing of the 3d Battalion, 34th Infantry.

Sergeant Wolsinski and two Japanese torpedo boats found in a cave near San Jose Point.

Lt. Col. "Big John" Erickson, Commander 3d Battalion, first to jump on Corregidor, with Lt. Dick Williams, leader of the Signal Corps combat photo team who jumped with the 503d.

General MacArthur, Colonel Kinsler (then Commander of the 503d), and party at the 503d base camp in New Guinea.

View of Topside during the drop of the 3d Battlion, 503d, on 16 February 1945.

Result of air strike on a cave on Topside.

Golf course Drop Zone.

Topside. Behind the "Mile Long" Barracks are the commissary and the hospital.

Golf course drop zone with swimming pool at right center.

U.S. Navy ship offshore ready to pick up paratroopers who might have been blown into the sea.

An LCT carrying the 3/34th Battalion Combat Team moving toward Black Beach. Paratroopers are still in the air over Topside.

wounded. The remaining Japanese, with some eleven wounded men, fled into the hills. The Philippine Scouts followed them and eventually tracked them down.

On 5 January, the 503d headquarters ordered Company B to return to base via a march to Mamburao and another LCI ride to San Jose. As the fortunes of war would have it, the same LCI that had delivered the company to Mamburao three days earlier was waiting to return them to San Jose. The troopers, once on board, tired after a long, three-day march and a fairly intense firefight, suggested to the LCI's sailors that they were something other than brave for leaving them only partially unloaded some three days earlier. In the ensuing brawl, neither side suffered severe injuries.

Although the ground combat on Mindoro was relatively light and produced few casualties (by the end of January the Western Visayan Task Force had suffered 16 men killed, 71 wounded, and 4 missing), offshore and overhead the situation was far different. The Japanese reacted to the Mindoro landings and buildup with aggressive sea and air tactics. On 21 December, just six days after the initial landings of the Western Visayan Task Force, the Japanese renewed their air assaults with an attack on the ships of a resupply convoy en route to Mindoro. The Japanese Naval Air Service, responsible for the attacks against the Mindoro operation, was reinforced by about fifty planes flown in from Formosa, raising its strength to about eighty aircraft. All of the planes were based on strips on Luzon within easy reach of Mindoro. The Japanese hit the convoy with about twenty kamikazes and virtually destroyed two LSTs and damaged two destroyers and a Liberty ship. The U.S. losses were 108 men killed or wounded. The Japanese lost at least ten planes.

The Japanese navy was not to be outdone. The Japanese Southwestern Area Fleet, whose headquarters was in Manila, organized a small fleet of two cruisers and six destroyers with orders to bombard the Allied beachhead on Mindoro and sink whatever shipping it could find unprotected in the Mindoro Strait. With this force, the Japanese had no intention of making a major effort; they hoped only to delay the development of the Allied base on Mindoro.

The surface strike force left Camranh Bay, Vietnam, on 24 December and was discovered the next day by Allied submarines operating in the South China Sea. The U.S. reconnaissance seaplanes then began tracking the force and reported on the twenty-sixth that the seaborne force was within easy striking distance of the Mindoro base.

Although the Japanese had no intention of making a landing on Mindoro, the U.S. High Command had no way of knowing that fact. On the contrary, the appearance of the fleet and unconfirmed intelligence reports of possible troop convoys steaming toward Mindoro lent credence to the possibility of an invasion.

The Allied High Command reaction was swift and positive. General MacArthur's headquarters alerted the 511th Parachute Infantry Regiment of the 11th Airborne Division on Leyte to prepare to jump on the San Jose airfield. (The 11th had just recently come out of the rain-soaked, muddy hills of Leyte and was re-equipping and cleaning up individually and collectively. Some of us, the author included, had gone nineteen days in the hills without taking off our fatigues, boots, or having shaved.) Lt. Gen. George Kenney, MacArthur's air commander, hurriedly reinforced his Mindoro air units and, by the time the Japanese ships were within striking range of Mindoro, had assembled on Mindoro a total of 105 planes of various types. The Western Visayan Task Force headquarters, with a sense of urgency, moved its headquarters from the San Jose area farther back into the surrounding hills.

The 503d command post stayed in place. Colonel Jones took a skeleton staff and went to the beach to check the defenses against the possible Japanese landings. He had previously assigned the 462d Parachute Field Artillery Battalion, equipped with pack 75-mm howitzers, to positions along the tree line near the beach and had directed each battery to support one of the infantry battalions in their defensive positions, sited to counter an amphibious landing. C Company, 161st Parachute Engineer Battalion, reinforced the infantry beach defensive positions, prepared previously by an engineer amphibious battalion, by stringing miles of double-apron barbed wire, burying special demolitions, and booby-trapping the wire with mines and Bangalore torpedoes. The amphibious engineers had also built dugouts along the beach that now provided adequate but cramped cover for the skeleton 503d staff.

About 2300 on the twenty-sixth, the Japanese ships began shelling the beachhead area and the airfields, which were about two to three miles inland. U.S. aircraft rose in the dark to attack the ships. Unfortunately, only the P-61s, of which there were few and which were searching for Japanese aircraft, were equipped for night operations. The thirteen B-25s, forty-four P-38s, twenty-eight P-47s, and twenty P-40s assembled by General Kenney had to use their running and landing lights as identification to each other and to locate the Japanese ships on the way to the Mindoro Strait under cover of bad weather.

The resulting firefight from ships and planes lighted up the night. The guns of the surface ships flashed and thundered, and their antiaircraft fire filled the skies with exploding shells as they sought to shoot down the attacking aircraft. After about forty minutes of shelling, the Japanese ships withdrew at high speed to the west, still under attack by the U.S. aircraft. The Japanese had done little damage to the shore installations, but near the beach, they did sink a Liberty ship and a PT boat. The Allies lost twenty-six planes, many of which were not lost to Japanese action, but to the fact that the pilots could not land on the Mindoro airfields that were under attack; many had attempted to fly to Leyte and crashed en route from lack of fuel and heavy weather on the way. The Allies had sunk one Japanese destroyer, severely damaged two cruisers, and damaged, at least in part, all of the other ships in the attack group.

On 28 December, the Japanese resumed kamikaze and conventional attacks against the U.S. ships on the beach at Mindoro and on ships on their way to reinforce the Mindoro base. They sank three Liberty ships, two LSTs, a destroyer, and two LCMs. They also caused three other Liberty ships to be grounded to prevent sinking. And during the dark of the night of 2–3 January, the Japanese attacked the Mindoro airstrips and destroyed fifteen P-38s and seven A-20s.

By the early part of January, the Japanese had lost fifty aircraft in the Mindoro area; thereafter, however, they almost completely reduced their operations against Mindoro and concentrated on the ships that were moving toward Luzon. All told, the total casualties for the Allied forces who were involved in establishing the Mindoro air base, including those from kamikaze attacks, were 475 men killed and 385 wounded. On Mindoro itself, the Japanese lost 170 men; 15 were taken prisoner.

By January, Mindoro was fully operational for the mission for which it had been seized: providing air bases for the aerial support of the invasion of Luzon. Mindoro was ideally suited for the mission: it was only about 115 air miles from Manila and had been cleared of its relatively few Japanese defenders. Major Allied air units on Mindoro included three fighter groups, two night-fighter squadrons, two medium bomber groups, three tactical reconnaissance squadrons, a photographic squadron, and an air-sea rescue squadron. Without the superb engineer effort that went into building the bases for these aircraft on Mindoro, there is no question but that MacArthur would have been unable to invade Luzon when he did.

Day by day, the 503d also prepared for a mission. In late January, the commander of the 503d did not know what that mission would be, but he knew that one must be in the offing. He reasoned that the war was reaching a climax in the Philippines. He commanded a battle-ready force of paratroopers who could mount up and be in combat in hours, and he had already been alerted for possible airborne operations. He had already been alerted on 25 January for a possible jump on Luzon; that alert was canceled within two days.

Col. Jones was alerted again on 3 February to jump on and seize Nichols Field just south of Manila. To the commanding officer of the 503d, this seemed like a sure mission because on that day, 3 February, the 511th Parachute Infantry Regiment had departed from the San Jose airfield to jump on Tagaytay Ridge south of Manila. It seemed only logical to the 503d staff that another regimental drop at Nichols Field would pinch the Japanese defenders between the 503d at Nichols and the 511th advancing north on Highway 17 toward Manila. Certainly two regimental parachute jumps so close together, both in distance and time, would confuse, surprise, and disorganize the enemy and hasten the fall of Manila.

With the alert of 3 February, Col. Jones put into motion all of the standard operating procedures of the regiment: weapons maintenance, parachute bundle preparation, radio checks, supply packaging, jump-stick alignment, plane assignments, takeoff schedules, and jumping procedures.

But that jump was not to be either. On the morning of 5 February, General Krueger's Sixth Army headquarters canceled the alert. This time, Sixth Army canceled with good and sufficient reason. On 3 February, General MacArthur sent a radio message to General Krueger outlining his plans for clearing Manila Bay. General Krueger's interpretation of the message from MacArthur was this:

> It envisaged the earliest possible seizure of Bataan to include Mariveles, and the seizure of Corregidor and the south coast of Manila Bay in the general Ternate area. Corregidor was to be taken by shore-to-shore assault, parachute drop, or both, as the tactical situation might indicate after effective air neutralization. Ground operations were to be carried out by Sixth Army. The Navy was directed to clear obstructions to navigation. The supply services were to develop the Port of Manila.

The "parachute drop" option in MacArthur's message caused Krueger to cancel the 503d's 3 February alert. He would need the 503d for this operation.

With amazing speed, General Krueger submitted his plan for the opening of Manila Bay to MacArthur's headquarters on 4 February. His plan

> provided for a reinforced RCT to drive down the east coast of Bataan Peninsula, while another RCT, plus an infantry battalion, mounted at Subic Bay, assaulted and seized the enemy positions in the Mariveles area on D-day. The plan further provided for a combined airborne and shore-to-shore assault against Corregidor on D plus 1. The airborne assault against Corregidor was to be made by the 503d Parachute Infantry Regimental Combat Team, mounted on Mindoro

by Eighth Army and transported to the objective area by
Fifth Air Force. Its attack was to be augmented by an assault
landing by a reinforced infantry battalion dispatched by water
from Mariveles.

The speed with which General Krueger and his staff worked
up a plan to open Manila Bay was the result of a couple of factors:
one, the staff had obviously anticipated the order from MacArthur's staff and had been in the process of preparing a plan for
a number of days; two, Lt. Col. Jack Tolson, who had been the
commander of the 3d Battalion, 503d, and led it on its jump
into the Markham Valley at Nadzab, was now a member of the
Sixth Army staff working for the G-3, General Eddleman, developing possible airborne plans throughout the area. Colonel Tolson
joined the Sixth Army staff on a temporary basis shortly after
the Nadzab operation ended on 19 September 1943. Prior to
the Noemfoor operation, he was transferred to the Sixth Army
headquarters but rejoined the 503d for the Noemfoor jump as
General Krueger's personal representative. In July 1944, after
the Noemfoor operation, Colonel Tolson was back at Sixth Army
headquarters and became more and more engaged in amphibious
planning and operations, especially for the invasion of Leyte.
He was with one of the corps for that assault landing. Later he
became involved and worked extensively on the Lingayen Gulf
invasion of Luzon and joined one of the corps for that amphibious
assault.

After the invasion of Luzon, Colonel Tolson remembers:

We continued working in Sixth Army on plans for an
airborne assault on Corregidor, and I was very much involved.
Generals Krueger and Eddleman were pretty well set on
our plans by the end of January 1945 and supported me
100 percent on the general concept. Prior to the jump, I
was sent to the staging area at Mindoro to be General Krueger's personal representative and Deputy Commander of the
Rock Task Force. This force was composed of the 503d RCT
and the 3d Battalion, 34th Infantry Regiment, 24th Infantry
Division.

Jack Tolson, seven and a half years out of West Point, was becoming one of the stalwart commanders and planners of the World War II airborne forces.[22]

Not to be outdone in speed of decision making, on 5 February 1945, the CinC, SWPA, General MacArthur, radioed General Krueger approving the plan Krueger had submitted only the day before. The CinC's radio message also announced 12 February as the target date. In addition, the message also directed Sixth Army to

> seize positions in the vicinity of Mariveles by overwater operations on D-day, in conjunction with overland operations southwest toward the Ternate area; seize Corregidor on D plus 1 by airborne forces mounted by Eighth Army in Mindoro and transported by Fifth Air Force to the objective area and by seaborne forces launched from Mariveles Bay; arrange general coordination of the operation and send to GHQ, SWPA, representatives of the task forces designated to support the operation.

The CinC message also directed the commander, Allied Naval Forces, "immediately, to assemble at Subic Bay the amphibious craft required for the operation, to transport and escort seaborne assault forces, and conduct the preliminary bombardment of Corregidor and the Mariveles area and of the North Channel shore of Manila Bay prior to the operation and during the landings," and ordered the commander, Allied Air Forces, "immediately to institute heavy preliminary neutralization of the defenses of Corregidor and of the south coast of Bataan Peninsula and to make plans to drop on Corregidor appropriate elements of the 503d Parachute Infantry Regiment designated by CG, Sixth Army."

The Sixth Army staff reacted again to the CinC's message with speed and confidence, an efficiency built up no doubt by

---

22. And to prove that the system works, before he retired, Jack Tolson became, as a lieutenant general, the commanding general of XVIII Airborne Corps and Fort Bragg, N.C., the number one "airborne" slot in the U.S. Army.

their continuing successes in the Luzon battles and by their prior, anticipatory planning. On 7 February, Sixth Army issued Field Order No. 48. It provided substantially for

> Sixth Army, supported by Allied Naval and Air Forces, to continue its offensive by seizing the Mariveles Bay area and Corregidor by shore-to-shore and airborne operations to assist in securing Bataan Peninsula and opening the entrance to Manila Bay, 12 February being designated as D-day, H-hour to be announced later.
>
> XI Corps to land not to exceed one RCT, reinforced, in the Mariveles area of southern Bataan on D-day, H-hour, to secure a beachhead and to establish control over the southern tip of Bataan; in conjunction with the amphibious assault in the Mariveles Bay area, to launch a vigorous attack to the south along the east coast of the Bataan Peninsula and destroy hostile forces encountered; to move one reinforced infantry battalion to the Mariveles Bay area on D-day, prepared for a shore-to-shore operation against Corregidor on D plus 1 in conjunction with the assault of the 503d Parachute Infantry Regiment [On 11 February, Sixth Army amended F.O. No. 48 to make the entire 503d RCT available for the operation, thereby giving the infantry artillery and engineer support by the 462d Parachute Field Artillery Battalion and Company C, 161st Parachute Engineer Battalion]; on D plus 1, employ the 503d Parachute Infantry Regiment in an airborne operation, as arranged with Eighth Army and Fifth Air Force, and by a shore-to-shore operation from Mariveles Bay, capture Corregidor; control of the 503d Parachute Infantry Regiment to pass from CG, Fifth Air Force, to CG, XI Corps, upon completion of this drop on Corregidor.

And brooking no delay from its subordinate headquarters, the Sixth Army order also directed that, on or before 10 February, the commanding general, XI Corps, "designate the troops (exclusive of the 503d Parachute Infantry Regiment) for the operation from those under his command and to submit a brief of his plan, inclusive of plans of close supporting naval and air forces, to CG Sixth Army, on or before 10 February 1945."

On 6 February 1945, Sixth Army alerted Colonel Jones and his 503d Parachute Infantry Regimental Combat Team to get ready for an airborne operation. Target: Corregidor.

The drama for the return to Corregidor was thus set by the methodical, grimly efficient staffs of Headquarters SWPA and Sixth Army. The actors had their scripts; now they began to study their roles and the stage. The men of the 503d, gearing up for their third combat jump in the Pacific area, wanted to play their parts like the seasoned professionals they had become. They were soon to learn, however, that the stage and scenery their superiors had selected for them was, to say the least, extraordinary for a paratrooper cast.

CHAPTER X
503d Planning and Preparation

On 6 February, when Sixth Army formally alerted Colonel Jones for the drop on Corregidor, the mission came as no great surprise to him. He had had, in a roundabout way, a strong clue that his regiment would be assigned Corregidor as its next objective.

In late January 1945, after the completion of the ground combat phase of the action on Mindoro, the 503d passed to the control of Eighth Army. George Jones was well aware that his men were spoiling for a fight, especially to help liberate Luzon, the most significant and most publicized part of the battle for the Philippines. Therefore, he tried to get a role for his regiment in the reconquest of Luzon. He recalls:

> We had had several weeks of rest and were ready to get back into action. Gen. Joe Swing, Commanding General of the 11th Airborne Division, and I had conversations about the 503d RCT being attached to the 11th Airborne Division for that division's jump on Tagaytay Ridge, advancing through Parañaque and on to Manila. It so happened that we were both in the Eighth Army, and we thought that this would get us back into action. We requested Eighth Army to attach the 503d to the 11th Airborne Division for the Tagaytay Ridge operation. Word came back that the request was not approved, but that the 503d would be assigned the mission to jump on Corregidor and to recapture it.
>
> As I recall, this word came the last of January and I

was immediately directed to report to G-3, Sixth Army, to assist in planning for the operation. Col. Jack Tolson, who had been Executive Officer of the 503d, had been reassigned to G-3 operations in the Sixth Army. I mention this because Jack not only did an outstanding job in helping with the planning of the operation, but he actually jumped with his old unit as the "Rock Force" Deputy Commander and was invaluable in getting the operation going.[23]

It was actually General MacArthur's SWPA headquarters (GHQ) that had sent the message denying Colonel Jones's request for attachment to the 11th in late January and informing Jones that General MacArthur intended to assign the recapture of Corregidor to his regiment. Sixth Army's 6 February alert order to the 503d confirmed the GHQ message and cleared the air about the 503d's immediate future.

A pending mission, especially an airborne one, heightens a parachute unit's sense of purpose, morale, and zeal. In effect, an impending airborne mission figuratively tightens all of a parachute unit's muscles. The collective adrenaline flows, chests rise, and men strut—at least mentally. At this point, the 503d needed a mission. The regiment was eager, well trained, and combat ready. Camp life on Mindoro had become boring, the food was dull, the training was often tougher than combat, the six cans of beer a week were warm, the dry season was beginning to cover the tents with dust from the dry bottom of the Bugsanga River along which they were camped, the humidity was depressing, and, after all: "There is a war on."

During late January and early February, the 503d had been alerted and then "stood down" a number of times. On 3 February, for example, Eighth Army alerted the 503d for a possible jump on 8 February near Nichols Field, outside Manila, to assist the 511th in its attack on Manila from the south.

The 503d had watched the 511th Parachute Regimental Combat Team of the 11th Airborne Division arrive at San Jose airstrip

---

23. Jones, letter to author, 11 June 1985.

from Leyte on 2 February, mount up in the C-47s that the 503d thought were there for their jump, and take off for a parachute operation on Tagaytay Ridge on 3–4 February, to open up Eighth Army's drive on Manila from the south. Lt. Gen. Robert Eichelberger, commanding general of the Eighth Army, very much wanted to beat General Krueger and his Sixth Army to Manila. Dropping the 503d on Nichols Field might have hastened Eichelberger's drive. But the 11th Airborne ran into the formidable Genko line near Manila, and the rapid advance of Eighth Army stalled on the outskirts of Manila near Parañaque. On 5 February, the 503d's alert was canceled. The morale of the 503d suffered, especially since the 511th was a "junior parachute regiment," having been activated after the 503d.

But on 6 February, the sagging morale of the troops began to build. Even though the troopers of the 503d had not been informed officially of the mission and the objective, they could sense that "something was up." For a couple of days, they had watched their officers attend meetings at the regimental command post, they had heard rumors that Sixth Army had already shipped in a topographic relief sand table model of Corregidor (true), and they had sensed an increased seriousness in the attitude of their officers.

The reasons why Corregidor needed to be retaken by what could only be a high-risk, airborne attack probably never entered the minds of the troops of the 503d. They had a mission and that was that. No one asked "Why?" They asked only "When?"

To the planners at SWPA and Sixth Army, however, an airborne attack on Corregidor embodied one of the basic principles of war: surprise. The planners correctly reasoned that the Japanese naval commander on the island, Capt. Akira Itagaki, would think the Americans "insane" if they tried to land paratroopers on that small, rocky bastion in Manila Bay. Another factor that caused the planners to think "airborne attack" was the difficulty of making an amphibious landing on Corregidor. They remembered the costly and almost-disastrous amphibious assault by the Japanese on the east end of Corregidor in 1942. The planners were aware of the obvious risks of a parachute assault, but they were also influenced by the GHQ estimate of only 850 defenders, which turned out to be grossly incorrect. Balancing all of the elements, the answer came out "parachute assault," to be followed a few hours later by an amphibious landing.

Even with the Americans attacking relentlessly toward Manila, there were good and sufficient reasons for the retaking of Corregidor. Its recapture would erase from the minds of the American people the dark memories of 1942: the tortured prisoners, the ignominy of Wainwright's surrender. Those were the inspirational reasons for retaking Corregidor.

In the minds of the Allied strategists, however, were also very practical factors. Without Corregidor, the Port of Manila could not be safely opened and used because there was too much risk from the guns the Japanese could employ against ships, especially unarmed freighters, steaming into the harbor. The planners also reasoned that in spite of the fact that the Allies enjoyed almost total air supremacy over Luzon, air power alone, even reinforced with substantial firepower from the Navy, could not subdue the defenders of the island, so many of whom were deep inside caves and tunnels. U.S. intelligence also was aware that the island harbored Japanese suicide "Q" boats, poised to attack Allied shipping.

Whatever the reasons for retaking Corregidor, whether General MacArthur's emotional one or the possibility of heavy shelling of ships in the harbor or the need to protect the amphibious landings on Mariveles, the mines in the channel between Mariveles and Corregidor and in the channel to the south, the 503d now had the mission to retake The Rock from the Japanese—on the ground, square yard by square yard, hill by hill, tunnel by tunnel, cave by cave.

Before Colonel Jones could give any specific and essential guidance to his staff and battalion commanders, he had to find out more about Sixth Army's overall plan for opening Manila Bay and the help he could expect from the Navy and the Air Corps. Sixth Army's order, which alerted the regiment for the Corregidor mission, also directed Colonel Jones to report to Sixth Army headquarters for a planning conference. Between 3 and 12 February, Sixth Army headquarters was located at the town of Gerono; on 12 February, it moved to the town of San Fernando. These towns were along Highway 3 and the railroad that ran from Lingayen Gulf almost due south to Manila.

On 6 February, Colonel Jones flew up to Sixth Army in a

light Army observation plane, landed near the headquarters set up in some makeshift Filipino buildings near Gerono, and contacted his former regimental executive officer, Jack Tolson, now working for the Sixth Army G-3, Brig. Gen. Clyde Eddleman. Jack Tolson briefed Colonel Jones on the Sixth Army plan for opening Manila Bay and the part that the 503d would play. Tolson pointed out the obvious fact that Corregidor had very few areas that were suitable for drop zones but asked Colonel Jones, at General Krueger's request, to fly over the island and recommend to the Sixth Army commander some locations where he thought he could jump his regiment. Tolson also mentioned that even with the scarcity of suitable drop zones, General Eddleman had concluded that an airborne attack was the only way to get troops on the island without heavy losses on the beaches. Colonel Jones remembers that "the fact that the famous Alamo Scouts, a reconnaissance unit of Sixth Army, had never been able to land on Corregidor, even at night, no doubt swayed General Eddleman's thinking. General Krueger made the decision [to jump a regiment on Corregidor] based on his G-3's recommendation." Jack Tolson also gave George Jones the latest aerial photos and maps that he had of the island.

George Jones flew back to his command post on Mindoro with a much clearer sense of the scope and character of his mission. But his feelings were ambivalent. On the one hand, the aerial photos showed clearly the magnitude of the operational difficulties; there were no cleared areas worthy of being described as drop zones. The idea of dropping his regiment on the bomb-shattered, rocky, hilly, and cliff-surrounded small island gave him a deep concern. On the other hand, however, the Sixth Army G-2 intelligence section had given him cause to believe that the job was manageable, once he got his battalions on the ground. The G-2's briefing was optimistic: about 850 first-line Japanese troops were on Corregidor. Unfortunately, the G-2 estimate of the enemy strength erred on the light side. Instead of 850 Japanese, in actuality, before the fighting would be over, more than 6,000 Japanese soldiers would be killed—or would commit suicide—on the island. Perhaps it was just as well that Colonel Jones was unaware of the correct figure of enemy strength as he mentally plotted how he would carry out his mission.

Both the intelligence sections, with their increasingly more accurate photo interpretations, and the Filipino agents missed the last-minute shipment of the Imperial Japanese Marines to Corregidor. But as it turned out, the five thousand difference between the initial guess at the enemy strength and the ultimate reality made little difference. MacArthur and Krueger had as usual selected the right men in sufficient numbers to get the job done.

On his return from Sixth Army on the 6th, Colonel Jones called a meeting of his regimental staff. He repeated to them the situation as he knew it and directed his staff to implement the regimental SOP, which outlined in detail for all units in the regiment the exact steps each commander and man must take to prepare for a combat parachute operation. The SOP had been fine-tuned after each of the regiment's combat jumps and by February 1945 was a well-known, complete, operational guide. He also made arrangements to fly over the island on the seventh in an Air Corps bomber, a B-25, so that he could pick out some drop zones for the approval of the Sixth Army commander.

Even before the 503d's alert for the Corregidor mission, General MacArthur's headquarters had directed the Air Corps to attack the island with sufficient air power to prevent the Japanese from using the pre–World War II guns against the shipping in the harbor. As a matter of fact, when General MacArthur outlined to General Krueger his plan for securing Manila Bay, he told him that the final decision on whether Corregidor would be taken by parachute assault, amphibious attack, or both, would await the results of heavy and concentrated aerial bombardment of the island.

Ever since his return to the Philippines, Corregidor must have weighed heavily on General MacArthur's mind. On 22 January, he had designated Corregidor as a target for aerial bombardment. But even before that date, in November 1944, two intrepid P-47 pilots of General Kenney's Fifth Air Force, returning from another mission, had found Corregidor irresistible and had launched their own personal, short-lived, strafing attack. They probably did little damage, but they did raise their own morale considerably.

When General MacArthur designated Corregidor a target for aerial bombardment, General Kenney suggested that the Air Corps take Corregidor by itself, from the air. General MacArthur hesitated a moment but then told him to go ahead.

General Kenney and his Far East Air Force gave the task a monumental effort. The attacks got under way on schedule on 23 January. B-24s of the Thirteenth Air Force's 307th Bomb Group began the aerial attack with heavy demolition bombs, focusing their attention on Topside and Malinta Hill. The liberators dropped their 500-pound bombs from seventeen thousand feet with deadly accuracy. Eighty-five percent of the bombs smashed into their targets. Tremendous blasts threw smoke and debris three thousand feet into the air. One string of bombs hit an underground ammunition dump, and the jubilant pilots watched the resulting explosions race along an L-shaped track as the ground above the ammo dump erupted.

Next came three veteran groups of the Fifth Air Force—the 90th's Jolly Rogers, the Ken's Men of the 43d, and the 22d's Red Raiders. B-24s of the Seventh Air Force joined in from bases in the central Pacific. Between 28 January and 7 February, the B-24s dropped nearly one hundred tons of bombs per day. The Japanese antiaircraft batteries were knocked out early in the campaign, and thereafter B-24 photo-recon planes could circle unmolested at three thousand feet.

Starting on 7 February, the bombers doubled their tonnage. After 7 February, A-20s, the Grim Reapers of the 3d Attack Group, joined in the assault. The A-20s concentrated on Battery Woodruff and Fort Hughes.

Then came the fighters—P-38s, P-47s, and the newly arrived P-51s—with 1,000-pound bombs shackled under each wing. They buzzed the island from all directions and dropped 133 tons of bombs in 134 sorties. They attacked such places as cave mouths, barracks doorways, gun pits, and tunnel openings. They also fired thousands of rounds of .50-caliber ammunition on their low-level runs.

On 12 and 13 February, the bombers shifted their attack to Mariveles in anticipation of the amphibious landing scheduled there for D-day, 15 February. But on the fourteenth and fifteenth, the A-20s and the B-24s were back to blast Captain Itagaki's defenders on Corregidor with the heaviest concentration of bombs to date.

In twenty-five days, Corregidor had been subjected to 3,125 tons of bombs in target areas that totaled just over one square mile. This was a record unmatched in any campaign in the Southwest Pacific.

The Navy began its attack on Corregidor on 13 February. Task Group 77.3, under Adm. R. S. Berkey, consisted of five light cruisers, nine destroyers, and several minesweepers. On the thirteenth, the task group concentrated its fire at the northern end of the island, where the Japanese strength seemed to be the most evident. But on the fourteenth, the ships of Admiral Berkey's task force were unable to silence all of the fire coming from Corregidor. Admiral Kincaid augmented Task Force 77.3 with three heavy cruisers and five destroyers. These ships arrived in the area at 1230 on the fifteenth and joined in the fusillade on Corregidor.

The success of the bombing and shelling is difficult to assess. One indicator was that when the B-24s first started bombing the island, the air crews reported that the antiaircraft fire was intense; during the parachute drop on the sixteenth, antiaircraft fire was light. But the overall casualties from the air strikes among the Japanese defenders are hard to estimate because most of the Japanese were in tunnels and caves during the raids. One important result of the aerial attack was that the Japanese were driven off the exposed high ground of Topside into the safety of the tunnels and caves. The drop zones for the paratroopers, beaten up though they were, were virtually free of the enemy, at least initially.

On 7 February, Colonel Jones flew over the island in the machine-gunner's seat in the nose of a B-25. He had the pilot make a couple of low runs over the island while he looked for suitable drop zones. He was a seasoned paratrooper used to dropping his men on fairly open, level, relatively long and wide DZs.

What he saw from the nose of the B-25 was even more dismaying than the aerial photos revealed and raised a few hackles on the back of his neck. Topside was littered with the debris of the bombings: downed trees, shattered concrete buildings, corrugated tin roofs, innumerable bomb craters, blasted rock outcroppings, and tangled undergrowth. There were two small clearings on Topside that he looked at but considered barely suitable as DZs: the rubble-strewn parade ground in front of the barracks, about 325 yards long and 250 yards wide; and an old, sloping, bomb-pitted, nine-hole golf course, about 350 yards long and 185 yards wide. Both of these areas were very close to bombed-out barracks, wrecked officers' quarters, blasted headquarters buildings, and debris-littered gun positions; their edges fell off sharply and were bordered by steep, rocky cliffs on the west and south. Colonel Jones considered these two areas hazardous, at best.

The only other open area that Colonel Jones could find on the island was Kindley Field, a prewar airstrip built as an emergency landing field for light Army artillery observation planes. It was about eight hundred yards long, on the far eastern end of the island, on flat ground, but on the narrowest part of Corregidor. Because the Japanese had not used it during their occupation of Corregidor, it was heavily overgrown. Nonetheless, and thinking of the jump casualties his troops might suffer if they were to jump onto the rubble of Topside, Colonel Jones decided that Kindley Field offered the only suitable drop zone on the island. And even that was barely acceptable. When he returned from his flight over the island, he immediately radioed General MacArthur's and General Krueger's headquarters the recommendation that Kindley Field be designated the drop zone for his regiment.

Whether General Krueger was aware that the Kindley Field recommendation came from Colonel Jones is uncertain; in all likelihood, Colonel Jones's radio went to Jack Tolson in Sixth Army's G-3 section, who passed it through General Eddleman to General Krueger. At any rate, General Krueger later wrote:

> I vetoed a proposal to make the drop at Kindley Field, at the eastern end of Corregidor, the only really suitable drop site available on the island. A drop there would have exposed the paratroopers to devastating fire from Malinta Hill and Topside. It seemed better to me to make the drop on Topside itself, where the Japanese were not likely to expect it to be made.

General Krueger was well aware of the hazards of the Topside DZs. He wrote:

> Aerial reconnaissance and photographs indicated only two practical drop areas on Topside: the parade ground and

the golf course, each a mere couple of hundred yards across. Their combined areas were extremely small for a parachute drop. . . . But since these two areas were the only ones available on Topside, their disadvantages had to be accepted and jump plans were made accordingly.

General Krueger summed up his reasoning for selecting an airborne operation as the best tactic for attacking Corregidor—and on the terrible drop zones on Topside, at that.

Although Topside was, indeed, an extremely rough area in which to make the drop, it offered us the best chance of surprising the enemy. Since the drop had to be made in the daytime, arrangements were made for the Navy and the Air Forces to bombard Topside thoroughly for several days preceding the assault, as well as on D-day, prior to H-hour. This bombardment was highly effective and contributed to the success of the airborne operation; but several naval escort vessels were damaged by enemy fire while their bombardment was in progress.

The amphibious landing to be made on Corregidor by an infantry battalion in conjunction with the airborne assault was considered essential to gain a beachhead, establish a supply base, and secure Malinta Hill. The landing seemed feasible, since it would be made while enemy forces were disorganized by the bombardment and the airborne assault.

The commanding general of Sixth Army had made his decision: the 503d would jump on Topside, and the 3d Battalion Combat Team (Reinforced) of the 34th Infantry of the 24th Division would land amphibiously on the beach at San Jose Bay on the south side of Corregidor at the foot of Malinta Hill. The die was cast; there was no further discussion of the location of the drop zones. There continued to be, however, a lot of talk on the 503d staff about the ruggedness of those tiny DZs.

All commanders involved in the operation began to plan in detail and to coordinate with the other commanders. Sixth Army held a conference for some of the commanders and their staffs on 6 February; the commanding general of XI Corps, Maj. Gen.

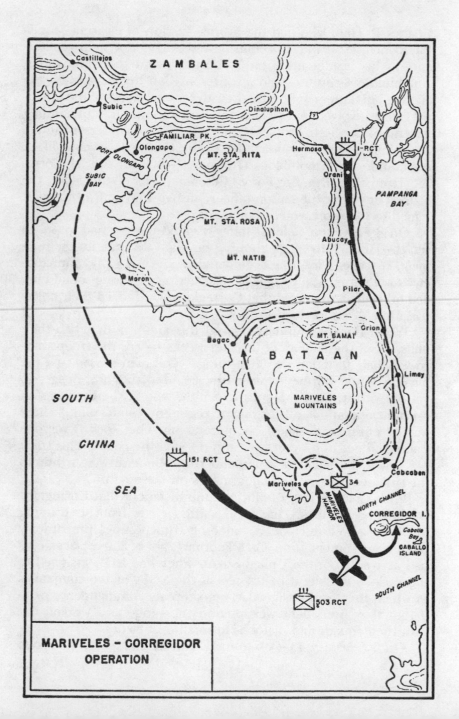

MARIVELES – CORREGIDOR OPERATION

Charles P. Hall, who had the overall mission of clearing Manila Bay to include the Bataan Peninsula and Corregidor, held a conference at his headquarters on 7 February; and the commander, Amphibious Group 9, held a conference on his flagship on the eighth. This latter conference drew the commanders of the principal forces involved in the Corregidor operation: the commanding general of the 54th Troop Carrier Wing; commander of the 7th Amphibious Forces; commander of the Cruisers, Seventh Fleet, commander of Amphibious Group 9, G-3 from the XI Corps, A-3 from the Fifth Air Force, Colonel Jones of the 503d, the Sixth Army airborne liaison officer, and various staff officers assigned to the represented commands.

On 8 February, Colonel Jones decided that he had to put to rest the rumors that were running rampant throughout the regiment. He called a meeting of his battalion and company commanders at his regimental command post, set up in a long squad tent, and officially announced that Corregidor was indeed their objective. Date of jump: 16 February.

When the commanders relayed this announcement to their units, all of the rumors of the past weeks faded; the troops narrowed their focus on the "real thing." The men sensed that the mission would not be a "piece of cake," but they were eager to get on with it. Capt. Magnus L. Smith, who at the time was an assistant operations officer on the regimental staff, said, "There was a sentimental aspect about retaking The Rock. Everyone wanted to get in on the show and do what he could. This spirit ran down the chain of command from General MacArthur to the riflemen, sailors, and tail gunners on the aircraft."

With Colonel Jones's official announcement that Corregidor was indeed its target, the 503d shifted gears from its training mode to a well-disciplined, smoothly functioning, preparatory phase for a combat jump. On 4 February, about 250 replacements had arrived from the United States. They had to be assigned to the various units and be trained in the SOPs of the companies to which they were assigned. The company commanders saw to it that they fired their weapons on the range and worked out with their squads and platoons in small unit tactics.

On 9 February, Lt. Col. John H. Lackey and his 317th Troop

Carrier Group, equipped with the C-47s that had recently dropped the 511th RCT on Tagaytay Ridge, moved back to Mindoro from their bases on Leyte. Colonel Lackey divided his 58 aircraft between the San Jose strip and the Hill strip because, he wrote, "of their proximity to the area where the 503d was billeted," and "in order to facilitate the loading, and to remedy the confusion that would inevitably have taken place on any one field that was large enough to handle the operation, as on each field it would be necessary to have adequate dispersal and loading areas for 29 aircraft and 500 men."

The 317th and the 503d had worked together before in Australia and on the Nadzab and Noemfoor Island operations. "The 317th was an old friend of the 503d," Captain Smith remembered, "having consumed many kegs of Australian beer together at Port Moresby in late 1942. The Commanding Officer, 317th was a personal friend of the RCT commander."

With the arrival of the 317th, the coordination between the troop carrier staff and pilots and the RCT staff and jumpmasters became close-knit. The staffs conferred daily and lived almost side by side during the days leading up to the jump. Colonel Lackey scheduled additional flight time for the troop carrier pilots who had not flown paratroopers before. The 503d staff and the 317th staff reviewed and updated their SOP for jumpmaster-pilot coordination prior to and during the jump. On the tenth, Colonel Jones and Colonel Lackey set up some small drop zones on a clearing near the San Jose strip and had all jumpmasters practice dropping short sticks of men on drop zones that were as short as the DZs on Topside.

When he found out where and how big the DZs on Topside were, Colonel Lackey had strong misgivings. Later, he wrote:

> The drop zones left much to be desired, but they were chosen as the most suitable drop zones on the island. There was considerable criticism [no doubt from older, experienced airborne planners] of the plan to drop airborne forces in these locations. It was said to be impossible, and, if executed, would be the greatest misuse of airborne forces yet conceived. The criticism was understandable.

During the 11th Airborne's attack on Manila from the south, Col. Orin D. "Hardrock" Haugen, the intrepid, courageous, aggressive commanding officer of the 511th, was mortally wounded by a Japanese 22-mm AA round fired while he and General Swing, the division commander, were conferring at the command post of the 511th's 2d Battalion. "Hacksaw" Holcombe was the 2d Battalion's commanding officer and had set up his command post in a house about 100 yards south of the Parañaque River Bridge. "Hardrock" had led General Swing to the second story of the building and was standing near an open window pointing out the progress of his troops along the street when a Japanese AA gun across the street blasted into Hacksaw's command post. One round shattered the side of the window. Only "Hardrock" was hit with the shell's fragments. He was subsequently evacuated to a hospital on Mindoro, where George Jones went to see him. Haugen and Jones were old friends who had been in the paratrooper business from its infancy. Jones went to the hospital on 11 February and told Haugen about the 503d's pending jump on Corregidor. Haugen, who had been stationed on Corregidor in the pre–World War II days, was astounded that anyone would have conjured up an operation involving dropping a regiment on that island. George Jones remembers Haugen's reaction. "Orin was very sick [and in fact died en route to the United States], but he had strength enough to look up at me and, looking very seriously into my eyes, say, 'George, they can't do that to you.' " But they could and did.

As D-day for the paratroopers neared, the planning and preparation for the jump increased in tempo. On 11 February, Sixth Army published an amendment to its Field Order No. 48 that made the entire 503d Combat Team, instead of only the three infantry battalions, available for the operation. This meant that the 462d Parachute FA Battalion, with its twelve pack 75-mm howitzers, and the 161st Parachute Engineer Company would also be part of the parachute force.

The pack 75s (the name derives from the fact that they were originally adapted for transport on pack mules) could be broken down into about nine basic loads of about 225 pounds each for mounting on six racks under the fuselage of the C-47s and in three doorloads, which the jumpmasters and another helper pushed out just before he jumped. As the doorloads were being thrown out, the jumpmaster released the loads in the racks under the plane by means of a toggle switch that he held in his hand. The six loads under the plane and the three in the door were all tied together on a daisy chain of nylon cord so that the pieces stayed together once they were in the air. On the ground, the artillerymen could find all the pieces because they were strung together. Each load, of course, had its own 24-foot individual cargo parachute. On the drop zone, the prime movers for the reassembled pack howitzer were about six burly cannoneers. (When the follow-up seaborne tail came ashore with heavy equipment, jeeps became the prime movers.)

On 11 February, Maj. Gen. William F. Marquat, a coast artilleryman who had been assigned to Corregidor in 1942 and who had left the island with MacArthur, arrived on Mindoro to answer any questions that Colonel Jones and his commanders and staff might have about the topography or defenses of the island. He was able to point out on the terrain model in Colonel Jones's constantly guarded briefing tent the exact location of various installations and what they looked like on the inside. Marquat said he was delighted with the plans for the parachute attack, that the Jap would make it costly any other way, and that he thought they'd get away with it in good style.

Sixth Army also detailed four enlisted men and two officers who had been stationed on Corregidor before the war to work with the regimental staff and commanders. And an American Japanese interpreter also arrived, ready to jump in with the regimental staff. The 503d already had three Filipino advisors qualified as jumpers on Noemfoor.

On the eleventh, Colonel Jones started indoctrinating all officers and senior NCOs on the plan of attack, using the sand table mock-up in the briefing tent. He said, "I am sure that this assisted us to get our troops together, but the smallness of the island and Topside, which was up the hill from wherever you landed, also helped us to get the show going once we hit the ground."

He remembers:

On Mindoro we were very busy in perfecting our plans for the jump, checking out all of our equipment and weapons, bringing to a razor-sharp edge our machetes, etc. This is normal on preparing for an airborne operation when you jump into any situation where you don't know what you are going to find opposing you on the ground. You expect to be outnumbered, outgunned, and surrounded!

At the time, he was totally unaware of just how outnumbered he and his regiment would be.

On 12 February, Colonel Jones and Colonel Lackey started flying their jumpmasters and C-47 pilots over Corregidor in the noses of B-25s that were making their daily bombing runs over the island. They got a very close look at the area during strafing runs across the DZs after the B-25s had dropped their bombs. And the strafing runs enabled the jumpmasters to put to rest the rumors that were prevalent in the 503d to the effect that the Japanese had planted antiparatrooper, sharpened poles and other antijumper obstacles on the likely DZs.

The rumors of the antiparachutist obstacles sprang from the fact that the 82d Airborne and the 101st Airborne divisions on their jump into Normandy on 6 June 1944 had run into *Rommelspargel* (Rommel's asparagus). The German General Rommel had fully expected that the Allies would use both paratroopers and gliders to precede their amphibious invasion. Therefore, he ordered his commanders of units behind the beaches to erect on all open fields what became known as *Rommelspargel*. These devices consisted of wooden poles six to twelve inches in diameter and eight to twelve feet long. The Germans planted these poles vertically to a depth of two feet and about thirty yards apart. Originally, the poles were designed to wreck gliders as they came in, powerless, for their usual crash landings. Later, Rommel decided to make them antiparatrooper as well. He ordered his units to attach mines to the tops of the poles and then to crisscross wires from pole to pole. If paratroopers landed in this web, they would detonate the mines and blow large numbers of themselves to death. This would be especially true with night landings. Rommel's order was not ignored by his commanders in the field. Rommel made an inspection of the area just behind the beaches in the spring of 1944 and later noted in his diary: "The construction of antiparatroop obstacles has made great progress in many divisions. For example, one division alone has erected almost 300,000 stakes, and one corps over 900,000."

As George Jones's jumpmasters and John Lackey's pilots buzzed the drop zones on Topside, they could see that the Japanese had not followed Rommel's tactics; what Lt. Col. John L. Erickson, commanding officer of the 3d Battalion, 503d, and Tech. Sgt. Thomas G. Mitchell, two of the jumpmasters, did see was every bit as chilling: the wrecked buildings, the blasted trees, the bomb-pocked parade ground and golf course, and the sheer cliffs bordering the minuscule DZs. One naive jumpmaster, after flying over the island, told his buddies on Mindoro that "the Japs are hardly garrisoning the place. Not a sign of human life anywhere up there."

One reason the Japanese had not bothered to prepare antiparatrooper defenses on Topside was that the commander of Corregidor, Captain Itagaki, did not expect an airborne attack, even though General Yamashita had ordered him to defend, what were in his opinion, likely airborne landing areas.[24] Nonetheless, even if Itagaki had expected an airborne landing on Topside, there was little more he could have done to make the DZs more inhospitable than the Allied Air Forces and the U.S. Navy had already accomplished.

Between 11 and 13 February, the entire RCT was briefed by platoon. Each platoon leader took his men to the briefing tent and pointed out the DZs, the platoon's zone of action, and the platoon's part of the mission immediately upon landing. The briefing tent also included bulletin boards on which the regimental staff had posted the latest aerial photos, diagrams of unit assembly areas, and maps outlining each unit's mission.

By 13 February, Colonel Jones had made the final decisions on his plan for the Rock Force. On that date, he issued Field Order No. 9, Hqs 503d RCT, a part of which explained the RCT commander's tactical plan:

---

24. General Yamashita made this statement in an interview with Sixth Army officers in August 1945.

The 3d Battalion, 503d RCT, with Battery A and one
(1) platoon of Battery D, 462d F.A. Battalion and 3d Platoon,
161st Airborne Engineer Company, attached, on 16 February,
will:

(1) Drop on Fields "A" and "B" at 0830I and secure
drop area.

(2) Upon being relieved by the 2d Battalion, advance
and seize the high ground approximately 600 yards NE of
the Hospital.

(3) Support the amphibious landing of the 3d Battalion, 34th Infantry by fire.

(4) Effect contact with 3d Battalion, 34th.

The 2d Battalion with Battery B and one (1) platoon
Battery D, 462d F.A. Battalion attached, on 16 February,
will:

(1) Drop on Fields "A" and "B" at 1215I and relieve
the 3d Battalion from defense of the perimeter around the
drop area.

(2) Exploit the terrain north and west of the Drop Zone.

The 1st Battalion with Battery C and one (1) platoon
Battery D, 462d F.A. Battalion attached, will:

(1) Drop on Fields "A" and "B" on 17 February at
0830I as RCT Reserve.

(2) Be prepared to exploit terrain south of the Drop
Zones.

Field Order No. 9 went on to direct that the Regimental Headquarters Company, Service Company, Headquarters of the 462d
Field Artillery Battalion, and the 161st Engineer Company drop
with the 1st and 2d lifts and perform the normal duties of administration, communications, supply, fire direction, demolition, and
medical service. The Regimental Executive Officer was directed
to stay behind, supervise the loading procedure, and then drop
in with the 3d lift on 17 February. Very wisely, Colonel Jones
directed the executive officers of the companies of the 2d and

3d lifts to jump in with the 1st lift so that they would be familiar with the situation and the areas of operations of their companies when the companies landed on Topside.

The order included the plan for the 3d Battalion, 34th Infantry, which would make an overwater movement from Mariveles, land on San Jose Beach on 16 February at 1030I, hold Malinta Hill, and make contact with the 503d on Topside. The 3d of the 34th came under the commander of the Rock Force, Colonel Jones, upon coming ashore.

The D-day situation is somewhat confusing. The Corregidor operation was a part of the overall plan to clear Manila Bay. Sixth Army's plan for the overall operation called for an RCT to drive down the east coast of Bataan while another RCT, plus an infantry battalion, mounted at Subic Bay, assaulted and seized the enemy positions in the Mariveles area on D-day. General Krueger's plan also provided for the combined airborne and ship-to-shore assault against Corregidor on D plus 1 (16 February). Therefore, D-day for the 503d was in reality D plus 1 for the Sixth Army overall plan.

The terse, stilted, stereotypical prose of military orders permits commanders briefly and succinctly to tell their subordinate commanders what their units are expected to do. But the very brevity of the operations orders belies and obscures the vast amount of planning, coordination, and details of execution that must take place for the operations order to be obeyed and the plan to succeed.

The airborne attack on Corregidor is an example of a complicated, difficult operation in reality, which, expressed simply in an operations order, seemed clear, neat, and uncomplicated.

The matter of dropping the paratroopers on the tiny drop zones on Topside is a case in point. World War II airborne commanders loved drop zones that were wide, long, relatively level, treeless, and big enough so that they could drop their troops from aircraft formations that fly over the DZ in a VOFV's, nine ships wide. This formation of aircraft permits the airborne commander to saturate the ground with men in the shortest time possible—achieving both surprise and mass. Obviously, such a method could not be used for the drop on the rubble-covered,

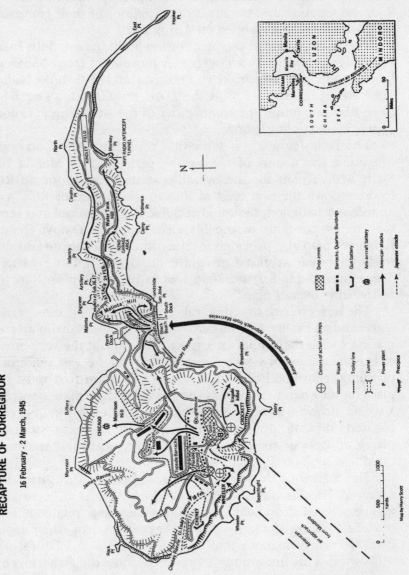

RECAPTURE OF CORREGIDOR

16 February - 2 March, 1945

Map by Harry Scott

inadequate, Topside drop zones. Colonel Jones estimated that his men would suffer anywhere from 10 to 50 percent casualties on the drop.

Nonetheless, as Col. John Lackey wrote after the war:

It was decided that a vertical attack was the only way to retake Corregidor—an amphibious operation was sure to be much too costly. The perplexing difficulty to be dealt with, was the size of the drop zones, as the largest was only 1500 feet by 400 feet. [In actuality, 1050 feet by 500 feet.] If parachutists descended perpendicularly the answer would have been a little easier, but, as the falling paratroopers are so much affected by the direction in which the wind is blowing and its velocity, a real problem existed. Wind drift might be defined as the distance in yards that each man will travel from the time he jumps from the aircraft until he has landed on the ground. The wind drift is figured as being equal to 2.8 yards times the altitude above the ground in units of 100 feet, times the velocity of the wind encountered by the parachutists in their descent in miles per hour. Substitute the facts that were encountered in the operation and the answer is not an encouraging one—

WIND = 18 knots = 20.8 miles per hour.
ALTITUDE = 600 feet
WIND DRIFT = $2.8 \times 6 \times 20.8 = 350$ yards
$= 1050$ feet

This means that each man dropped would drift over a space of 1050 feet, from the time he leaves the aircraft until he has made contact with the ground. At this point let me call your attention again to the fact that the largest drop zone was only 1500 feet long. The distance that the jumper will require in making his landing is also in direct ratio to the ground speed of the aircraft, and the time taken by each stick [a stick is the number of men who leave an airplane on any one pass over the drop zone] to make their exit from the troop carrier aircraft. The air speed of the plane was 110 miles per hour, and the velocity of the wind was 20 miles per hour, which gave a ground speed of 90 miles per hour or 44 yards per second. This added another 44 yards for each second required by the men to make their exit on each pass over the drop zone. Assuming that 4 seconds were required for each stick to leave the aircraft [this would be the minimum time necessary], the landing pattern would cover 528 feet. This distance of 528 feet, added to the wind drift of 1050 feet, will result in a distance just a few feet longer than the longest drop zone selected for this operation. Figures in this case did not lie—it was impossible to place all of the paratroopers in the area, and yet it had to be attempted. Even at the worst, it was a better solution than any of the other methods advanced for retaking the island—less costly in manpower, and more likely to succeed. But the only possible chance of success lay in complete coordination and cooperation of the air and airborne units. Colonel George M. Jones and the air force commanders were well aware of the problem, and agreed every man could not be expected to land in the drop zones, but felt that the zones selected were the best that the "Rock" offered, and that with the closest cooperation existing between the jumpmasters of the 503d RCT and pilots of the 317th Troop Carrier Group, the majority of the troopers could be placed in the selected areas. And through the planning, the great necessity for team work was stressed to all members of the units, and later paid dividends as proven by the results.[25]

After Colonel Lackey and his staff put down their slide rules, they decided upon a number of factors: the planes would have to fly over the DZs in a flight pattern of single ships in trail with 25-second intervals between each plane; the planes over DZ A, the parade ground, would fly in a counterclockwise direction, and the planes over DZ B, the golf course, in a clockwise direction; the direction of flight would have to be from southwest to northeast because the best line of approach—west to east—would crowd the two lines of planes over the DZs and would bring the planes too quickly over Manila Bay, increasing the likelihood that men

---

25. Lackey, "The Rock Operation, or The Return to Corregidor," monograph, Armed Forces Staff College, 1948.

would drift into the water or over the cliffs; the drop altitude
over the DZs would be 1,150 feet, or 600 feet above Topside;
each plane would drop a stick of eight men per pass; each jumpmaster would count four seconds after the pilot turned on the
green light over the go-point before he left the plane; the fifty-
eight planes in each lift would fly the 1-hour-and-15-minute flight
from Mindoro to Corregidor in a V of Vs so that en route the
planes would be more closely massed and thus more easily protected by fighters; and, finally, Col. John Lackey would fly the
lead aircraft with Colonel Jones in the cockpit beside him so that
they could control the jump from above and make any fine-tuning
to the jump plan precisely when needed. As events were to prove,
the presence of Lackey and Jones in the command ship over
Corregidor during the drop of the first lift proved to be prescient
and significant.

Colonel Jones recalls:

Our detailed planning called for very precise control of
two serials of C-47s flying one after the other in a wide circular
pattern to deliver eight men on each pass over the two drop
zones, one a small beaten-up golf course and the other on
Topside a postage-stamp-sized parade ground. Col. John
Lackey, the Air Force Troop Carrier Commander, and myself
flew above the jump planes and through inter-plane communications, actually controlled the jump. In the plan, in order
to allow for the wind, approximately 22 knots an hour, blowing across the island that morning, we had the jumpmaster
of each stick count a number of seconds after passing over
the shore of the island [the go-point] to insure that the plane
was well over the drop zone and that the chutes would land
reasonably close to the intended mark, after the wind had
operated on the descending chutes.

One problem peculiar to airborne units preparing for a combat
operation is the supply of personnel parachutes, cargo parachutes,
and cargo containers. The Parachute Maintenance Platoon of the
503d had arrived from Leyte on 6 February, just in time to receive
Sixth Army's alert for the Corregidor operation. Unfortunately,
the platoon's location on Leyte had lacked shelter and ship-unload-

ing facilities, and the weather, mud, and saltwater had seriously deteriorated the RCT's parachute supplies and equipment. With the alert, however, the platoon went on a 24-hour work schedule fabricating slings and containers for supply drops and packing personnel chutes for the three thousand plus paratroopers who were scheduled to make the jump. With the round-the-clock work and the donation of 1,500 personnel chutes from the 11th Airborne Division, the platoon managed to have equipment and personnel chutes ready by the sixteenth.

Colonel Jones planned to resupply his troops on Corregidor both by air and water—when possible. Initially, each paratrooper jumped in with one unit of fire for his weapon, four K-rations, and two canteens of water, among other things. The ammunition for the mortars, pack 75s, and other crew-served weapons were dropped in separate bundles with the assault force. Medical aid men dropped with each platoon, carrying as much aid equipment as possible.

Colonel Lackey allotted twelve C-47s for daily resupply from Mindoro, continuing on a daily basis until the beach was cleared and supplies could come in by ship. The regimental S-4, Capt. Robert M. Atkins, planned to have a detail gather the aerial resupply bundles and put them in a dump on Topside near the old barracks. As events turned out, this was resupply under very hazardous conditions.

Maj. Lester H. Levine was the adjutant of the regiment. After the war, he attended the Advanced Infantry Course No. 1 at Fort Benning and wrote a paper on his experiences on the Corregidor operation. In the rather formal prose of that paper he wrote:

> Supply plans included a detail of three officers and fifty men who were to bring, on D minus 4, supplies and equipment to the airstrip in the Subic Bay area. These supplies and equipment consisted of the squad kit bags, one unit of fire of 75-mm ammunition, flamethrowers, and communication equipment; from Subic Bay the detail was to transport these items via water on D plus 2. The squad kit bags, actually Air Corps parachute bags carefully labelled for rapid identification, contained for each man in the squad a blanket, one

pair of jump boots, one set of coveralls, fatigue cap, two pairs of socks, and one pair of drawers.

In reality, the plan for the resupply of the regimental combat team by water was not quite so formally prepared. Colonel Jones remembers that he took "one special action that was somewhat unusual":

It so happened that I had a number of people in the Combat Team who had been shipped from the United States as replacements. Some of the men were just plain "knuckle heads" and had very bad disciplinary records. They were quick to get into trouble in my well-disciplined organization. They were in the stockade with charges against them, awaiting trial. They had already been removed from jump status. I appointed five special courtsmartial which operated for about 10 to 12 hours a day for about a week, seeing that justice was done to all of these men. The stockade was full! The big question in my mind was how I could use these people on the operation without putting them back on jump status.

It came to my attention that we would need to be resupplied amphibiously over the beaches on Corregidor. Accordingly, I came up with this plan: I sent for Smitty, a lieutenant who, too, was on my black list, having gotten himself in some sort of trouble. When Smitty reported to me, the conversation went something like this: "Smitty, I think that you know how you stand with me, don't you?" He responded, "Yes, I do, Colonel. I know that I don't stand very well with you." I then said, "Okay, Smitty, now that we have that understanding, here's what you are going to do—you are off jump status, and I've got a number of other people who are off jump status, and, as you know, most of them are in the stockade. I'm not about to let you and those people in the stockade be left out of this operation. I've always thought that it takes "one of a kind" to command a bunch of people like you are going to command. I want you to organize a logistic support unit of this stockade population. With this unit, you will see that the Rock Force is adequately supplied by boat.

Now, I'm expecting you to do a good job, and I'll tell you now that if you do a good job, I will decorate you and any of the men that you recommend! And, of course, if you don't do a good job, you are in deep trouble." I am glad to report that Smitty, who was a good leader, did an outstanding job handling this bunch of "wayward souls" in his provisional unit. Smitty was decorated for his fine performance, as were several of those in his unit.

. . . I had long since had the nickname of "The Warden" in my organization. Perhaps this incident was only another measure of why I had been given that nickname.

By 14 February, Colonel Jones, Colonel Lackey, and their staffs had worked out most of the details of the mission. Colonel Jones had even selected the northern end of the mile-long barracks on Corregidor for his command post. The operations officer of the RCT, Maj. Ernie Clark, contacted the Navy liaison officers on Mindoro and from them learned of the capabilities and procedures for obtaining naval gunfire when he needed it. He also arranged with the Navy to have PT boats close offshore during the drop to pick up any paratroopers who might be blown into the water—a very likely possibility given the size of the DZs and the expected winds across the island. The RCT staff also arranged with the Navy to have air-sea rescue units standing by during the flight to the island and to have liaison parties of Navy and Air Corps control personnel jump with the regiment to provide close naval and air-fire support.

Lt. Dick Williams was a photographer who headed a Signal Corps Photographic Team in the Philippines. In early February, he was assigned on temporary duty to the 503d. He was, at first, not exactly sure of the 503d's mission. Two days before the 503d was scheduled to jump on Corregidor, Lieutenant Williams and his five-man team flew into the San Jose strip and started looking for the campsite of the 503d. He remembers:

The 503d Parachute Regimental Combat Team's encampment had not been easy to find on this blistering, tropical day on Mindoro Island, one of the larger of the Philippines. We were happy when our jeep struggled over a mound and the bivouac area came into view. It sat right in the middle of a dried-up streambed amidst rocks, tall grass, and dust simmering in the noonday sun. The camp covered acres with rows upon rows of dirty brown pyramidal tents forming company streets, battalion headquarters, and, at the far end, the row of long tents which should be regimental headquarters, our goal.

Ours was not the only vehicle headed for the center-cog of this emergency outfit on February 14, 1945, and, as I commanded a Signal Photographic Combat Team, it proved a task to get into the tent of Col. George M. Jones, commanding officer of the 503d. It took less time for me to report and get instructions on the forthcoming mission. It was rather a shock also to find that the regiment had been alerted for a mission to take place within the next forty-eight hours. The colonel was brief and to the point when he took my GHQ orders for assignment to his unit: "Draw combat equipment and cots for my men; let me know how many men will be jumping; see Colonel Erickson of the 3d battalion for further instructions and assignment."

Lt. Dick Williams was in for another shock—he would parachute onto Corregidor, and it would be his first jump ever.

On the afternoon of the fourteenth, The Warden called a regimental formation. The troops assembled by company and battery on the dusty parade field adjacent to the pyramidal tents they lived in. The tents had not yet been struck. The men wore their fatigues, web belts, and jump boots and carried their individual weapons. This was a rare formation for a unit in a combat zone, and as a matter of fact, it was the last regimental combat team formation of the 503d during World War II.

After the adjutant's "At ease," Colonel Jones read a commendatory message from General MacArthur that praised them for their past victories in the Pacific War and, in typical MacArthur style, bade them good fortune on their next, most important, mission. Colonel Jones then spoke briefly; he took only five minutes. His voice was strong, clear, and deliberate. One of his officers described him when he spoke as "erect, rugged, slightly tense . . . altogether a very soldierly and courageous leader."

He expressed his faith in the RCT's ability to accomplish the very difficult mission they were about to undertake, wished them well, and told them that they were about to make airborne history. The bugler sounded "Retreat" and "To the Colors," and the troops, with chests raised and morale high, marched off the field to their company areas. The climax of the afternoon was the issue, at 1800, of a beer ration—six hot cans per man. The troopers relaxed—thirty-six hours away from the most unique airborne operation in the relatively brief history of parachute troops.

At 1000 on the fifteenth, D-day for the start of the operation to open Manila Bay to Allied shipping, the 151st RCT, reinforced by the 3d Battalion, 34th Infantry, went ashore in LCVPs at Mariveles after Fifth Air Force B-24 Liberators had bombed the beach area and destroyers of Admiral Struble's Task Group 78.3 moved in for close support. The 151st met some Japanese machine gun and rifle fire but moved rapidly inland. An LSM carrying the 24th Reconnaissance Troop struck a mine and caught fire, resulting in some casualties and the loss of the unit's equipment. During the night of 15–16 February, the 3d Battalion of the 151st beat off an attack by about one hundred Japanese and killed about sixty of them. By the eighteenth, the 151st had made contact with the East Force moving down the east side of Bataan, at Limay.

The East Force was the 1st RCT of the 6th Division. It had moved out of Orani on the fourteenth and, by dark of the next day, had probed south to Orion. East Force had met little opposition until the night of 15–16 February when about three hundred Japanese attacked the 1st's perimeter near Orion. The RCT beat off the attack in a wild battle, sometimes involving hand-to-hand combat. But that Japanese attack marked the end of organized Japanese resistance in southern Bataan.

The next day, General MacArthur had a narrow escape from either injury or death. He was visiting the East Force's zone, and he and his party drove south along the Pilar-Limay coastal road to a point almost five miles ahead of the 1st Infantry's front lines. There were apparently no Japanese in the area, but a Fifth Air Force P-38 patrol spotted the column of vehicles far beyond the front lines and assumed, naturally, that they were Japanese. The patrol leader asked for permission to strafe and bomb the vehicles. General Chase, commander of the 38th Division and of the 151st operating along the south and east coast of Bataan, decided to check the identity of the vehicles before giving permission to the P-38s to strafe. General Chase's hesitancy was fortuitous—the check showed that there were only Americans in the vehicles, General MacArthur among them. The party turned back and headed for safety behind the 1st RCT's lines.

On the fifteenth, the 503d RCT went about its preparations for the jump the next day. Newsmen and photographers arrived to record the preparation for and execution of this unique attempt to reclaim the symbol of the U.S. humiliation of three years previous. The commanders briefed the pilots and jumpmasters one more time. The 503d troopers struck all of the pyramidal tents except those that were used for storing gear each man left behind in individual duffel bags. The Parachute Maintenance Platoon issued personnel parachutes and equipment bundles to the men of the 2d and 3d battalions and their reinforcements. The men packed the bundles and checked all of the webbing and the parachutes. They also once again very carefully cleaned and oiled their weapons. The supply team issued two white phosphorous and two fragmentation grenades to each man. The artillerymen cleaned their pack 75-mm howitzers and broke them down into the individual loads for subsequent mounting onto the pararacks under the bellies of the C-47s.

John Lackey completed his preparations for the first drop—the 3d Battalion at 0830 the following morning. He remembers:

A parking plan for the planes was decided upon which would not interfere with the normal operations of the airstrips (San Jose and Hill) and also be one which would cause little confusion when the hour for loading arrived. . . . Loading of aircraft is perfected by having many dry runs to be sure that all equipment and personnel are properly placed. After several practice runs, it was decided that all troops of the first lifts would be loaded in trucks in the airborne area at 0600 arriving at the airstrips at 0630, allowing 30 minutes for final checks before emplaning at 0700.

In the 503d area, the jumpmasters completed their flight manifests and turned them in to the regimental command post. The regimental staff passed out to all company commanders the parking plans at Hill and San Jose (sometimes called Elmore) strips and the flight plans of Lackey's 317th Troop Carrier Group. Platoon leaders continued to take their platoons to the briefing tent to make certain that each man knew his unit's mission and exactly what he was expected to do once he landed amid the rubble of Topside. In their spare moments, the troopers wrote letters, and the chaplains conducted services—which were abnormally well attended.

By evening, the 503d was as ready as its chain of command could make it. And to keep his paratroopers' minds properly focused on the morrow's mission, Colonel Jones arranged to show his men, in their outdoor theater, captured Japanese films that depicted the Japanese attack on and the surrender of Corregidor in 1942. The film showed the Japanese maltreating American POWs and stomping the American flag into the ground. It also emphasized again the ruggedness of the terrain and did nothing to make the paratroopers think they were going to fight an enemy that believed in and followed the Geneva Convention. Like all American troops fighting the Japanese, they believed that Japanese were uncivilized, brutal, sadistic subhumans to whom they could not and would not surrender. As a result, they found it very easy to kill Japanese.

On the night of the fifteenth, the men of the 503d bedded down as best they could. Having struck their pyramidal tents and turned in their cots, they slept, what little they could, lying on their packs on the ground.

Reveille of the 3d Battalion and its attachments was at 0530 on the sixteenth. The NCOs had little trouble rousing the men and getting them organized. Breakfast was not the usual steak and eggs before a combat jump—in the 503d area it was dehydrated eggs, soggy pancakes, and coffee, eaten in the dark by the quivering light of a gas torch. After breakfast, the men assembled by stick with their equipment, including parachutes, weapons, and musette bags; then they climbed aboard trucks for the short ride to the loading area. Each truck carried twenty or twenty-one men, one planeload of jumpers. Each truck was numbered with the same number as the chalk number on the plane for which it was headed. Thus, there was little confusion in getting the troopers to the correct aircraft.

At planeside, the trucks halted by their assigned planes, and the men scrambled down to the ground with their heavy gear. Next, the crew chief of each plane issued each man a "Mae West" life preserver, because a long leg of the flight would be over water, and, additionally, there was the possibility that a jumper might be blown into the sea near Corregidor if the jumpmaster did not "go" at the proper point. Next the men put on their web equipment and then their main and reserve parachutes and slid their rifles down through their webbing. They lined up in reverse order of jumping. On the ground, each man got an equipment check from the jumpmaster and the man directly behind him. By 0650, the men had completed donning their Mae Wests, entrenching tools, equipment packs, parachutes, ammunition pouches, and weapons. Then the order came down the line of C-47s to "mount up." Still in reverse order of jumping, the troops duck-walked—no other word adequately describes the gait of a fully equipped and combat-loaded paratrooper wearing about eighty pounds of gear—to their planes, climbed up the four steps to the interior, and took their seats along the canvas jump seats that paralleled the inside of the fuselage.

At 0700, the first plane, piloted by John Lackey, with George Jones in the cockpit, started its takeoff roll. It was followed in rapid succession by the other twenty-eight planes from that strip. On the other strip, the planes also began their takeoffs. By 0715, the planes were in formation over San Jose and had begun their 75-minute northwest flight to Corregidor.

Even as the C-47 column was approaching Corregidor, the heavy bombers of the Fifth Bomber Command were continuing their daily pounding of the island. Twenty-four B-24s blasted known and suspected gun positions with 500-pound bombs, eleven B-25s hit antiaircraft gun positions and the entire south coast with 260-pound fragmentation bombs, and thirty-one A-20s bombed and strafed wherever they found targets.

Naval bombardment had begun on the thirteenth in conjunction with the bombing and minesweeping operations in preparation for the seizure of Mariveles. During the morning of the sixteenth, cruisers and destroyers blasted the south shore of Bottomside, where Lt. Col. Ed Postlethwait was to lead his 3d Battalion, 34th Infantry, ashore at 1030. Navy ships stood by for calls for fire from their control teams, which would parachute in with the 503d and come ashore with the 34th. The PT boats, which were standing by to rescue errant paratroopers, cruised along the cliffs and machine-gunned any shore batteries they could identify. And as the C-47s loomed larger on the horizon on their way to Corregidor, seventy A-20s stood by to suppress any antiaircraft fire and to hose down the sides of Corregidor adjacent to the drop zones and the eastern end of the island.

The troopers neither knew nor cared that they had been or would be under a number of commanders in a very short space of time. For their loading and staging, they had been under the command of Lt. Gen. Robert Eichelberger of Eighth Army; when they boarded the planes of the 317th Troop Carrier Group, they had been under the command of the commanding general of the Fifth Air Force, Maj. Gen. Ennis C. Whitehead; when they hit the ground, they were under the control of Lt. Gen. Walker Krueger, Sixth Army commander and Gen. Charles P. Hall, commanding general of XI Corps; and once Colonel Jones hit the ground on Corregidor, he would be the commander of the Rock Force, the 503d RCT and the 3d Battalion Combat Team, 34th Infantry.

None of these command arrangements really concerned the troops of the 503d. They were seasoned troops, most of them battle tested, most of them combat jumpers, and all of them ready and willing to get on with their jobs. The glamor of the paratrooper and his shiny jump boots, the mystique that was attached to him as the modern version of the dashing cavalryman, the camaraderie that had been built up during months of overseas training and fighting—all of this, yet none of this, truly affected the combat-loaded paratroopers on their way to Corregidor. They were just anxious to "stand up" and "hook up" and "go."

CHAPTER XI
The Assault

On Friday, 16 February 1945, at 0825 Lt. Col. "Big John" Erickson, commanding officer of 3d Battalion, 503d RCT, crouched in the open jump door of a C-47 flying at 1,150 feet above the waters of Manila Bay. The pilot held the plane at 110 knots on a northeasterly course. Erickson, loaded with his combat gear and parachute, filled the jump door opening. He hung onto the sides of the jump door on the left side of the plane, stuck his head and shoulders out into the slipstream as far as he could, and tried to pick up his jump target a few miles ahead. The wind rippled his face, tugging strongly at the steel helmet whose strap was firmly buckled to his chin, and forced him to squint as he tried to see what was beneath and ahead of his plane. Erickson's plane was the lead ship in one of two long, single-file columns of C-47s flying to Corregidor.

Behind Erickson sat twenty-one paratroopers on bucket seats along both sides of the plane. On the right side of the plane just next to the jump door opening in which Erickson crouched were two small lights—one red and the other green. Erickson pulled his head in from the slipstream and saw that the pilot had just switched on the red light, which told Erickson that the go-point was about five minutes away.

Erickson turned to his men and shouted, "Stand up and hook up." Eight paratroopers, who had been sitting in the bucket seats along the left side of the plane, immediately struggled to their feet, ground out their cigars and cigarettes, buckled the straps of their helmets, faced to the rear of the plane, and snapped the fasteners of their parachute static lines (which would automatically pull the parachutes from their backpacks once they left the plane) to the anchor cable that ran the length of the plane's interior. They continued to hold the snap fasteners in their left hands until they were about to jump out the door.

Erickson stuck his head out into the slipstream again. In the distance, he could see his target—Corregidor. Even though his plane was still a few miles away, Erickson could make out The Rock's prominent features, which he had seen when he flew over the island in a B-25 and which he had studied so thoroughly and so recently on the sand table and terrain model on Mindoro: Topside, the bulbous head of the tadpole, about 550 feet in elevation; Middleside, its slopes gradually falling to Bottomside, with its small docks on both the north and south sides and the site of the demolished barrio of San Jose; and Malinta Hill, rising to about 400 feet, just to the east of the waist of the island at Bottomside. The narrow and relatively low tail of the island pointed out toward Manila.

Corregidor was covered with smoke and dust from the pre-invasion bombings. The blasted and shattered buildings on the island, the smoke and dust in the air told Erickson that the Navy and the Air Corps had done their jobs. He realized that it was now up to the 503d and the 3/34th to finish the job. Little did he know at that moment, however, that there were about six times as many Japanese on the island as the intelligence experts had estimated and that thousands of the enemy were alive and holed up all over the island.

Those thoughts were not uppermost in his mind at this moment, however; what concerned him now was finding the go-point, counting the prescribed four seconds before he jumped, and getting all of his stick onto DZ Alpha—the parade ground.

By the time the C-47s were on their final approach to Corregidor, they had strung out in two long lines of single ships in trail, about five hundred yards apart, twenty-five or twenty-six planes per column.

Colonel Erickson pulled his head back inside the plane once more and shouted, "Check equipment." Each man checked his own static line to make certain that it was snapped securely to

Monkey Point after the Navy radio tunnel explosion.

Paratroopers using white phosphorous grenades working on a cave on Topside. 16 February 1945.

Air strike on Topside. View is toward the southwest. Bottom of photo shows Bottomside with North Dock on the right and South Dock, where the 3/34th will land, on the left.

Long Barracks with chutes scattered on and near the Parade Ground.

Drop zone over the wrecked quarters. Theater is in the upper right corner.

Pacific War Memorial

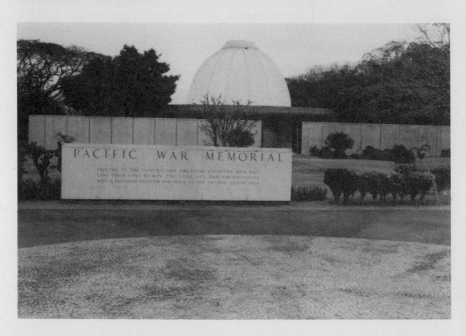

the anchor cable and that it was not under his arm. Then he checked the static line of the man in front of him to make sure that that static line was clear and not snarled under his parachute harness—a situation that would prove fatal on a jump because if a paratrooper jumped with his static line under his harness, the static line would try to pull the parachute out of the backpack under his harness—a no-win situation.

Next, Colonel Erickson yelled, "Sound off for equipment check." The last man in the stick shouted "Eight, okay" and tapped the bottom of the man in front of him. That man shouted "Seven, okay" and tapped the next man. When the count got to Erickson, he yelled, "Stand in the door." Each man shuffled to the rear of the plane and as close to the man in front of him as he could get so that when the stick jumped from the plane, it would be as tight a group as possible—but not so tight that the men became entangled. Closing up was especially important in today's operation, given the size of the DZs and the wind conditions, about twenty-two knots over the DZ. That wind speed would be enough to cancel ordinary training jumps—even on a DZ three miles long.

Erickson was now just seconds from leading his stick of eight men out of the plane. He looked out once again and could see the cliffs of Topside rapidly approaching. A few seconds later, the pilot switched on the green light, ordinarily the signal to "go." But in today's operation, the green light meant only that the pilot was over the go-point—the western edge of the concrete emplacement around Battery Wheeler. Erickson saw the green light go on, and, as planned, started his deliberate count to four seconds: one thousand, two thousand, three thousand, four thousand. Then he yelled "Go" and leaped from the plane. He was closely followed by T/5 Arthur O. Smithback and Pfc. Stanley J. Grochala. Time: 0833, just three minutes behind schedule.

Erickson felt the opening shock and then tried to get his bearings. His target had been the parade ground, but when he looked down, he saw that he was not going to make it. The 22-knot wind and the jump altitude of 550 feet were causing him to drift rapidly near the cliffs about one hundred yards to the west of Battery Wheeler. After just one or two oscillations of his chute, Erickson hit the ground in a bone-jarring crash. "Considering

They were, fortunately, ineffective. Father Powers had sense enough to send some men to the top of the hole to prevent the Japanese from rushing their position. Later, they crawled toward their assembly area and sent a litter team back for the doctor.

One of the 503d's surgeons had been in one of the planes that dropped on the parade ground. He was actually the last man in the second stick to jump from that plane. Later, he wrote:

> The first eight men of our plane-load were already hooked up within the cabin while the jumpmaster stood beside the door watching for the "Go" point. It was a tense moment for him, since his own and his men's lives hung upon the second he chose for this command to jump. The chutes of the previous planes, swinging downward, showed that the wind was even stronger than we had feared and that our jumpers were thrown backward in the direction from which we came. Our C-47 pilot was flying his course "dead on the nose." A man has no time under these circumstances for emotional thought; neither courage, fear, indecision, nor recklessness should sway him. He must be as objective as the second hand of a clock. Having crossed the point of the Battery, the jumpmaster started counting, in deliberate tones: "One thousand . . . two thousand . . . three thousand . . . The first jumper's hands were gripped backward on the outside door. His head was projected slightly into the windy blast. His legs were slightly crouched, for a spring. The other seven men pressed closely, in single file, behind him. "Four thousand . . . five thousand . . . six thousand." The jumpmaster had added two seconds to the expected count in order to compensate for the estimated force of the wind. But now was the moment. "Go." In swift, uninterrupted succession, the jumpers leapt out, and their static lines rattled along the anchor cable. Before there was time to tell it, the place where the men had stood became unbelievably vacant.
>
> Below us, as we banked for a turn, the complete panorama of the Island lay exposed. There, rose the perpendicular cliffs; there, the rough, shell-blasted Top-side; there, the narrow waist of the beach; and there, the towering mass of Malinta Hill still smoking from the bombs so recently dropped

upon it. There, the parade ground and the tiny golf course were littered with chutes, while still others in mid-air floated down on them. From our flight, we could see no fire fights, no smoke or grenades or mortars, though it was too early to expect a heavy action. The crumbling wreckage of demolished buildings offered the most forbidding sight. They were crowded in a spectral palisade around our "drop zone"; and already some of them were festooned with chutes where some of our unfortunate jumpers had landed.

. . . Major Stevens had stepped to the door the moment the first stick had completed their exits. He kept his eyes fixed on their chutes as they swung to earth. The picture was confused by other planes who were following us and dropping their "sticks" of jumpers but Stevens marked the spot where our men came down, and swiftly made his calculations. "The wind must be stronger than they figured, for they landed short of the parade ground," he yelled in the ear of his first jumper, loud enough to be heard above the engine's roar. "I'm going to hold you to a count of eight; then we'll pitch out the bundle, and you follow it." Stevens was an unusually clear-headed leader. No amount of excitement could cloud his judgment, and he was as cool now as if he were playing a poker hand, though the stakes were higher than he had ever bid before. He supervised the men as they dragged their 200-pound jump bundle to the door and nosed it just far enough out to make ready for the final push. By the time we had half rounded the circle, the jumpers of our second group were all hooking up, my own place being end man. From the door, Stevens signalled down the line. We could not hear him distinctly, but we understood the expected order, "Check equipment." Each of us made the routine tests of our snaps, and of the packs worn by the man in front of each of us. Then we stood waiting, the left hand grasping the hook of the static line along the anchor cable, and the right hand free to catch hold of the side of the cabin if the plane should rock. I made a last feel for the grenades in my pouch to see that I could reach them in a hurry, then for the string with which to inflate my Mae West jacket if I should need it for a water landing. These were clear, and so was my knife, in case I should have to cut my way clear of the straps. The handle of my reserve chute was set just right for an emergency pull. My .45 automatic was secure in its holster. O.K. I was all set to go.

Our pilot made the same expert approach as before, undismayed by the knowledge that a few Jap snipers had swung a machine gun in our direction. Major Stevens had noticed it as he looked down from the open door, and he had seen some tracer bullets breezing close to the path of our flight. The plane just in from us had swung out of line and turned away, its left engine trailing smoke. But we, inside the cabin, were ignorant of all this, and perhaps it was just as well, for nothing could be done about it anyway. Despite the impression so many people hold, a parachutist is completely defenseless while in the air. Any attempt on his part to fire back at the ground would be out of the question. . . . Suddenly, Stevens swung his arm, and immediately the jump-bundle was heaved overboard while we followed it automatically, almost before there was time to think. The one great worry to a man in the rear of the file is that someone ahead of him may stick in the door, or some obstacle may block his exit, in which case he will have to push his way through by any means available. Fortunately for me, no such delay occurred, our men all being expert jumpers. Without further incident, we found ourselves dangling in the free air over Corregidor.

The descent came easily, in spite of the wind. Seeing that I was heading uncomfortably close to the battered concrete roof of a building, I collapsed one side of my chute violently and this avoided too much drift. Just as the earth seemed about to hit me, I released my hold, and the chute again jerked open to its full diameter, thus easing the jolt of the fall. Once on the ground, the wind caught my chute so hard that I was dragged up a slope about ten feet; but, before I could manipulate my ropes to correct this, the chute caught against a high bush and gave me time to release the awkward snap-fasteners of my leg and chest straps. Others, who continued to drop all around me, were going through similar experiences. Owing to the skill and judgment of our jumpmaster, we had been lucky enough to escape all hazards, and to land unhurt on the parade ground itself. Now, there was work to be done.[26]

The plane that had to turn out of the column because of the smoking left engine was the only one in the first lift that did not drop its cargo of paratroopers as planned. That plane carried the 3d Battalion's demolition section, commanded by 1st Lt. Bill Blake of Ronceverte, West Virginia, or, in his idiom, West—by God—Virginia.

Bill Blake was one of the best-liked officers in the regiment, according to one of the doctors. "He was known among us as a sort of hillbilly sage, with a shrewd Will Rogers type of humor through which he often pointed out the folly of wisdom, and sometimes impressed us with wisdom of folly," the doctor remembers. "His rough-cut features and thick, unkempt hair helped to emphasize his role of a rustic philosopher with which he often amused us. One of his sergeants said when we had heard that Blake's plane had crashed, 'You needn't worry about the lieutenant, sir. The trouble ain't made that that man don't know the way out of. He's the cussedest know-how man I ever knowed.' "[27] Lieutenant Blake was going to need every ounce of his "cussedest know-how" to extricate himself and his men from their present dilemma.

When his plane was ten minutes from the go-point, Lieutenant Blake had already alerted his men that they were coming up on Corregidor for the first pass. The men were stretching their legs, putting on their helmets, checking their equipment, and two of the men were pushing the first bundle to the door, ready to toss it out on the command "Go." Bill Blake remembers that he "was sweating out the red light that would let me know we were three minutes from the go-point."

At about seven minutes from his drop zone, Blake, standing in the door of the C-47, saw that there "was hot oil, burning carbon, and pieces of the motor flying by." He immediately rushed

---

26. Anonymous, "Combat Over Corregidor."
27. Ibid.

to the cockpit for an emergency and very hasty conference with the pilot. By this time, the pilot had cut the engine and fanned out the fire, but "it was still throwing oil and all that stuff." The plane had been at an altitude of 1,300 feet, ready to slide down to 1,150 feet for the jump. But because of the dead left engine, the plane was slowly losing altitude in spite of the pilot's fight to keep it level and straight.

Blake pleaded with the pilot to make one pass over Corregidor, and he would jump all of his men at once instead of in the three sticks as planned. But the pilot said that he could not keep the plane up long enough to get to Corregidor, and he pulled out of the column and headed for Nichols Field, a part of which was still in Japanese hands.

Blake went back to the cabin and told the men what was going on. They were unhappy that they were out of the formation and headed either for the water or a crash landing somewhere near Nichols Field. With his plane steadily losing altitude, the pilot ordered Blake to jettison everything that was not bolted or welded to the plane. First went the door bundles, then two flame throwers, then the radios, and then the machine guns. Then the men started on any of the plane's equipment that was movable. Out went the radios, radar, door, steps, litters, brooms, food, and "everything that wasn't nailed down." In spite of these efforts, the plane continued to lose altitude; the pilot ordered Blake to throw out more gear. Blake had the men strip themselves of all of their personal equipment—rifles, web gear, ammunition, steel helmets, musette bags, and their own food. Blake remembers looking out the door, and he swears that he got a direct hit on a PT boat with a case of 10-in-one rations. But they were still losing altitude. Next Blake ordered the men to take off their reserve chutes and throw them out. He insisted that they keep their Mae Wests in the very likely chance that they would have to jump into the water somewhere between Corregidor and the mainland.

Blake went back to the cockpit and told the pilot that they were going to jump "no matter what." He had spotted a Liberty ship beneath the plane, and he saw other boats scattered along the bay. He believed that if they jumped they would have a good chance of being picked up. He felt that the odds were far better than sticking with the plane and crash-landing in the water. But when he got to the cockpit, he was overjoyed to spot land in front of him. He could see a saddle between two ridges and rice paddies beyond. The pilot said that he would crash-land the plane in the paddies. Blake told him that "right there is when we leave the plane."

The crippled plane, now smoking also from the right engine, was wallowing along at about five hundred feet altitude when it crossed the ridge. Blake went back to the cabin and had all twenty-six men stand up and hook up and close in the door. There was no need for an equipment check because they had no equipment left to check except their main parachutes. The men were remarkably calm and cool; they knew the danger of jumping from below five hundred feet with no reserves, but "they didn't look any different than they had many times before when I had jumped them in combat or a 'Sunday' jump."

Blake swatted the number one man on the rump and yelled "Go," at the top of his lungs; he left. The rest of the long stick followed without the slightest hesitation. "It was one of the most beautiful jumps I have ever seen," Blake later said. "I had hooked up first and then jumped last. I know that not ten seconds passed from the time I yelled 'Go' until the last man was out. I think I uttered the most fervent and reverent 'Thank God' I ever uttered in my life when I felt that opening shock."

In spite of the low altitude and the haste with which they left the plane, none of Blake's men was injured on landing in the rice paddies, although they had been blackened with the oily soot from the smoke through which they had to jump. Blake and his men had landed in the southern part of Bataan. After he gathered his men, Blake marched them to Mariveles and wrangled a boat ride to Corregidor the next day. And the pilot of the plane managed to nurse the stricken plane all the way to Nichols Field outside Manila. He was lucky on three counts: he landed safely, his gas tanks were just about empty, and that very morning the 511th Parachute Infantry of the 11th Airborne Division had cleared Nichols Field of the Japanese.

Another surgeon of the 3d Battalion of the 503d was Capt. Logan W. Hovis. He was in the first stick to jump from the second plane over Drop Zone B, the golf course. He was in the middle of the stick, rather than the jumpmaster, because Colonel Erickson, his battalion commanding officer, wanted to be sure that his battalion surgeon had a good chance of landing uninjured on the drop zone, rather than drifting over a cliff or landing on some buildings. As planned, the 120-pound doctor landed in the middle of the golf course, but the wind, gusting from twenty to twenty-five knots, dragged him across the rocky terrain. He did not try to collapse his chute because he "did not want to risk injuring his hands"—which he knew he would need in the days to come. As it turned out, the other battalion surgeon had sustained a severely fractured ankle on landing, had then been pinned down behind a fallen tree trunk for a time by enemy fire, and had had to be evacuated. That left the 3d Battalion with only one surgeon at a most crucial time.

Hovis's chute finally snagged on the remains of a tree at the edge of the field. But he had become so ensnared in his parachute lines that he could hardly move. Shortly, however, Lt. Don Ziler came by and cut him out of his chute.

Dr. Hovis made his way across the golf course to the lighthouse, which was located at the highest point of the island, and, as previously planned, set up his aid station. He and his medical section were very busy shortly tending the wounded and the injured. His medics had a difficult time transporting the wounded and the jump casualties because the equipment chutes and bundles carrying the litters had drifted over the cliff into the bay. But the resourceful aidmen improvised litters by using blown-out doors and blankets attached to poles, and just plain piggybacked the wounded men to the aid station. Sometime during that first day on Corregidor, Colonel Erickson told Dr. Hovis to move his aid station from the lighthouse to one of the ruined officers' quarters along officers' row. Erickson wanted the lighthouse for his command post, and it was much too crowded with the wounded and injured for double use as a command post.

After the last plane in the first lift, which dropped Erickson's combat team, made its last pass, Colonel Jones, aloft in the command plane, strapped on his equipment and his parachutes and asked Colonel Lackey to fly him over the parade ground DZ. Ordinarily, he would have been the first man to jump, but he correctly foresaw that he would be more useful to the 3d Battalion if he remained airborne and adjusted the battalion's jump patterns for greater accuracy.

At about 0940, Colonel Jones and his orderly jumped out over the parade ground. And this was a singular moment for the Rock Force because once Colonel Jones touched down on Corregidor, he was in command of the force, his own regiment plus the 3d of the 34th.

Colonel Jones's landing was not without mishap:

> We landed in a sheared-off tree area short of the parade ground, which was our target for landing. A four- or five-inch tree stump took the flesh off the inside of my thighs on each leg, which was somewhat painful, but did not require any attention from the medics. I have often joked that I was fortunate that the contact with the tree was not higher up on my anatomy or it might have changed my voice from bass to soprano.
>
> At any rate, my orderly sustained a broken ankle, but we moved to Topside, and he had the presence of mind to take into his personal custody a case of "liberated" Santori Japanese scotch. He turned this over to me and immediately qualified as a hero. He was soon evacuated from the island for treatment, but that Japanese scotch, which was very light, certainly served its purpose to get Ernie Clark, the operations officer, and me through the operation.

For the next hour, the men of the 3d Battalion plus the artillerymen of A and D batteries of the 462d and the Engineers of the 3d Platoon of the 161st continued to drop on the island, at the mercy of the northeast wind, which blew them back along their flight path. That fact plus the stubbornness of Capt. Itagaki proved fortuitous to the ultimate success of the 503d's mission.

Because of the strong wind, some twenty-five men of I Company, targeted to land on the golf course, drifted about three hundred yards southeast of the DZ over the cliff near Breakwater Point and landed in some scrub-covered hillocks two hundred feet or so above the water's edge. They quickly got out of their chutes, assembled, and started to move along a trail that led to

Topside. At a turn in the trail, the lead man of the I Company group saw about eight or nine Japanese standing near the trail, staring intently to the south over Geary Point. The lead I Company man immediately waved his arms, quietly motioning the men behind him to deploy. They started shooting and throwing grenades immediately at the startled Japanese, who scattered but returned the fire. But the Japanese fire was too little, too late. In short order, most of the Japanese were killed. One I Company man was injured. But with almost unbelievable good fortune, one of the dead Japanese was Captain Itagaki. One who survived the attack and was captured was Itagaki's aide.

Captain Itagaki and his staff were at an observation post, an outcropping on the cliff well below the level of Topside, to watch the progress of Col. Ed Postlethwait's 3/34 Combat Team around Geary Point. One of Itagaki's officers on the north side of Corregidor had seen the 3/34th load up in landing craft in Mariveles Harbor at about 0800 that morning. He alerted Itagaki, who then moved out to the Breakwater Point observation post from his command post in Malinta Tunnel. He was evidently so intent on watching the landing craft below him that he missed the parachute drops on Topside—an event that he had previously deemed unbelievable. That the noise of the aircraft overhead had not grabbed his attention is equally unbelievable.

Coupled with the immediate loss of the overall commander of the Japanese forces on the island was the capture of the Japanese communications center on Topside, located in the old bombproof telephone exchange, by some of Erickson's men, who had landed near the center. All of the Japanese wire communications from the tail of the island, from Malinta Tunnel, from the defensive positions in the ravines, and on the beaches all around the island fed into the center. But none of the outlying positions was connected laterally. Therefore, with the capture and destruction of the center, the various elements of the defense could not communicate with one another. These two events, early in the battle, effectively stole from the Japanese, so reliant on centralized control and authority, their ability to mount coordinated attacks or to defend their positions with any overall supervision and coordination.

Almost all of the paratroopers who jumped on The Rock that day had unusual experiences in making a jump under circumstances so different from other jumps. The great majority survived; others were killed or severely injured.

Pfc. Jesse S. Castillo of C Company of the 161st Engineer Company was in the first lift on a plane headed for the golf course DZ. When his jumpmaster, Lieutenant Burt, had the paratroopers stand up and check equipment, Castillo found to his horror that he had not buckled his leg straps. When Lieutenant Burt asked, "Are you ready?" Castillo yelled at the top of his lungs, "Noooooo." Castillo knew that if he jumped with his leg straps unbuckled, he would fall through the harness when he got his opening shock.

Fortunately, the plane missed the DZ on the first pass. Castillo enlisted the aid of his assistant machine gunner, Pfc. Thomas Gambrell, to help him secure the straps. By the time of the second pass, Castillo was ready. When he went out the door, his chute opened properly. Just as he got his opening shock and was facing the door of the plane, he saw a man jump whose chute never opened. Castillo watched him plummet all the way to the ground. When Castillo hit the ground, he ran about one hundred yards to the point where he saw the body land. It was his assistant, Thomas Gambrell. Sergeant Lindsay, in the same plane, also died when his chute malfunctioned.

B Battery of the 462d Field Artillery Battalion jumped on the parade ground. In the jump, Pvt. James Manning was killed by small arms fire just as he left the plane, and Pvt. Robert Reisinger was killed by a sniper just as he hit the ground. 2d. Lt. Robert Allen of Headquarters Battery was killed after his chute carried him over a cliff, where he got hung up on a tree. He was an easy target for a Japanese sniper.

Lt. Edward T. Flash was the 2d Platoon leader in F Company of the 503d. His stick jumped on the golf course, which, according to Lieutenant Flash, "was just below the Corregidor lighthouse and included a large olympic-size swimming pool. Our aircraft made three passes, extremely low, dropping approximately three troopers each pass. Each time we passed over the golf course the floor of the aircraft was riddled with bullets, splinters flying everywhere. Three men were wounded in the legs on the first pass. Two men insisted on jumping, but the third man was bleeding profusely and had to return with the aircraft to Mindoro." The entire platoon landed on the golf course. Flash "hit like a brick right next to the swimming pool. . . . As I unbuckled my parachute harness, individual Japanese riflemen started at us. We actually had to return fire and fight our way to our assembly point."

Flash also remembered another oddity of the Japanese defenses and their unique way of escaping the paratroopers. "My platoon sector of the Topside perimeter was a long administrative building just above the railroad tracks in the low ground of Wheeler Point. The first day on the perimeter we had Japs hiding in American autos, trying to coast from Topside to Bottomside. I distinctly remember it was a red roadster with a rumble seat which had been parked in front of the officers' quarters."

Maj. Arlis E. Kline was the commander of the 462d Field Artillery Battalion. He and his executive officer, Maj. Melvin R. Knudson, and his sergeant major loaded up with the 3d Battalion and jumped in on the first drop in order to get onto the island ahead of the bulk of the 462d and prepare positions for the followup batteries. Major Kline, unfortunately, made a late jump and landed on the roof of the barracks directly beyond the parade ground DZ. He rolled off the roof, fell three stories to the ground, and landed hard in rubble of rocks and corrugated roofing surrounding the base of the building. He smashed his face, broke a number of bones, but survived the shock of his landing. Major Knudson took over command of the battalion.

Capt. Emmet R. Spicer was a doctor with the 462d Field Artillery Battalion. He came in with the first wave and made a successful landing. One of the officers in the battalion, Lt. Jack Russell, remembers Doc Spicer "as an excellent doctor, a fine officer qualified as both a medic and an artilleryman and all that is fine in the term 'southern gentleman.' "

He epitomized those traits and qualities on the drop zone just after he landed. First, he set up his aid station, then he reported to the regimental surgeon, and then he returned to his own station on the edge of the parade ground near the barracks. On his way back, he saw one trooper in pain, lying on the DZ. He gave the trooper first aid—the man had lost an eye from a stray sniper shot—and had him delivered to the regimental aid station. There were other wounded—both through jumps and sniper fire—whom he treated even while under sniper fire himself from the Japanese who were now—about an hour after Erickson landed—beginning to edge out of their caves and tunnels and fire their machine guns and rifles at the still-disorganized paratroopers.

The DZ was littered with the equipment bundles, abandoned parachutes, and many injured paratroopers. Captain Spicer made his way among them. One of the wounded men told Captain Spicer that there were more injured men in a gully to the west between the two drop zones. Unfortunately, it was far from clear of Japanese. Nonetheless, Spicer decided to go down into the gully to help the men there. Capt. Albert L. Tait of Headquarters Battery of the 462d remembers the last time he saw Doc Spicer. "He said there were wounded soldiers in there [the gully] and he was going in. That was the last time I saw Doc alive."

No one knows exactly what happened to Doc Spicer, but when they found his body the next morning, attached to it was a medical tag like those he had used so often on other wounded troopers. Spicer had written his name, rank, and serial number and included in the proper place on the form his own diagnosis: "GSW [gunshot wound], perforation of the left chest. Severe. Corregidor. 16 February 1945." He had failed to include only the time of death.

When a patrol found him the next morning, he was dead—and the wound was precisely as he had diagnosed. He had given himself a shot of morphine, smoked a last cigarette, and drunk the last of the precious water in his canteen. He was posthumously awarded the Silver Star.

The troopers of the 3d Battalion Combat Team would, if asked, certainly have agreed with Itagaki's appraisal of Topside as totally unsuitable for a parachute landing. Without a doubt, Topside was "the worst jump field ever used for an airborne operation." Fortunately, the casualties did not reach the 50 percent estimate made by Colonel Jones prior to the operation. But the injury rate was significant nonetheless. The men had landed for the most part around and away from the designated drop zones and crashed onto large chunks of concrete, snagged themselves in trees, bounced off the roofs of shattered buildings, drifted over the cliffs, and fallen into the countless bomb craters that had turned the area into a moonscape. One terribly unfortunate trooper had a streamer—a partially opened chute—and had plummeted into the empty Fort Mills swimming pool. When the aidmen found his body, his blood had saturated his parachute.

In Erickson's battalion, some 1,000 men jumped onto Corregidor; of that number, 750 were available to fight. Some were policing up bundles from the DZ; others were severely injured. "But," Colonel Erickson said, "it should be remembered that we did not consider a man a casualty unless he was immobile as a result of broken bones or was suffering shock as the result of wounds or injuries. Otherwise, he was treated, bandaged, and continued to fight."

By about 1000, Erickson's companies and the artillery battery had assembled most of their men and a good part of their equipment. They began to accomplish their immediate tasks—clearing the area around the DZs, occupying the high ground that overlooked the roads leading up from Middleside and Bottomside, and establishing a perimeter that included both of the DZs, the "Long" barracks where the regimental command post was located, the old hospital to the north of the barracks, and the Middleside barracks.

In clearing the Middleside barracks, H Company killed three Japanese hiding in the building. After moving through that area, Capt. Joseph M. Conway, the H Company commander, sent a platoon as far as Morrison Hill, which overlooked Chicago Battery. The platoon took the battery from the rear.

G Company, under Capt. Jean P. Doerr, secured the area overlooking Ramsay Ravine and set up a pair of .50-caliber machine guns from D Battery of the 462d in time to support the landing of the 3d Battalion, 34th Infantry, making its landing at South Dock.

Back on the parade ground, at about 1100, two men from the regimental headquarters company, T/5 Frank Arrigo and Pfc. Clyde I. Bates, climbed up one of the few still-erect telephone poles near the parade ground and attached to its top a U.S. flag that flew there day and night for the rest of the campaign. I Company secured the drop zones in preparation for the next lift—the 2d Battalion, 503d, Service Company, B Battery, and a machine gun platoon of D Battery, 462d.

At 0800, while the paratroopers of the 503d were aloft on their way to drop on Corregidor, BLT #3—3d Battalion, 34th Infantry (Reinforced)—began loading at Mariveles into twenty-five LCMs of the 592d Engineer Boat and Shore Regiment, their transportation for the jarring, two-and-a-half-hour ride across the North Channel, separating Corregidor from Bataan, and around the west and southwest corners of The Rock. Destination—Black Beach, Corregidor, a narrow, 200-yard-wide beach in front of the by-now obliterated Filipino village of San José. Before the war, it was known as South Dock. Before their departure, their commanding officer—Lt. Col. Edward M. Postlethwait, a tall West Pointer, class of 1937, and thirty-four at the time, gave his troops some last-minute advice. "There's no place to go, once you're there," he said, "but forward. We simply take a hill at all costs and stay there until we've killed all the Japs or the Japs have killed all of us."

Weldon B. Hester, the Red Cross field director with the 34th Infantry Regiment was present when Ed Postlethwait briefed his battalion on the coming operation. He said that Ed Postlethwait's next statement "raised the hair on the back of my neck." Postlethwait finished his briefing with these words: "The only reason you will not reach the top of Malinta Hill is because you are dead or incapable of putting one foot in front of another."

Postlethwait's overall mission was clear, if not easy to accomplish: seize and occupy Malinta Hill and clear out Bottomside, thus effectively cutting Corregidor in half. This barrier across the island would prohibit the Japanese on the tail from getting to Topside and would permit the 503d to clear Topside without worrying about attacks from Malinta, Bottomside, or the tail.

General Krueger stated Postlethwait's mission even more clearly. He said later: "The amphibious landing to be made on Corregidor by an infantry battalion in conjunction with the airborne assault was considered essential to gain a beachhead, establish a supply base, and secure Malinta Hill. The landing seemed feasible, since it would be made while enemy forces were disorganized by the bombardment and the airborne assault." (Army commanders have a distinct way of putting battalion commanders' missions in precisely clear and simple prose, as if each battalion task were untroubled and seemingly effortless.)

As the amphibious soldiers, crowded and huddled down in the wells of the LCMs, made their way around Geary and Breakwater points, they watched the skies overhead. They saw the C-47s making their circular flights over the DZs, and they watched in fascination as the paratroopers dropped out of the planes and drifted in and slammed onto Topside. They could see hundreds of chutes draping the cliffs and the trees where the paratroopers had been blown by the winds. They sailed past destroyers and cruisers that were still pinpoint-shelling parts of the island around its perimeter. And they watched the Air Corps planes strafe and bomb the edges of the island, paying particular attention to the area where they were about to land.

XI Corps planners, in selecting the South Dock area for the landing of Postlethwait's battalion combat team, estimated that the Japanese would expect an amphibious attempt either at the more obvious North Dock (because it was closer to Mariveles) or on the tail of the island, which was more open and flat. The planning staff hoped that by landing at South Dock they would catch the Japanese at the point of their weakest defenses against an amphibious landing. The staff also hoped that the parachute assault, coupled with the air and naval strikes all around the island, particularly in the Bottomside area, would divert the attention of the Japanese and permit the 3d Battalion, 34th, to make a relatively easy, if not unopposed, landing.

The column of twenty-five LCMs, in waves of five ships each, rounded Geary. There they picked up their Navy escorts, rocket ships that would precede them to the landing beach and fire salvos of missiles at the caves and possible enemy defensive positions that overlooked or dominated the South Dock area. Before the first wave landed, three Navy destroyers, only five hundred yards offshore, blasted the caves with salvos from their 5-inch guns. The rocket ships moved even closer to the landing beach and loosed salvos of fire-trailing rockets with deadly accuracy against the shore points. In spite of the fire, however, one of the rocket ships took four hits from a 3-inch gun on shore. She did not sink but kept on firing her 40-mm guns and machine guns and then went up on the advanced firing line and fired her rockets.

The XI Corps planners were almost, but not perfectly, on target in selecting South Beach as the best area for the assault of the 3d of the 34th. The first wave of five LCMs hit the beach at 1028, two minutes ahead of schedule. They had received some machine gun fire from the cliffs just east of Ramsay Ravine, and three of the LCMs were hit, but none of the men was wounded. The first wave went ashore without further opposition or casualties. The infantrymen scrambled out of the beached landing craft and raced across the sand. As they ran, they noticed that the Japanese had mined the beach with antivehicle mines whose noses they could see sticking above the sand. But they raced ahead, carefully avoiding the mines or any trip wires that might have connected them.

The next four waves of boats met more fire than had the first. One boat in wave three took forty machine gun bullets, and another took a direct hit from a mortar round. The last two waves took even more hits from the Japanese, who were now recovering from the pounding by the destroyers and the rocket ships. Most of the fire came from machine guns in Ramsay Ravine, Breakwater Point, and from cliffs at San Jose Point, just at the southwest corner of Malinta Hill. Amazingly enough, however, losses among the amphibious troops were slight—only two men were killed and six wounded in the landings. Postlethwait's boat was in the third wave and was the one that had taken forty hits. A Japanese 20-mm round had also killed the coxswain of his boat and one other man aboard.

The vehicles that came in on the LCMs of the fifth wave were not able to escape the 130 mines that lined about 125 yards of the beach. First, an M-4 Sherman tank of the 603d Tank Company, and then a 37-mm antitank gun of its Anti-Tank company were blown up. By the time the fifth wave had hit the beach, the Japanese were recovering rapidly. They enfiladed the beach with machine gun fire from both flanks and dropped mortar shells into the vehicles trying to get away from the area. One mortar knocked out a truck.

At this point, there was a great deal of confusion on the beach. An engineer NCO organized a party to mark a lane through the mines and another bulldozed stalled or wrecked trucks and jeeps out of the way. By 1053, all of the LCMs had unloaded their cargos and were pulling back out to sea. Unfortunately, the mortaring and the mines had disabled almost half of the vehicles that tried to land with the fifth wave.

In spite of the cross fire on the beach—from the west near Ramsay Ravine and from San Jose Point in the east—by 1100 the first two companies ashore, L and K, had raced and scrambled onto their objective, Malinta Hill. They had expected to fight a fierce battle for that summit, but they reached it with no losses. Once on top, Capt. Frank Centenni, commanding officer of K Company, said simply, in disbelief, "I'll be damned." They had accomplished a large part of their mission in record time—in sharp contrast to the terrible loss of life that the Japanese had experienced three years earlier in their amphibious assault on the tail of the island.

The reason for the success of the parachute and amphibious landings was undoubtedly surprise. One of the Army's astute military writers, Robert Ross Smith, said in "Triumph in the Philippines":

> Surprise was complete. The lack of opposition to the first parachute drops and to the initial landing waves at Bottomside can be attributed both to the shock of preparatory naval and air bombardment and to the fact that the Japanese had not expected a parachute attack. Evidently, circling bombers and fighters of the Allied Air Forces had kept the Japanese under cover while the LCMs and escorts approaching from Mariveles apparently diverted Japanese attention from the in-coming C-47s. Indeed, since the C-47s resembled "Betty" bombers of the Japanese Army Air Force, the Japanese naval troops on Corregidor may have assumed that the troop-carrying aircraft were more American bombers. In turn, the para-

chute drop diverted Japanese attention from the amphibious craft moving on Corregidor. Obviously, confused by the coordinated assault, the Japanese did not know what to do first. By the time they had recovered their wits sufficiently to take meaningful action, the 3d Battalion of the 34th and 503d Infantry Regiments had secured their initial objectives with negligible combat losses.

While L and K companies of the 34th had been scrambling to the top of Malinta Hill, the other three companies in the 3d Combat Team went about their tasks: seizing Bottomside; helping to unload equipment; and blocking the west entrance of Malinta Tunnel, the Navy tunnels on the south, and the roads running around the sides of Malinta Hill.

On Topside, Erickson's first mission was to clear the drop zones for the arrival of the 2d Battalion combat team of the 503d, due to begin dropping at 1215. Initially, there was light opposition on the DZs from the Japanese—a few small and uncoordinated teams of Japanese armed with light machine guns and rifles. Erickson's men dispatched them or killed them with little difficulty. But this was in no way a sample of what was to come. The paratroopers may also have been lulled into a false sense of security— given the light initial opposition and the fact that the bulk of the enemy was still hidden underground in the myriad caves, tunnels, ravines, and blasted concrete buildings and gun pits that surrounded Topside. The Americans were still thinking in terms of 850 to 1,000 Japanese when, in actuality, there were about 6,000 of them, living like moles underground.

Given the high rate of jump casualties on the first drop, and unaware yet of the large number of Japanese actually hidden on the island, Colonel Jones considered canceling the drop of his 2d Battalion Combat Team, having it land at the San Marcelino airfield above Subic Bay, and moving over water in LCMs to the beach area secured by the 3d of the 34th. But even though he had made the decision, he was unable to cancel the drop because of communications difficulties back to Mindoro. As it turned out, given the steadily increasing attacks by the Japanese on Topside, it is probably just as well that the 2d Battalion Combat Team came in by parachute as planned. By midafternoon, the tempo of the enemy assaults began to increase.

The same aircraft that had dropped Erickson's battalion had returned to the airstrips at Mindoro by 1000. After the planes landed, the crew chiefs refueled them, performed any necessary maintenance, moved them to the parking and loading areas, and lined up the planes by chalk serial number. Maj. Lawton B. Caskey, commander of the 2d Battalion Combat Team, had his battalion ready to load by 0830.

Capt. Henry W. "Hoot" (of course) Gibson was the commander of B Battery, 462d, which was slated to jump with and support Caskey's battalion on Corregidor.

Going back to Corregidor would be a unique experience for Hoot Gibson. He grew up at the U.S. Navy base at Cavite, about ten miles to the east of Corregidor, across Manila Bay, where his father worked for the Navy. "As a kid," he says, "I went to Fort Mills, Corregidor, to participate in swimming meets with the Army kids there. I knew the island very well, and I passed this knowledge on to my officers and men." When he landed, he would be shocked at the devastation wrought on the once-beautiful island.

The fifty-one planes in the second lift carried the 2d Battalion, 503d; a detachment of the regimental headquarters company; Service Company, 503d; Battery B of the 462d; and a .50-caliber machine gun platoon of D Battery, 462d. Jumping with this group was Lt. Col. John J. Tolson, formerly commander of the 503d's 3d Battalion when it jumped on Nadzab. He was now assigned to the G-3 Section of the Sixth Army, and as when he jumped at Noemfoor, he was General Krueger's personal representative on the island. In addition, he was the Rock Force's deputy commander.

Major Caskey led his battalion onto The Rock at 1240 on the sixteenth, about twenty-five minutes behind schedule. In one sense his jump was better than the 3d Battalion's: by the time Caskey and his battalion were jumped, the procedures had been refined, the jump altitudes and go-points had been fine-tuned, and even with a wind of more than twenty knots, most of the

2d Battalion landed more or less on the drop zones.[28] Ten of his troops did drift over the cliffs and were rescued by PT Boat 376. In all, on both drops, PT Boat 376, with Lts. Raymond P. Shafer and Charles Adam manning their flimsy rubber rafts, got the men to shore even though they were under fire from Japanese in caves along the cliffs.

In another sense, however, the 2d Battalion Combat Team had a harder time of it than did the 3d Battalion. In the first place, the Japanese were now aware that an airborne operation was taking place, even though they grossly overestimated the number in the assault airborne force. (One of the few POWs taken said that the Japanese had estimated that eight thousand men were in the parachute forces.) The Japanese were able to get out of their holes and hiding places because the Air Corps and the Navy could no longer bomb Topside at random. They had established bomb lines inside of which they could not fire; but inside those bomb lines were hundreds of the enemy.

The second lift, therefore, took more antiaircraft fire, and the paratroopers descending and struggling on the ground to get out of their chutes took more machine gun and sniper fire than had Erickson's battalion. Some of the fire at the second lift came from a Japanese 20-mm antiaircraft gun and two American .50-caliber machine guns that had dropped wide of the DZ. The Japanese quickly put the machine guns into action against the descending and assembling troopers. In both drops, the Japanese killed some ten men either in the air or on the ground before they could get out of their chutes. Some of these were men who had been blown over the cliff and had landed near the caves that honeycombed the cliff area. Ten other men were killed on the two jumps—three who had malfunctioning parachutes and seven who crashed so violently into concrete buildings that they were killed outright.

A lot of the Japanese fire that harassed the 2d Battalion while it was assembling was coming from the area around Wheeler

---

28. Unfortunately, Lt. Col. Jack Tolson broke his foot on the jump but did manage to avoid evacuation for four or five days.

and Cheney batteries. One victim of this fire was T/5 Lloyd S. Allen, a medic with the 462d Parachute Field Artillery Battalion, who was treating a wounded man in a bomb hole and needed more plasma. He spotted a medical equipment bundle a few yards away from the hole where he was treating the wounded trooper and dashed out to retrieve the bundle but was cut down by Japanese fire on his return.

Lt. Donald E. Abbott was the executive officer of Company E, 2d Battalion, 503d. "If there is any assignment in the service which is more of a 'fifth wheel' than the post of Company Executive Officer, it could only be that of Assistant Platoon Leader, another post that I held for a seemingly endless time," he recalls. "That post, however, let me participate in the first-wave assault that I would otherwise have missed." George Jones saw to it that the executive officers of the companies and batteries in the second wave jump in with the first so that they would be on the ground when their units arrived, they would be somewhat acclimated to the situation, and they would have been able to reconnoiter their unit's locations before their arrival.

Abbott jumped in with a plane carrying part of the regimental headquarters. He was leading the third stick out of the plane, and he had noticed that the first two sticks had drifted well south of their DZ, the parade ground. So he took it upon himself to extend the count. When the green light came on, the C-47's crew chief started pounding on his leg, thinking that he had frozen in the door and was not going to jump. But Abbott waited until he was two-thirds of the way across the parade ground before he leapt.

I first hit in a jumble of rubble that had been thrown around by earlier bombing and then bounced several times before I managed to stop my chute with the help of a couple of men who had already landed. A few feet more and I would have been pulled over the side of Battery Wheeler. . . . Had I jumped only an instant earlier, I would have landed over the edge and probably taken part of the stick with me. . . .

Luckily, we met with very little opposition from the Japanese at the time of our jump because they were mostly in their holes down the sides of the island escaping the heavy bombardment from the air force and the navy which had preceded our landing. While the time between leaving the door of the C-47 and landing on the ground was short, I remember looking to the east on the way down and seeing a B-25 making a run on the center of the island in the vicinity of Malinta Hill. If the Japanese had attacked in force at the time we were recovering from the jump, we could have been wiped out. They, however, had been told that a parachute landing was impossible because of the lack of places to land, and as a consequence, they had set up all of their defenses to protect against a landing from the sea.

In the midst of the confusion and disorganization that always follows a mass parachute jump—as the troops recover their bundles, find their assembly areas, and get organized into units— Lieutenant Abbott found a spot of tranquillity and calm.

I could not have been on the ground for an hour when I was checking the area northwest of the barracks and came across a 75-mm howitzer section from the 462d Parachute Field Artillery Battalion. The men had already found a supply of liquor that the Japanese had stored somewhere in the barracks and were passing around a bottle. They had their gun set up and were ready to fire but were, by that time, feeling no pain and invited, "Hey, lieutenant, how about a drink of this brandy?" Paratroopers, in general, had a great talent for finding something to drink in the least likely places.

The company that probably experienced the most difficult landing was E Company, on the second drop. E Company had loaded up at Elmore airstrip on Mindoro at 1105; the lead plane began dropping its paratroopers at 1244. Capt. Hudson C. Hill was the company commander of E Company. When his plane got over the go-point, Battery Wheeler, Hill counted the required seven seconds and then jumped. Seven seconds was not enough. He landed on the ruins of a three-story concrete building to the south of his drop zone, the parade ground. When he hit the top of the building, his parachute collapsed, and he crashed through the ruins of the building to the floor. His most serious injury was the loss of seven teeth, either knocked out or broken off. He concluded that "the loss of the teeth was a fair exchange for possible death had I landed outside of the building." He and a number of his men had landed in an area that was swept by intense machine gun fire from pillboxes near Cheney and Wheeler batteries. Some fifty men of Companies E and F were trapped in the three buildings along the western edge of the parade ground.

About a hundred yards to his west, Hill could see several men trying to get out of their parachute harnesses while trying to avoid the heavy enemy fire. Some of the men around them were already dead, still in their parachutes. Two of his men ran out of the building in an effort to help the injured and the men in the exposed position. One of them was machine gunned before he had gone fifteen yards. The other was seriously wounded and managed to get back to the cover of the building.

About the same time that these two men scrambled out of the building, fourteen Japanese soldiers ran out of a dugout near Battery Wheeler and attacked with bayonets the men lying on the ground, "even those lying helpless on the ground." Almost every man in Hill's building opened fire on the Japanese and drove them back to their hole. Hill yelled to the men on the outside to lie flat on the ground until he could get help to them. He assigned men in the building fields of fire to keep the Japanese from returning.

One of the dead men lying to the west of Hill's position was S. Sgt. Edward Gulsvich, the platoon sergeant of Company E's 60-mm mortar platoon. Sergeant Gulsvich had been hit by Japanese fire while he was still in the air, but he was still alive when the Japanese "attempted to spear the jumpers on their bayonets as they landed." Singlehandedly, Sergeant Gulsvich killed fourteen of the enemy with his Thompson submachine gun before he was finally killed by cross fire from two machine guns covering the area. He was later awarded the Distinguished Service Cross.

Captain Hill used his SCR 536, a handheld radio with a short range, to contact Lieutenant Abbott. He told Abbott of the situation and the need for fire support to drive off the Japanese and knock out their pillboxes so that Hill and the men with him could get out of the building and get on with their mission—securing the perimeter in the north and northwest corner of the drop zone and being prepared to attack James Ravine on order. Hill directed Abbott to get the artillery to fire point-blank at the pillboxes near Cheney and Wheeler as soon as possible. At 1400, Hill and the men holed up with him in the buildings heard the welcome sound of the 75s whistling overhead. A few more rounds aimed directly at the pillboxes silenced the enemy machine guns.

At 1450, Hill was able to lead his men and the others from other companies of the 2d Battalion up across the parade ground to his company assembly area in the northwest corner of the parade ground. It took him about forty minutes to gather and assemble what men were available. When his platoon leaders reported in to him, he found that he had lost one officer and thirty-seven men; his effective strength was six officers and ninety-five men. Of his losses, five had been killed in action, twelve wounded, twelve injured, and eight missing. The eight missing men had drifted over the cliffs; Pfc. John F. Romero had organized them and led them back to Topside by daybreak of the seventeenth. They had met only slight enemy fire on the cliffs around Topside.

Hoot Gibson's plane was about halfway back in the string of C-47s that was jumping on the parade ground. He recalls:

We had decided on using a small building on the south end of the DZ as our go-point. And I told my jumpmasters to add a few seconds to the jump order because the pilots said they were encountering head winds and some of the early drops were missing the DZ and drifting into the cliffs and the water.

We got our red light about ten minutes out, and the men quickly checked equipment. All were excited but eager to go into action. The plan was to fly in single file and discharge half our personnel and the paracrates [which held the pack 75s broken down into parachutable loads under the plane's fuselage] on the first pass, circle around and drop the remainder of the stick on the second pass.

As we approached the go-point, I could see the bulk of the parachutes were south of the DZ and, as we passed over the shack, I counted about five seconds before I yelled "Go" and released the bundles. As we circled, I could see that the stick was dropping in the DZ and, on the second pass, I did the same thing and led the stick out. We dropped about eight men on each pass.

I landed in the DZ and rolled into a large bomb crater and became entangled in my parachute shroud lines. A trooper passed by, and I yelled at him to give me a hand. He did and cut my lines so I could extricate myself. The DZ was full of men running to their bundles. There was no firing although I could hear some rifle fire in the ravine to the south of the DZ.

Each artillery battery dropped six 75-mm pack howitzers as we did not know what our losses would be. My men recovered all six of our howitzers plus two of A Battery's. When I received the report from my section chiefs of our personnel and equipment status, I headed for battalion headquarters in the old barracks to report to the battalion commanding officer. When I got there, I found Major Kline [the battalion commanding officer] on a stretcher with his head all bandaged and his arms in slings.

I returned to my unit, which was assembling on the east end of the DZ, and I picked the last officers' quarters in that row as my command post. My 1st Sergeant, Eddie Powers, reported that two men were missing. . . . We also had a few minor injuries, such as sprains, bruises, cuts. They received first aid at the battalion aid station and reported back for duty. There were many there with broken bones and cuts.

The jump casualties for the 2,050 men who jumped during both battalion drops were high but less than the more pessimistic guesses of the 503d's staff before the operation. Total jump casualties were some 280, or approximately 13.7 percent, some 11 percent lower than the planners had been willing to accept. Of the 280 casualties, 210 had been injured on landing and another 50 wounded in the air or by enemy fire on the drop zones. About 180 men had to be evacuated and hospitalized. Three men were killed when their chutes malfunctioned, 2 when they crashed into concrete buildings, and 15 were killed by Japanese fire before they could get out of their tangled chutes.

By about 1400, Major Caskey had assembled enough of his battalion to begin to take over the duties of perimeter defense around the drop zones from Colonel Erickson's 3d Battalion. Erickson's battalion had already cleared the parade ground DZ and had then gone into Topside barracks to the north of the parade ground to clear it out. The barracks by this time was clear of the Japanese, but the H Company soldiers did find a rather important cache—especially since the water supply was nil—a few cases of saki and liquor. The H Company commander, Capt. Joe Conway, very wisely immediately put a guard on the booty. Next, he cleared the gutted hospital, which was three hundred yards to the north of and behind the main barracks.

When the 2d Battalion took over the perimeter defense mission, generally an uneven circle running roughly along the 500-foot contour line, Colonel Erickson tackled the next part of his mission—clearing the rest of Topside and making contact with the 3d of the 34th at South Dock and around Malinta Hill. He moved H Company to the high ground northeast of the hospital. H Company ran into little opposition. It killed three Japanese stragglers in the old Middleside Barracks, and then Conway sent a platoon onto Morrison Hill, which permitted the platoon to take Chicago's gun pits from the rear. The platoon found some "very fine defensive positions," according to Capt. Magnus L. Smith, who was an assistant operations officer on the regimental staff. "Why the Japs gave up these positions without a fight is known only to the oriental mind."

G Company had earlier moved into the old U.S. AA gun pits five hundred yards west of the South Dock, just to the north of Ramsay Ravine. From these positions, the company could support the landing of the 3d of the 34th on Black Beach. G Company also set up some .50-caliber machine guns in buildings on the east side of the golf course to help suppress any Japanese fires against the 34th. G Company, from these positions, could also interdict the road leading from Bottomside to Topside. But even though there had been actual contact between a patrol of G Company and the 3d of the 34th at 1630, the road from Bottomside to Topside was still not secure. This fact prevented Colonel Jones from evacuating his wounded and injured to South Dock, where they could be transported to hospital ships, and it also prevented resupply to the 503d across the South Dock. The 503d still had to rely on aerial resupply by the twelve C-47s that Colonel Lackey had allocated for this purpose.

I Company, after it had assembled on Field B, the golf course, manned the eastern edge of the perimeter and was in position before 1000 so that its machine guns, spotted on the 250-foot contour line, could help support the landings of the 3d Battalion of the 34th. When they were relieved by the 2d Battalion, two platoons of I Company moved into Ramsay Ravine and set up positions along the same level—the 250-foot contour line.

By midafternoon, the Japanese were cautiously emerging from their underground caves and tunnels and becoming much more active around the perimeter of Topside. The greatest concentration of fire and enemy troops was still in the Cheney and Wheeler Battery areas and in the ravine between. The Japanese covered the parade ground with heavy concentrations of machine gun and rifle fire and kept up a steady volume that pinged and ricocheted off the concrete sides of the long enlisted-men's barracks. The fire on the drop zones became so heavy by late afternoon that the regimental supply officer, Capt. Robert M. Atkins, and his section had to abandon their attempt to recover the supply bundles that littered the two drop zones.

Because of the inherent disorganization of parachute units immediately after a drop, even under the best of circumstances, and the Corregidor jump was at the opposite end of the spectrum, paratroopers are then obviously at their most vulnerable. And for some reason, the western edge of the 503d's perimeter, overlooking Cheney and Wheeler batteries, was weak and lacked depth all day long on the sixteenth.

Had the Japanese been aware that there were only about two thousand men on Topside, and many of them not yet organized into their fighting formations, they could have raised havoc with the attacking force. The death of Captain Itagaki and the loss of their communications were factors that were almost pure luck for the 503d. Even though the attacks of the Japanese on the afternoon of the sixteenth were increasingly heavy, they were obviously uncoordinated. The attacks lacked control and unity and were more in the nature of banzais—many more of which were to bedevil the 503d and 3/34th's soldiers before Corregidor would be secure. All day on the sixteenth, the two thousand men of the 503d on Topside and the one thousand men of the 3d of the 34th across Bottomside were very susceptible. But the Japanese were confused, disorganized, leaderless, and out of communication, one unit with another. Their defenses, well dug in along the beaches and lower levels of the cliffs, had been aimed at repulsing an amphibious attack—not a combined airborne-amphibious assault. So the 503d and the 3d of the 34th—the Rock Force—went about their missions, still actually unaware of the size of the enemy force that outnumbered them approximately two to one, even after all of the Rock Force was ashore. Good training, aggressive patrolling, and coordinated actions saved the day. A little luck helped.

By midafternoon, Hoot Gibson had B Battery of the 462d assembled and in firing position on the east end of the golf course drop zone. Up until this time, there had been few calls for artillery fire. But when the Japanese machine gun started firing and kept the supply section off the DZ, Hoot Gibson "pinpointed the machine gun fire coming from a hill near Wheeler Battery southwest of our position." Gibson ordered the first section of his battery to disassemble a pack 75 and carry it to the second-story porch of the officers' quarters he was using as a command post. A concrete railing around the porch gave the gun crew some protection. He felt that he could not fire the weapon on the ground because the gun crew "would have been exposed to the machine gun fire."

When the gun was ready to fire, Gibson went up to the porch to direct its fire. Directly in front of the gun and obscuring his vision toward Wheeler Battery was a cargo chute that had caught on a roof overhang. A couple of men tugged on the chute but failed to budge it. Pfc. John P. Prettyman jumped up on the railing, gave it a strong pull and released the chute. But before he could get down from the railing, a Japanese machine gun fired a burst that caught Prettyman across the chest. He fell to the ground mortally wounded.

Captain Gibson recalled:

This inspired all of us. All caution went out the window. I ordered one round of time fire, estimating the range to the target and using the tables for the fuze setting. We got an air burst slightly over, so I reduced the fuze setting a few seconds, and we got a short round which impacted on the hill. We fired for effect and fired several·rounds which gave us a mix of air bursts and impact bursts. We continued to sweep the hill and the wooded areas around it, firing round after round of high explosive. They poured shell after shell into that hill for about fifteen minutes when I ordered them to cease fire. The MG fire ceased, and no more fire came into the DZ so that the troops once again continued to pick up bundles and supplies.

Pfc. Prettyman was awarded the Silver Star posthumously, although Capt. Gibson thought that he deserved a much higher award for his gallantry. "It was again an act of valor without thought of its consequences," he wrote later. "A job had to be done, and he did not hesitate to do it. He gave his life that others might live. He was a brave soldier."

The Topside Barracks, even though it was still under enemy sniper and machine gun fire from caves and pillboxes and old revetments to the south and west of the parade ground, was like a magnet, drawing into its tattered and shattered structure the command posts, medical sections, communications centers, fire direction centers, and air and naval gunfire support teams of the Rock Force. The 503d regimental command post, the 503d Medical Section, Headquarters and Fire Direction Center of the 462d Artillery Battalion, Service Company of the 503d, the 2d Battalion command post, the 6th Air Support Party, and the 592d Joint Assault Signal Company all made their way into the spacious, if open-aired, rooms of the old barracks. "It was better than trying to dig into the rock of The Rock," one battalion staff officer said.

In short order, the barracks began to take on the look of a functioning command post. In typical military fashion, one of the sergeants found some old brooms, the clerks swept out the offices, hardy types shoveled out most of the debris, and scrounging supply sergeants found desks and chairs (one of carved teakwood) reasonably intact. Radios were set up and functioning, maps were tacked up to the walls, reports began to come in, and wire communications were being laid to the subordinate command posts, the only major one of which, the 3d Battalion's, was outside the Topside Barracks. Erickson had set up his command post in the old lighthouse to the east of the golf course DZ. The S-2 of the regiment looked at some documents taken from seven dead Japanese near the barracks, and for the first time, Colonel Jones began to find out just who he was fighting. The documents identified the dead as members of a naval unit. One staff officer remembers that they "were all well fed and equipped."

By late afternoon, Colonel Jones was beginning to feel that his task force had the situation well in hand, although he was not yet aware of the true extent of the enemy on and under the rocks of Corregidor. He knew that the Japanese had not launched any coordinated attacks, the 3d of the 34th was well dug in on Malinta, and the two battalions of the 503d had established a fairly tight perimeter around Topside. He reasoned, therefore, that it would be illogical and derelict of him to permit the 1st Battalion Combat Team to jump onto Corregidor the next morning, as scheduled, and subject themselves to the same order of casualties suffered by the first two battalion combat teams. Therefore, at 1830 he got off a message to General Hall at XI Corps, under whose immediate command he was operating, recommending that the jump for the next morning be canceled and that the 1st Battalion Combat Team be flown from Mindoro over Corregidor, where they would drop their supply bundles, and then fly to the San Marcelino airfield near Subic Bay, where they would land and transfer to landing craft for the trip back to Corregidor, with a landing at South Beach, the same one used by the 3d of the 34th.

General Hall approved the recommendation, but Maj. Robert H. Woods, commanding officer of the 1st Battalion did not get the message until 0700 the following morning. But it was in time to cancel the drop. The paratroopers, some no doubt disappointed at not making the combat drop on Corregidor and well aware that the other two battalions would taunt them about their method of entry into combat, were simply passengers as the C-47s overflew Corregidor.

By the evening of the sixteenth, the 2d and 3d battalions had formed a fairly tight perimeter around Topside. Most of the supplies had been picked up from the DZ, but Captain Atkins felt that the supply report he gave to the regimental staff that evening was "somewhat meaningless." Most of the men had eaten the food they jumped with; the real shortage was water. The two canteens each man brought with him went fast in the heat of the tropical sun. There was no water supply on Corregidor that they could get to; the men would have to wait for the resupply drop of the C-47s or until ships could dock at South Dock and the road from Topside to Bottomside could be cleared. But for the moment, they were parched.

By 1700, part of the 3d Battalion had pulled back into the perimeter on the east end of Topside, and the 2d Battalion manned the west and north sides. The machine gunners put their weapons into defensive positions, checked their fields of fire, and settled in for the night. The artillery and mortars set up their positions inside the perimeter on the parade ground and registered on points around the perimeter from which they could shift fire on an attacking enemy force. They also fired harassing fires on ravines and other likely avenues of approach to discourage the enemy and keep him off balance. The 592d JASCO men, in communication with the Navy ships offshore, arranged for the Navy to fire parachute illuminating star shells overhead at regular intervals throughout the night. Visibility under the star shells was "good," according to Hoot Gibson.

During the early evening hours, the regimental commander had a staff meeting in a room in Topside Barracks designated the Operations Center. The battalion commanders knew their missions: "they had been given a sector and told to kill all of the Japs in it." Colonel Jones got reports on casualties, the supply situation, and the exact location of the units in and around the perimeter. At this meeting, as well as in subsequent commanders' meetings, Colonel Jones gave each battalion commander a mission and then he asked the commander what help he needed to do the job. "It then became the task force commander's job to coordinate the firepower and logistical support necessary to complete the job," according to Captain Smith. The weapons report that evening was somewhat discouraging: the field artillerymen had only five weapons operational out of the nine they dropped. Two were damaged on landing and two were under such heavy fire that they could not be retrieved the first day.

The Air Force and Navy liaison officers also arranged for fire for the next day's attacks.

The battalion commanders returned to their command posts and laid out the plans for the next day's operations. Colonel Erickson called his company commanders into the lighthouse and put out his orders: G Company was to hold its position above San Jose Dock and White Beach, send out patrols, and support the amphibious landing of the 1st Battalion, which would be landing at 1345 the next day; H Company would have Morrison Hill as its objective; I Company would attack toward Breakwater Point and clear out all the enemy and seal any caves they came across with the help of the regimental demolition section. (Blake and his demolition section in the errant C-47 would arrive by boat at South Dock on the seventeenth also.)

The 2d Battalion commander similarly gave orders to his company commanders for the next day's operations. His companies would move out from the perimeter and clear the area to the south of the DZs, particularly in the troublesome area around Wheeler Battery.

When darkness fell over Corregidor that first night of the operation, the four or five men in each of the foxholes and firing positions around the perimeter were alert to every noise around them. At least one man in each position, on shift, was awake all night. The others slept only fitfully. Each man on guard had a helmet ready to smother a grenade if one were thrown into the hole. He had his rifle or machine gun pointed toward possible enemy lanes of approach. He had some form of communication back to his squad leader. He heard the mortars and the artillery firing their sporadic harassing rounds at the unseen but suspected enemy. And he thought occasionally about the rumors which had it that the Japanese had mined the entire island with tons of explosives. Maj. Lester H. Levine, the 503d adjutant, remembers the rumor clearly. Corregidor was "prepared for destruction by carefully located demolitions, which could be detonated electrically and remotely. Everyone held his breath."

The first day, except for the jump casualties, had been relatively easy on the men of the Rock Force; the succeeding days would be far more costly, more difficult, and more agonizing. Even though cornered and hopeless, the Japanese would not think of surrendering. Death was the only honorable way out.

General Krueger summed up the situation on Corregidor tersely but accurately. He said:

> By nightfall of 16 February our troops had secured Topside and Malinta Hill. And they had disrupted the enemy's communications and cut his forces in two. But while our troops now held the dominating terrain features of Corregidor, the task of dislodging the enemy from a multitude of strongpoints, tunnels and caves still remained; and this involved some of the bloodiest fighting of the entire Luzon Campaign.

For the 503d Regimental Combat Team and the 3d of the 34th Combat Team, the worst was yet to come.

CHAPTER XII
The Japanese React

The night of 16–17 February was clear, the sky was star-studded, and the soft, tropical breezes cooled the thirsty, tired, hungry paratroopers and infantrymen who lay quietly in their foxholes along the perimeters or who sat up awhile, in shifts, watching for any signs of the enemy, who, they knew, preferred to attack at night in catlike stealth and graveyard quiet. Even the fat, blue flies that were beginning to become a major problem as they fed on the bloated, unburied enemy bodies and proliferated at an alarming rate, seemed to quiet down and stop bedeviling the troops with their constant buzzing and massed attacks on their bodies and food. At another time, this night would have been perfect for something other than war.

The 503d, deployed generally around Topside's perimeter along the 500-foot contour lines, would have a relatively easy time of it this night: the Japanese moved around, probed the outer flanks of the position, and lobbed in a few mortar rounds. But the 3d of the 34th would not be equally neglected; they caught the full brunt of the night's attack.

Captain Centenni and his men of K Company were resting uneasily in a small, tight circle atop Malinta Hill. Without much difficulty, Centenni had reached his objective—the northern reaches of Malinta Hill—before dark and had sent his third platoon around the base of Malinta to secure Malinta Point on the northern shore of the island. L Company was adjacent to K Company on top of Malinta on the south and southwest slope.

The historian of the 3d of the 34th put it this way:

> The whole afternoon [of the 16th] was swathed in peculiar quiet for K Company, atop northern Malinta Hill. A brace of squads were sent out to a brace of knolls to effect a more or less integrated line, extending from the company perimeter on the southwest to the 3d Platoon on the northeast. There was nothing to do but sit tight. A similar situation existed on the southern half of the tunnel-ridden hill. L Company performed the "holding" part of its mission.
>
> At first, it appeared that A Company's first platoon—out on its roadblock—was going to experience the warmest night. Scarcely had the fat blue flies that swarmed over the island begun to retard their buzzing, when the platoon, constantly under fire, saw a great section of the cliff about them lurch into the night with a deafening roar. The Japs had mined it—filled it so full of explosive charge, that when the fuse was touched off and the charge blew, it sent the rock, designed to fall across the road, blocking it, over the heads of the troops below, and on out into the bay. Only impotent chips and dust fell on the road and the A Company men.
>
> The night's really bloody paragraphs were written where the day had left blank pages—on the north of Malinta Hill by K Company.[29]

Just before midnight, the two squads that Centenni had sent out to the two knolls, nicknamed Goal Post Ridge and Little Knob by the K Company men, came under an intense attack by the Japanese. Centenni could hear the shouts of his beleaguered men and the staccato fire of rifles, grenades, and machine guns on the two knolls below him. Shortly, the telephone line to the two squads and the 3d Platoon went out. The Japanese from the west side of the hill fired their pesky knee mortars into K Company's main perimeter.

The men on the northern edge of the perimeter heard a

---

29. Operation M-7, After Action Report, 3/34th Infantry Regiment, undated, p. 139.

man struggling up the slope toward them. Fortunately, they held their fire. In a moment, Pvt. Rivers P. Bourque staggered into the perimeter carrying on his back a man with a mangled leg and helping another whose blood was dripping from numerous wounds. A few moments later two more men struggled up the slope and crawled into K Company's position.

The information that Centenni was able to gather from the exhausted men was bleak: the Japanese had attacked both the squads on the knolls and the 3d Platoon. Bourque reported that the Japanese had killed or wounded every man of the squad on Little Knob except himself and Private Cassie, who had volunteered to stay behind on the knob with two wounded men. The other two men who had made it to Centenni's lines were from Goal Post Ridge, where the enemy had killed nine of the eleven men in the squad. The Japanese attack, by knocking out the two squads, had driven a wedge between the 3d Platoon out on Malinta Point and Centenni's main position atop the hill. But before Centenni could do anything about trying to rescue the wounded on Little Knob or to try to fill the gap left by the slaughter of his men on the knolls, his own position came under heavy attack. "The night exploded in fury and death," according to Jan Valtin, the unit historian.

To the men on the perimeter of K Company, the Japanese assault was simply impossible. But the Japanese did not know that. They had climbed straight up the nearly perpendicular northwest slope of Malinta Hill almost hand over hand. They came with all of "the fury of the damned—in the epitome of the 'Banzai' tradition." The Japanese Imperial Marines, for that is who they were, were armed with a wide assortment of weapons—everything from their own bayoneted rifles to spears to captured American shotguns. K Company let them crawl to within close range and then opened fire with every weapon they had. Cpl. Daniel Smith hurled grenades and saw them crumple a group of the screaming enemy. Pvt. Adolph Neamend emptied his M1 into "the wide open howling mouth of a Jap . . ."

Pvt. Ray Crenshaw kicked away a grenade and then shot its thrower with his Garand. The cliffs the Imperial Marines had climbed were so steep that, when the men were hit, they fell straight down into the faces of those crawling up the cliff behind them, or they fell straight to the bottom of the gorge below. For almost three hours the Japanese came in twos, threes, and fours. They were like men possessed. The falling bodies of their fellow marines did not deter those below. They moved them aside, picked themselves up, and climbed up again and again. Their last rushes took them to within ten feet of the K Company perimeter. Centenni and his men held; the attack stopped when there were no more Japanese marines in that area to clamber up the cliff. It had lasted for an hour and a half.

At dawn the next morning, the men on the northwest corner of the tiny K Company perimeter looked down and counted thirty-five bodies at the base of the hill. More may have been dragged away.

Colonel Postlethwait was deeply concerned about K Company's position and the wounded men who might still be alive on Goal Post Ridge and Little Knob. At daylight, Centenni sent a patrol across the saddle toward the 3d Platoon to find out what had happened and to bring back the dead and wounded. The eight-man patrol made its way to Goal Post Ridge, where it found one man still alive; but heavy enemy fire killed four of Centenni's men in the patrol and prevented the patrol from getting to Little Knob. Obviously, the Japanese still controlled the area between K Company's perimeter and the 3d Platoon on the point.

Centenni decided to lead the next patrol himself—he wanted to bring in all his wounded and find out what was going on. He led the patrol out of the perimeter and had gone but a few yards when a Japanese rifle cracked. Centenni fell forward over a little hump in the ground just out of the view of the rest of the patrol. The men returned the fire "viciously," crawled to within inches of their company commander, and tried to retrieve his body. But the Japanese tossed three grenades almost on top of Centenni, and covered his body with fire. The patrol had to leave him there.

The 3d Platoon had also been attacked during the night of the sixteenth and the early morning hours of the seventeenth. Even though the platoon succeeded in beating off the attack, it still remained isolated from the rest of the company. And Sgt. Lewis Vershun, Pvt. Emil Ehrenhold, and Pvt. Ronald Paeth, manning an outpost a few hundred yards from the 3d Platoon and above the North Shore Road, were in even worse straits. These three men would be out of contact with the rest of the company until 23 February, but during that time they fought off repeated night attacks by the Imperial Marines. The three intrepid and lonely soldiers killed twenty-three of the enemy in the last Japanese charge toward their position.

During the seventeenth, I Company of the 34th set about clearing the enemy from positions to the west of Bottomside and at the base of the hills that rose up to Middleside and Topside. The company commander personally led the attacks. His men used flamethrowers, rifles, grenades, and bazookas. He and his men dug out the entrenched Japanese in position after position along the base of the mountains. By the end of the day, I Company had killed at least thirty-one Japanese and holed up many more uncounted ones.

Even though the night of the 16–17 had not been as hard on the 503d as it had been on K Company of the 34th, the night did bring some Japanese probes to the 503d perimeter and fatalities on both sides. At daylight, the paratroopers found both their dead and the fallen Japanese lying out in the open. The troopers picked up their own men and carried them and their wounded into the medical aid station in the long barracks. Unfortunately but unavoidably, they had to leave the Japanese where they were. It was not long before the bodies bloated and began to smell. The blue flies grew fatter and infinitely more numerous. No man who fought on Corregidor has ever forgotten the stench of decaying bodies or the waves of flies that were like a swarming, unnerving pestilence.

While I Company of the 34th was working the lower levels, G and I companies of the 503d had been attacking from Topside down toward the I Company, 34th, men. Colonel Jones was most interested in opening the main road, which snaked down along the contour lines from Topside to the beach at South Dock so that he could evacuate his wounded, get additional food, medical supplies, ammunition, and water and link up with the 3d of the 34th, which was under his command. As long as the main road from Topside to South Beach was closed, Colonel Jones and his 503d men atop Corregidor were isolated and totally dependent on John Lackey's C-47s for all of their resupply—including water, a necessity that was becoming scarcer and scarcer as the troops fought and sweated under the searing tropical sun. Most men had long since drunk their two canteens of water.

To assist in opening the road from the South Beach to Topside, on the seventeenth Colonel Postlethwait used three armored vehicles in a role for which their designers had probably never intended them. He formed one of his undamaged Sherman tanks and two of his M-7 self-propelled 105-mm howitzers into a clanking, armored posse to run the Japanese-controlled main road to Topside. Sgt. William Hartman and Cpl. Mike Nolan were two of the volunteers who made the run, bringing to the paratroopers on Topside much-needed blood plasma and other desperately essential supplies. They gunned their behemoths past uncleared caves and tunnels from which the Japanese fired a steady beat of small arms against the hulls of the vehicles. Fortunately, the Japanese along that stretch of road had no antitank weapons.

The three armored vehicles made their way to the 503d aid station in the main barracks to the cheers of the paratroopers in and around the barracks. Sergeant Hartman loaded up two seriously wounded troopers and, when he found out how desperate even the medics were for water, volunteered to make another round-trip. He and Nolan ran the gauntlet a second time, occasionally stopping on the way up to make a 90-degree turn on the road to fire point-blank into a cave or tunnel opening. Once safely back at the South Dock, Sergeant Hartman tried to count the bullet scars on the hulls of his tank and howitzers. After the count got to two hundred, he gave up.

By the morning of the seventeenth, the paratroopers were developing a system for routing the Japanese out of caves and tunnels that would stand them in good stead throughout the rest of the campaign. With variations, it would be used by all of the units of the Rock Force in digging the molelike enemy out of their holes, caves, and tunnels.

Lt. Bill Blake, who had jumped his planeload of paratroopers on Bataan after his plane's engines caught fire and then made his way back to Corregidor on the morning of the seventeenth, commanded the demolitions section of the 503d. Lt. Bill Miller and his platoon from I Company of the 503d had been assigned to clear out a section of the main road from Topside to Bottomside. Blake and his section went along with Miller and his platoon on the road-clearing mission. The section of the road that Colonel Erickson had assigned to Miller was along a cut in the cliff of Topside, facing toward the east and Malinta Hill. The Air Corps had bombed the area, and the Navy had shelled it until it resembled a working quarry rather than a road. But the caves above the road still harbored live enemy. Like so many of the caves, tunnels, pillboxes, and concrete gun emplacements that honeycombed the island, the Japanese could get far enough back in them to protect their lives, if not their hearing and their sanity.

In the face of the hillside cut just above the road Miller was trying to clear were the caves manned by the usual diehard Japanese. Miller had lost a couple of men trying to get around to the front of the caves so that they could bring some direct fire to bear on the openings. But he was having little success in knocking out the caves. Lieutenant Blake volunteered to give it a try. He brought his section down a draw toward the caves while Miller's men, with sporadic rifle and Thompson submachine gun fire, kept the Japanese pinned in their holes.

Blake found six caves within a stretch of about ten yards along the bank. Because the cave openings were so close together, Blake decided to try to neutralize three cave openings at once. Miller and his platoon shifted their automatic weapons fire to the other three caves while Blake and his section went to work on the first three.

Blake and two of his men, Parsons and Anderson, crawled up to within five yards of the cave openings. The Japanese tossed out a couple of grenades, which exploded within ten feet of the trio. The only injury was to Anderson, whose lower legs collected a few pieces of metal. Then Blake tossed a white phosphorous (WP) grenade squarely into one of the cave openings. As the smoke poured out of the cave, he tossed another WP grenade at the cave mouth, but this one missed. It ricocheted off the side of the hole and showered white phosphorus over the men near the cave. They were not deterred. Hidden by the smoke, Anderson moved up with his flamethrower and sprayed the three caves with steady streams of flame. Nine Japanese with their clothes on fire rushed screaming out of the three caves. They almost knocked Blake over, and some of the flaming napalm on their bodies actually set fire to Parsons's uniform. He doused it quickly. Miller's men, who had been covering Blake's operation, shot all nine Japanese as they raced past them in flames.

Blake wrote of the incident later:

Our first operation had been a success. We sealed those three and before we could get to the others, one lone Nip came to the entrance with a white rag. A couple of trigger-happy boys drove him back in the cave two or three times, and it sounded to me as though the other Nips inside were trying to haul him back. He was screaming his bloody head off, and finally I persuaded the men to let him come out. The concussion from the blasting of the other three caves had fixed him. He couldn't hear a thing and was bleeding from his eyes, ears, nose and mouth. Apparently these caves were all entrances to one main chamber and the concussion had done him in. . . . We closed the other three caves and called it a day's work well done. This was only the first day in that sector and before the operation was over, Parsons and his section had closed forty-three caves along that one side of the hill. We finally got it on a Yankee production line basis so that we could take care of them in bulk. Two well-placed WPs, a 3-second burst of napalm, followed by a 20-pound satchel charge did the business. We were closing six and eight caves with two flamethrower refills. There were many instances like this one.

H Company of the 34th had established a defensive position around the battalion's initial beachhead on South Beach. At about 0500 in the dark of the morning of the seventeenth, two parties of the Imperial Marines appeared "from out of nowhere" and attempted to infiltrate H Company's position. The 2d and 4th platoons of H Company succeeded in beating off the attacks. At daylight, the men of H Company counted some fifty bodies "lying in the rubble a stone's throw away." Curiously, the squads that had thrown back the assaults were machine gun squads, but not one machine gun had been fired. "The Yanks," according to the unit historian, "did the work with carbines and grenades."

A Company of the 34th had two platoons helping to man the beachhead perimeter. Those platoons managed to kill twenty-three Japanese who had tried to swim around the South Dock and infiltrate the beachhead by water. The busy riflemen of the 34th gave the Japanese an "A" for effort and ingenuity but an "F" for intelligence.

At 0830 on the morning of the seventeenth, Colonel Lackey led his group of C-47s across Topside once more. This time, however, two aspects of the trip differed from the previous day's aerial operations: one, no men jumped, and, two, the Japanese AA fire was far more intense. Because Maj. Robert H. "Pug" Woods, the boyish-looking commander of the 1st Battalion Combat Team of the 503d, had received word to abort his drop after he had fully loaded his planes for the expected parachute operation, he and Colonel Lackey decided to fly over Topside, drop the prepacked supply and equipment bundles from the doors and pararacks of the C-47s, and then airland the troops at San Marcelino near Subic Bay.

As the planes were making their equipment drops, however, Japanese antiaircraft fire from the vicinity of Wheeler and Cheney batteries was extremely heavy; sixteen of the forty-four planes in the formation were holed, and five of Lackey's airmen were injured. Thus, Colonel Jones's decision to abort the drop and bring Woods's Battalion Combat Team in by water was proved wise. The paratroopers would have been hit by a lot more enemy fire on the second day than on the first because the Air Corps planes and the Navy ships would not have been able to support them with their intensive suppressive fires as they had been able to do on the sixteenth.

Shortly after dawn, the two 503d battalions on Topside began to fan out from their tight perimeter of the night of the sixteenth. In so doing, they came across situations in which the artillerymen of the 462d Parachute Field Artillery Battalion would be of great help to them using their pack 75-mm howitzers in a relatively unconventional manner, quite different from the indirect fire role for which they had trained so ardently. Supporting artillery fire, to the conventional cannoneers, meant lofting indirect, heavy concentrations of fire over the heads of the friendly infantry onto the enemy positions to pave the way for the infantry to overrun them. Topside fighting, however, would introduce the artillery-men of the 462d to relatively new and unique methods of fire, which grew out of the uncommon combat techniques required to defeat the unconventional Japanese defenses. The new method was direct fire, and for a change it put the artillerymen in the front lines with the infantry.

In an area to the south of the parade ground not far from Wheeler Battery, a platoon from E Company of the 503d trapped a large number of the enemy in a concrete bunker that had one small door and one tiny window. The infantrymen were not able to force them out or to neutralize the bunker. The platoon leader called for artillery support. Hoot Gibson provided it—directly.

Hoot and his men hand-carried and man-dragged two of his pack 75-mm howitzers to a rise about two hundred yards from the bunker. The infantrymen covered the door and the window with small arms fire but could not get in close because of the Japanese fire coming from the openings. Gibson remembers:

[I] pointed out the target, namely the door and the open window to each gunner and ordered one round of HE [high explosive]. We could see the trajectory of the shell, and we adjusted the range accordingly. The next rounds penetrated both the doorway and the window. I then ordered both pieces to continue to fire, alternating HE with WP. We could see the flashes of explosions inside the bunker and thick white smoke poured from both openings. We lifted the fire and the infantry sent a patrol toward the bunker. They encountered no fire as they moved in. They came out later and signalled that all the Nips were dead.

I took both gunners with me and we went into the bunker with the platoon commander. We found bodies all over. The infantry found some still alive but dazed. Some of the uniforms on the Japs were smoldering from the white phosphorous fragments. We counted 85 dead.

Unknown to me, Colonel Jones, the regimental commander, and Major Knudson, my battalion commander, had witnessed this action from Topside Barracks, which was behind us. I was later awarded the Silver Star for this action. . . . My point here is that this action was observed, but there were many individual acts equally as heroic, or more so, that were not observed or reported. It was a job that had to be done, and you went along and did it without any idea that it was out of the ordinary. I recommended both gunners for heroism because they remained at the pieces in full view, setting the sights while the rest of the section was in defilade until needed to load the piece.

By the seventeenth, Colonel Jones had divided Topside into two sectors for the elimination of the enemy by his two battalions already on the island. Erickson's 3d Battalion drew the northern half; Maj. Lawson B. Caskey's 2d Battalion got the southern half. He gave them a mission that was simple to understand: "Kill all of the enemy in your areas."

Because of the initial disposition of Capt. Hudson C. Hill's E Company, 2d Battalion, on the northern edge of the perimeter overlooking James Ravine, which was in the 3d Battalion sector, Hill assisted the 3d Battalion in its attack on Morrison Hill and the areas around it. Hill's principal task was to attack James Ravine with three objectives in mind: one, destroy the enemy in the underground infantry barracks, which were known to be dug into the cliffs on the west bank of James Ravine; two, check out the serviceability of the freshwater pumping station, which, according to the men who had served on Corregidor before the war and were now with the 503d, was somewhere at the base of James Ravine; and, three, locate and destroy the electrical mine-control system that the Corregidor veterans believed was also somewhere in James Ravine.

The third part of Hill's mission was especially vital to the U.S. Navy. The Navy had observed, somewhat apprehensively, that whenever any of its ships sailed between Bataan and the northern shore of Corregidor, mines often exploded in their paths. The Navy concluded, logically enough, that the enemy had the ships under observation and that the Japanese observers were in all likelihood watching them from James Ravine.

The attack on James Ravine was typical of the fighting that lay in the days ahead for the paratroopers of the 503d and the infantrymen of the 34th. The ruggedness of the terrain, the size of the island, and the defensive tactics of the enemy—scattered and static as they were in small groups in countless caves, holes, emplacements, tunnels, and ravines—rules out any large-scale maneuver by even company-size units. The action gradually evolved into a series of platoon and even squad-size attacks. At night, however, the units withdrew into a tightly connected perimeter of battalions. Colonel Jones's plan for clearing Corregidor was now clear: the 3d Battalion, 34th Infantry, would secure Malinta Hill and contain the Japanese on the eastern end of the island while the 503d cleared Topside and Middleside. Then the 503d and the 3d of the 34th together would move east and overrun the tail of the island.

James Ravine was a narrow, precipitous defile averaging about 300 feet in depth, gouged by nature out of the sheer northern cliffs of The Rock. The ravine floor was more or less triangular; about 10 feet wide at the base of the cut, widening to about 150 feet at the beach. The only way to get from the top of the ravine to the bottom was by following a narrow road, which, in years gone by, U.S. engineers had carved out of the walls of the ravine. The road gradually followed the contours of the sides of the ravine down to its floor. At the bottom of the west wall of the ravine were the entrances to the underground "infantry" barracks and a powder magazine. The pumping station was sited at the eastern edge of the ravine near the beach. A concrete pillbox, built deep inside the ravine at about its narrowest point, covered the beach and the road as it descended to the beach.

Captain Hill decided to launch his attack on the ravine at 0800 on the morning of the seventeenth with a reinforced platoon led by Lt. Joe Whitson. Whitson led his platoon down the road on the east side of the ravine and in an hour had advanced about halfway down the slope. At that point, the platoon ran into heavy machine gun and sniper fire from the vicinity of the concrete pillbox. It took the platoon another hour of individual maneuvering around the pillbox to knock it out. The platoon moved ahead about fifty yards, where they again came under heavy machine gun fire from four machine guns halfway up the west slope of the ravine. Whitson recognized the folly of going farther against that kind of fire. He pulled the platoon back, and Captain Hill brought in 81-mm mortar fire, a section of light machine guns, and the deadly accurate fire of a destroyer lying offshore to blast the machine gun nest. It wasn't until 1610 that afternoon that Lieutenant Whitson was able to pull his platoon back from the trap that the Japanese had sprung on him.

Before he attacked the ravine again the next morning, Captain Hill had the air controller with the regimental headquarters direct an air attack by P-47s loaded with napalm and 1,000-pound demolition bombs against the defenders halfway down the ravine and along its bottom. At 0730, after the air attack, Hill sent two platoons down the road, one on the east and one on the west side of the ravine. "The Japs bitterly contested every foot of advance made," according to Captain Hill. By 1700 that afternoon the company had been able to reach a point on the roadway just above the entrance to the underground infantry barracks in the west side of the ravine and only halfway down on the east side. Captain Hill followed the pattern that was developing for combat on Corregidor: he broke contact and pulled the company back into the battalion perimeter for the night.

On the morning of the nineteenth, Lieutenant Colonel Erickson requested an air strike to assist Hill's attack. Within an hour and a half, fighter planes based on Mindoro were on target, blasting the Japanese caves. Hill then launched another attack against the stubborn defenses along the lower reaches of the ravine. But he did not get under way until 0900, a circumstance that proved propitious for Hill's E Company. "The lateness of the hour must have confused the Japs," Hill wrote later. The platoons met no resistance until they had reached the limits of their advance of the eighteenth. There the point men of the platoon in the lead found three abandoned Japanese machine guns set up in firing positions and with full boxes of ammunition on the ground beside them. It was now already 1015 because Hill's advance had been "extremely cautious."

Down in the bottom of the ravine, Hill heard a loud commotion of men running and scurrying without regard to cover, concealment, or stealth. The next thing Captain Hill heard was a barrage of fire from his platoon in front of the entrance to the underground barracks. "Japs were streaming out of the entrance to the underground barracks. It was slaughter. Sixty-five Japs were killed before they stopped coming. Apparently they were rushing out to man their defensive positions. Why they had not maintained security is a secret known only to the Japanese," remembered Captain Hill.

Now that his company had the Japanese in the ravine cornered in the underground barracks, Hill proceeded to eliminate them. He directed a couple of fire teams to keep fire on the entrance while his demolition men placed demolitions around the tunnel entrance and in the ventilation shafts. Then he had his men pour napalm from five-gallon cans, which they had brought along for this purpose, into the ventilation shafts. Finally, he ordered the demolitions blown. "The resulting explosions ended for all time organized resistance in James Ravine," he wrote. He was not quite correct.

Captain Hill had now accomplished the first of his three missions: elimination of the Japanese in the underground barracks and along the sides of James Ravine. Next, he set out to check the serviceability of the pumping station on the beach just north of Morrison Point. Colonel Jones had had faint hope that the pumps might be in working order or, at least, repairable. There was no such luck; the pumps had been destroyed beyond all hopes of repair. Hill immediately radioed the regimental headquarters the discouraging news.

Hill's third mission was to locate the electrical mine-control system that almost certainly was located somewhere in James Ravine. Hill sent out squad-size search parties to try to locate the cave that housed the system. He cautioned the men to use great care around the beach because it was heavily mined with Japanese horned mines. At 1620, on the nineteenth, one of the squads searching for the system came across it in a cave just on top of the entrance to the underground barracks. And even though Hill had thought that he had killed all of the enemy in James Ravine when he blasted the underground barracks entrances and ventilation shafts, there were still some Japanese alive in the mine-control cave. One of his men was killed during a brief firefight, but his squad eliminated fourteen Japanese who were alive in the caves. "The Thompson submachine gun was again proved to be a very potent weapon," Hill said later.

The mine-control system consisted of about one hundred knife switches, connected in series to a power source of six storage batteries, each about the size of a GI footlocker. From the switches, leads ran to a cable about six inches in diameter. The cable went underground and then to the mines planted offshore. Captain Hill and his men made short work of the mine system. They blew it up.

After he had accomplished his three missions, Captain Hill continued to mop up and close caves in James Ravine for the next three days. During that time, 10 of his men were killed or died of wounds, and 11 were wounded. His men killed 211 of the enemy by actual body count, and he estimates that there were 250 more of the enemy sealed in the nineteen caves his company closed. He destroyed some 173 enemy rifles and 5 machine guns. The strength of his company, which had started out on Mindoro with 134 officers and men, was down to 75.

While Hill and his company were working their way through the jungle and the enemy-infested caves of James Ravine from the seventeenth to the twenty-second, the rest of the 503d companies on Topside went about the task of clearing their areas with the same sort of tactics used by Hill and his E Company.

At dawn on the seventeenth, Capt. Joe Conway launched his H Company, 503d, in an attack on the highest terrain on the island, Morrison Hill. By 1000, against very light opposition, he had reached his objective. Conway was pleasantly surprised that the enemy had not defended more stoutly this important and critical piece of high ground, the possession of which gave the 503d a piece of commanding terrain and would logically permit the expansion of the perimeter on Topside.

I Company, under Capt. Lyle M. Murphy, had the mission on the seventeenth of clearing the area from the vicinity of the lighthouse on Topside down toward Breakwater Point. His task turned out to be more difficult than Joe Conway's. The terrain over which I Company fought was rugged and traversed by only a few trails. Murphy used his company in patrols—sending one patrol along the high ground running parallel to the trails and another along the trails. The Japanese contested the patrol's advances almost every foot of the way. Numerous caves indented the cliffside, and one overlooked another. The troops found that while they were covering the entrances to one cave, they would receive fire from another. They learned rapidly that they had constantly to be on the alert for cave openings, almost always heavily and cleverly camouflaged. The troops soon learned that around every bend in the trail they could expect to be fired upon by yet another bunch of Japanese from yet another cave. They also found out that the Japanese would sacrifice long fields of fire in order to retain concealment. In spite of these obstacles, by 1400 that afternoon, Murphy and company had fought their way along the trail to a point directly above Breakwater Point and about halfway down the cliffside. This position put the company between E and D companies of the 2d Battalion.

Sometime around midday on the seventeenth, Colonel Jones managed to get to Bottomside to meet with Colonel Postlethwait. In addition to the two self-propelled howitzers and the tank that had made their way to Topside on the seventeenth, later in the day two jeeps had also run the gauntlet. Each jeep had pulled a trailer loaded with five-gallon cans of water. To the thirsty paratroopers, Christmas came on 17 February that year. The regimental S-4, Capt. Bob Atkins, used one of the jeeps and trailers to collect scattered bundles around Topside; the other, even though it had made it up the road to Topside, had taken too many hits on the road and was unserviceable. But the one that was operational took Colonel Jones to Bottomside for a meeting with Ed Postlethwait.

The ride down the road to Bottomside was not without its hazards. Colonel Jones remembers:

The enemy was holed up in various and sundry places throughout the island, including the buildings along the road. But, as I recall, there were not very many running around who did not seek the security of caves and other compartments around our heavy guns throughout the island, such as Wheeler Battery. I don't remember much of what the discussion was between Ed and myself, except to congratulate him and thank him for moving on to Malinta Hill and to remind him that his occupation of Malinta Hill was his primary mission as it would cut the island in half, and the troops of the 503d would take care of the enemy on Topside and Middleside as the first order of the day and then we would go on from there. As I recall, Ed was very happy that he was part of the Rock Force and was determined to do his job.

Starting on the morning of the seventeenth, the units of the 503d began their systematic cleanup of Topside. A pattern emerged. At first light, the troops would leave the night's perimeter and attack positions they had previously cleared. Just before dark, they would leave those positions and return to the perimeter. During the night, the Japanese would return to their previously held positions but always in fewer numbers. According to one of the regimental staff officers, Maj. Lester H. Levine, the regimental adjutant:

> The principle employed was to exploit during the day but withdraw at night. During the night the enemy would return to the locations at which he had suffered such heavy casualties during the day (cumulative total first day—364), and the good hunting would commence in the morning.

It soon became clear to the troopers of the 503d that "each position occupied would have to be destroyed, and every cave and pillbox sealed off."

The system for attacking the smaller caves and bunkers began to follow a set sequence. Capt. Magnus L. Smith, who was the regimental assistant operations officer, described the method of attack this way:

> The infantry would assault a position, kill all of the Japs if they could. When the enemy would hole up in the numerous caves and bunkers, the Infantry would cover the entrances with fire while an Engineer or Demolition Team would either seal the cave with TNT or burn them out with their flamethrowers. It was during this period that our people used a little trick which was effective and became popular throughout the rest of the fighting. The high wind on the Island caused a heavy draft in some of the caves which caused the flamethrowers to blow back into the face of the operator. To solve this problem they just gave the enemy position a

squirt of napalm and gasoline—unignited. A WP grenade was then thrown into the position, which ignited the napalm. Out came the Japs, sometimes on fire, and were cut down by our weapons. On many occasions when the resistance was light, our Infantry would drive the Nips underground and move on. The Engineers followed close behind with explosives, and then pushed on behind the Infantry. By the 23rd of February our troops had attacked and sealed 164 caves and bunkers on Topside.

The attack and reduction of the larger fortifications such as Batteries Geary, Hearn, Smith, and Wheeler presented more-formidable obstacles. The underground portions of these concrete-and-steel-reinforced blockhouses were virtually impervious to artillery and naval gunfire. In addition, their underground interiors were honeycombed with tunnels, storerooms, baffles behind the entrances and exits, and built with many exits, some overrun with vines and brush or concealed behind rubble. The enemy within these fortifications had to be forced out into the open or somehow killed within them.

The attack on Battery Wheeler at the southern end of Topside was typical of the hard fighting and ingenuity that were required to subdue one of the massive gun emplacements. In the Wheeler attack, troopers of Major Caskey's 2d Battalion, 503d, surrounded the battery from covered positions but kept up a steady volume of small arms fire on all of the entrances. Hoot Gibson sent one of his pack 75s to the area to cover the main entrance with direct fire. In the event that the Japanese had closed a steel door, the pack-75 shells would smash it. The regimental demolitions section accompanying the 2d Battalion would already have fashioned some homemade explosive devices. These consisted of a five-gallon water can filled with gasoline and napalm with six to eight WP grenades and two blocks of TNT taped to the sides of each can. Then the demolitions men tied the "bomb" to each of the ventilator shafts that they could find at ground level. Next, the demolitions crew would light a three-second fuze that dropped the can down the shaft. Another fuze would go off fifteen seconds later. The resulting fire not only burned the enemy within but also used up all of the oxygen in the bunkers. The Japanese either died of asphyxiation, burns, or gunfire if they tried to escape from the underground caverns. Nonetheless, Battery Wheeler was so formidable and extensive that it required three days of constant attention before it was reduced.

In the morning hours of the seventeenth, the 1st Battalion, 503d, plus C Battery and a platoon of D Battery of the 462d Parachute Field Artillery Battalion air-landed on the San Marcelino airstrip near Subic after having dropped their bundles from the C-47 doors and pararacks as they flew over Corregidor at 0830. Maj. Robert B. Woods's battalion combat team deplaned, loaded up on trucks, and moved to the docks at Subic, where they mounted APDs (attack personnel destroyers) and left immediately for the South Dock at Corregidor, the same area where the 3d of the 34th had landed the previous day. The landing was not without incident. At 1400, as the APDs tried to land, heavy and sustained automatic and sniper fire from some caves on the east face of Topside cliffs covered the entire beach with intense fire and forced the landing craft to pull back. A Navy destroyer, *Claxton,* lying offshore, took the cave mouths under fire with pinpoint accuracy from her 5-inch guns. G Company, 503d, and the 34th also helped neutralize the Japanese guns. In a short time, Major Woods and his troops made it to shore, but not before six of his men were killed in the landing.

It was almost dark by the time the 1st Battalion, 503d Combat Team was completely ashore. Because the road to Topside was still not safely traversable, Colonel Jones ordered Woods to move into a perimeter on Bottomside and to move to Topside on the morning of the eighteenth.

By nightfall of the seventeenth, the 503d had pulled back into a perimeter that had been slightly expanded from that of the previous night. The 2d Battalion's zone generally encompassed the Long barracks, the prewar administrative buildings, the officers' quarters, the hospital, and the two drop zones; I Company of the 3d Battalion was part of the 2d Battalion's perimeter; H Company was in a company defensive position on Morrison Hill, and G Company was in a perimeter on the eastern side of Topside cliffs between the lighthouse and Middleside.

The 34th spent the seventeenth consolidating its positions and sealing caves around Malinta Hill. But for K Company, the beleaguered company atop Malinta Hill, the day was "scorching, miserable, and quiet." The company had finally re-established communications with its 3d Platoon on Malinta Point. The K Company men could hear firing all day long from the 3d Platoon, which had spotted a waterhole where the Japanese from Engineer Point came to get water, apparently their only source. All day, according to the unit historian, "they picked off Nips by ones and twos."

Colonel Postlethwait had ordered his battalion to "sit tight"; K Company sat. He had no spare units with which to reinforce K Company. Most of their canteens were empty, and the "big blue flies buzzed and lit and stuck and persisted and swarmed." A Company cleaned up pillboxes and maintained its roadblock at the southern tip of Malinta Hill. I Company mopped up the west flank of the battalion zone and returned to the vicinity of the beach. L Company maintained its position atop the southern half of Malinta Hill.

Once again, on the night of 17–18 February, it was K Company that took the brunt of the Japanese attacks in the 34th area. During the night, some of the enemy ran into booby traps set by A Company's roadblock platoon; other minor skirmishes punctuated the night with intermittent fire all over the island. But it was in K Company's area that the relentless Japanese attacked again with a frenzy that was inhuman, beastlike, and suicidal. The historian reported:

> They came on cat-feet at first. A K Company officer (Lt. Henry G. Gitnik) who'd won his commission on Leyte in the field . . . heard a small sound, lit a flare. Yanks peered over the edges of their foxholes to look down the mountainside and looked straight into the faces of Japs 15 or 20 feet away.
>
> The leaders were eliminated. The others were out of grenade range. Their swarming, creeping forms were lashed into demoniac fury by the American fire from above. They charged like rampant baboons, screaming and squealing.
>
> By weight of numbers, they pressed in. K Company wanted that, for it meant they could bring grenades to bear.

In the battle that followed, Lieutenant Gitnik, who had replaced Captain Centenni as the K Company commander, was killed by a grenade. Lt. Robert R. Fugitti took over the company. There were only two other officers left in K Company: Lts. Albert S. Barham and Albert J. Cruver. K Company had only twenty-eight able-bodied men left on the hill. Lt. Barham knew that his men needed more grenades. "I'm going to get more grenades or bust," he said as he took off for L Company's perimeter. Long minutes later, he was back with eight grenades, all that L Company could spare.

The officers and NCOs checked what was left of the company: eight men in the 1st Platoon, nine in the 2d, and eleven in the Weapons Platoon; the 3d Platoon was on its own on Malinta Point. There were a few clerks, cooks, and linemen to help man the perimeter. There was a total of thirty-eight men and three officers "and the whole northern half of Malinta Hill to hang onto." K Company had had three company commanders in as many days.

At 0300, the Japanese came up the hill again. K Company had only the eight grenades that Lieutenant Barham had been able to scrounge.

It was a monstrous, bloody, twisting turmoil of flesh and sweat and shells and hot lead and cold steel. They kept coming until 0400. Then they had spent themselves.

K Company counted off again. Thirty-three men—three officers fit for duty.

Before them and below them on the churned-up limestone of Malinta Hill, 150 Jap cadavers stared unblinking into the dawn.

The first two days of The Rock assault were over. The 503d and the 3d of the 34th had established patterns and techniques for fighting a burrowing, fanatical, relentless enemy who would not surrender, no matter the odds. Colonel Jones came slowly but surely to the realization that the intelligence estimates of enemy strength were wrong by a factor of at least five. He knew now that he and his men sat, literally, on a powder keg that might explode anytime. He realized that the only way he could recapture

Corregidor was by killing all of the enemy, no matter how much of the island he held aboveground.

Ed Postlethwait also recognized the enormity of the threat to his battalion and the precarious position in which he found himself. He knew that the enemy was not defeated—especially after he heard the depressing report from K Company, battered but still holding its position atop Malinta.

For all of the Rock Force, the coming days would be action packed: the paratroopers and the infantrymen of the 3/34th would be subject to crazed banzai charges, horrendous and crippling underground explosions, savage hand-to-hand combat, and more and more casualties. The worst was yet to come on The Rock.

CHAPTER XIII
Banzai

By the third day of the operation, 18 February, George Jones understood far more clearly the extent, the difficulty, and the hazards of retaking Corregidor than he had known just a day and a half before when he crash-landed onto the rocky Topside, jumping from John Lackey's command C-47. He also sensed that he was facing a far more fanatic enemy than any intelligence had revealed to him before the start of the operation. Even in the first thirty-six hours, his units had reported individual acts of Japanese self-destruction; but in the next two weeks, the Rock Force would witness massive banzai charges, which the Japanese seemingly knew would fail, and group, ceremonial suicides. Even the combat-hardened paratroopers would be aghast at the Japanese penchant for monstrous self-destruction.

By the eighteenth, the road from Topside to Black Beach at South Dock was still not completely free of enemy fire, but it was reasonably open and provided the 503d an avenue off Topside that eased their problems considerably. In the first place, the 503d medics could now evacuate wounded men to the beach for further transport to hospital ships and medical facilities ashore. Until now, the sick and wounded had been lying on the concrete floor of the Topside barracks. Their blankets were salvaged parachutes. In the second place, the 18th Surgical Portable Hospital was able to make its way to Topside and set up its facilities adjacent to the Regimental Aid Station on the first floor of Topside Barracks. This added medical help lessened the burden on the overworked surgeons of the 503d, who until the arrival of the 18th had operated only with the medical equipment with which they and their aidmen had jumped in. And in the third place, the 1st Battalion of the 503d, which had landed amphibiously on Black Beach the previous day, was able to join the regiment on Topside.

The 1st Battalion's trip up the winding road was not a simple road march. The battalion met some resistance at a number of places along the road, and it took "Pug" Woods until noon to close his troops within the regimental perimeter on Topside. Undoubtedly, the men of the 1st Battalion thought they were now in relative safety; unfortunately, Pug Woods and a large number of his men would never make it off the island. The Japanese would subject the 1st Battalion to an explosion that would cripple their ranks.

The opening of the road to Topside also eased the water-supply problem for the paratroopers on the high ground. During the first two days of the operation, water was the most critical need of the paratroopers. The weather was hot and humid, and the fighting conditions simply "dirty," according to Maj. Harris T. Mitchell, Sr., who was John Erickson's battalion executive officer. He remembers:

> Although we urged the men to go easy on water, we became short. It was tough to see resupply of water go into the ocean. This was not the fault of the resupply units. The wind was constantly changing direction and speed. They finally got it to us by dropping it at about a hundred feet or so. I recall we found some water standing on top of an old water tank. It was covered with a green slime but we sent some men to the top and passed canteens to them. They would scrape the slime back and fill the canteens. We would then drop in halazone tablets and pass them on.

Bennett Guthrie reported that "many cans of water dropped from planes were damaged on landing. . . . Troopers would suck on pebbles, share a tongue-moistening swallow of water with a buddy, and even shake the canteens of the fallen enemy for water. Tongues would swell and parched lips would crack in thirst."

Once on Topside, Pug Woods made his way to the long bar-

racks and reported to George Jones for his mission. With his 3d
Battalion now in place, Jones could reassign sectors of responsibility on Topside. He gave Pug Woods responsibility for clearing
out the southern zone of Topside; to Major Caskey, he assigned
a sector of Topside from the north to the southwest; and to John
Erickson, he gave responsibility for an area from the north to
the southeast.

While Colonel Jones was rethinking his plan of attack, the
Japanese were also rethinking theirs. The senior Japanese officer
left on Topside was a Japanese naval officer, Lieutenant Endo.
He was well aware of the desperate situation facing the remainder
of his defenders. They were holed up in hundreds of scattered
small dugouts and caves; they were in the massive concrete battery
emplacements of Geary, Wheeler, and Cheney; their communications were virtually nonexistent because of the bombing and the
occupation of the high ground by the 503d. Endo was cut off
from the southern part of the island by Postlethwait's men, and
like General Wainwright's desolate and isolated men three years
previously, they were also desperately in need of water. A prisoner
later reported that in Malinta Tunnel the Japanese were living
on canned juices and the water that seeped through the rock
walls. After they had captured the island, the Japanese had failed
to repair the extensive water systems of Corregidor and had, instead, established only four water points. There were some springs
in Cheney and James ravines, but the paratroopers eventually
captured them for their own much-needed water supply.

Lieutenant Endo of the Japanese Imperial Marines had arrived
on Corregidor in October 1944. He commanded about six hundred
marines spread among four fortress batteries equipped with ten
150-mm naval guns that the marines had brought in with them
in October.

Prior to the arrival of the American forces on Corregidor,
Endo and his 150-mm guns had caused Rear Adm. R. S. Berkey
a considerable amount of trouble. Berkey's naval task force was
charged with supporting the landings on both Mariveles and Corregidor and of clearing the mines in the channel between Corregidor and Bataan. To support these operations, Berkey brought
in a force of five cruisers and a number of destroyers. On 13
February, he began the difficult task of clearing the mines from

the bay. The minesweepers worked ahead of the cruisers and destroyers that blasted Corregidor with 6-inch shells from the light cruisers and smaller shells from the destroyers. Berkey had his force divided into two groups: one worked the channel between Corregidor and Bataan, and the other cleared the South Channel and fired on The Rock from that location. But Endo was not yet ready or authorized by Captain Itagaki to take the naval task force under fire.[30]

In the North Channel, Berkey's minesweepers' paravanes cut free hundreds of horned mines that the destroyers behind them then destroyed by fire. Many of the mines were U.S. Navy Mark 6As that the Japanese had not swept and that they had incorporated into their own defensive fields for guarding the entrance to Manila Bay.

Endo's silence confounded Admiral Berkey. Berkey was aware that Endo and his marines were on Corregidor because his intelligence had told him that the Japanese had sent 150-mm naval guns to Corregidor; Berkey could not understand Endo's failure to retaliate. Berkey, an experienced sailor in the Pacific naval war, knew from his previous experiences on Saipan that the Japanese would have tunneled the guns into the vertical cliffs of Corregidor and used the hanging vines and the dense jungle growth to camouflage the openings. This is exactly what Endo had had his men do. But Itagaki would not let Endo shoot with so much U.S. naval power at such close range.

At sunrise on the morning of the fourteenth, Berkey, whose forces had spent the night in Subic Bay, returned to clear the rest of the North Channel and Mariveles Harbor. This time, Itagaki gave Endo permission to shoot. At 0933, Endo opened fire on the minesweepers, who promptly radioed to Berkey that they were under attack. The destroyers covering the minesweepers quickly forced Endo's guns to stop shooting. But Endo was far from finished.

At about noon, a group of minesweepers began to clear Mariveles Harbor. The destroyers *Hopewell* and *Fletcher* were covering the sweepers and were ready to attack any Japanese guns that

---

30. Itagaki was killed on the sixteenth.

might open fire from the Mariveles Harbor area and to sink any mines that the minesweepers would cut loose. At about 1330, the *Fletcher* was dead in the water to lower a boat to scuttle a buoy that her gunners did not seem to be able to finish off. Endo recognized an opportunity when he saw one. He directed the fire of one of his 150-mm batteries against the *Fletcher*. The first rounds bracketed the destroyer, and his second salvo blasted the destroyer's forecastle, killing five sailors and wounding six.

Berkey's ships more than repaid Endo in kind. Observers on the *Phoenix*, Berkey's flagship, had spotted the fire, dust, and smoke from Endo's last blast in the cliffs to the west of Morrison Point. Two destroyers followed the lead of the *Phoenix* and bombarded Endo long and accurately enough to force him to cease fire. But he was still not out of action.

At about 1400, Endo's guns took the wooden minesweeper, *YMS-48*, under fire, scored direct hits, and started a "mortal" blaze aboard her. The destroyer *Hopewell*, racing to the rescue of the crew of the minesweeper, took three hits from Endo's accurate guns. The results were serious; six men were dead, eleven wounded; *Hopewell*'s stack had been holed; the torpedo mount damaged; and the ship's sonar, telephone, and forward lighting system knocked out. When Berkey got the damage reports, he was more than annoyed; he was livid.

He ordered the *Phoenix* and her supporting destroyers to open fire at maximum rate at Endo's guns, a number of which had now been plotted. In the next eight minutes, a thousand 5- and 6-inch shells struck Endo's guns, silencing him once more. For the rest of the day, the ships kept up a harassing fire to prevent Endo's uncommonly accurate gunners from manning their pieces. The Navy's firing blew away a great deal of the camouflage around the guns, permitting Berkey's observers to spot precisely three of the troublesome 150s. The spotters picked up three more along the shoreline but were unable to detect the other four. Berkey was still not finished with Endo and his pestiferous guns. Berkey knew that he had to continue the minesweeping and that he would have to support the next day's landings at Mariveles. So Berkey sent Endo's coordinates to the Fifth Air Force with a request for "glide and dive-bomber attacks by P-47s."

Early on the morning of the fifteenth, Berkey and his cruisers left Subic to escort the landing craft carrying the infantry to their landings at Mariveles Harbor. At first light, as the cruisers neared Corregidor, Berkey ordered them to fire a slow, steady fusillade against the cliffs hiding Endo's guns. At 0730, Endo fired once and brought down the wrath of the entire naval task force. Endo backed off. At 0900, the P-47s arrived and fired up Endo's gun positions with both high explosives and napalm. The *Phoenix* was not to be outdone. Her gunnery officer fired single shots, carefully and patiently aimed, at Endo's caves. One of them hit the "jackpot." One 6-inch shell went "right down the throat" of the masonry-lined tunnel that concealed the most dangerous of the 150-mm guns. Endo was almost, but not quite, finished. At about 1040, he fired another round, which hit an LSM at the waterline and disabled it. After that final, uncannily accurate shot, Endo gave the command to cease firing.

By the eighteenth, Lieutenant Endo's battery of naval guns were completely silenced; he and his remaining marines were not. True to their code of chivalry, Bushido, with its unchanging ideal of martial spirit and the fearless facing of the enemy, and their almost total unwillingness to surrender under any circumstances, they planned to attack again and again, until they had left themselves the only other recourse—suicide. On Topside on the eighteenth, Endo sent a runner to his scattered command with the message: Charge the enemy at 0600 on the nineteenth.

With his three battalions now assigned sectors of responsibility, George Jones could see a pattern of combat developing. One of his staff officers, Maj. Lester H. Levine wrote:

The pattern of ground action became very familiar and effective, aided and abetted by the enemy's own actions of blowing himself up in his underground arsenals. Direct fire of the 75-mm artillery was used as the ground assaulting fire on enemy emplacements; this fire was frequently coupled with naval and/or aerial strikes. Immediately after the assaulting fires had lifted or were being lifted, the aggressive and vigorous ground assault began. This ground assault was conducted by patrols, supported by the battalion heavy weapons (60- and 81-mm mortars) and field artillery, 75-mm howitzers and accompanied by demolition personnel.

By 2400 on the eighteenth, the systematic reduction of enemy in caves and strong points accounted for 1,090 enemy dead on Topside.

Colonel Jones personally was getting a better feel for combat on Corregidor and what he had to do to maneuver his Rock Force to secure Corregidor. He was a man who "seemed to be everywhere," according to Major Mitchell. "Every time you would look up it seemed that he was there." 1st Lt. Edward T. Flash, platoon leader of the 2d Platoon, F Company, 503d, wrote:

> In retrospect, I look at then Colonel George Jones as the General Patton of the Pacific Theatre. You could always see him right in the middle of the action, helping wherever and however he could. He marched with us on the trails and even helped the troops carry equipment. The Rock Force had no vehicles in battle. We jumped and carried everything we needed on our person—weapons, ammunition, rations, water, radios, whatever. We even placed our dead and wounded in our own ponchos, strapped to bamboo poles, cut with our machetes and carried them for miles on jungle trails to the aid station.

Pfc. Jesse S. Castillo was a member of C Company of the 161st Engineers. On the morning of the eighteenth, he and his squad were ordered to accompany medics with plasma to wounded troopers below the cliffs to the south of the parade ground. Recently, he wrote:[31]

> When we left the command post and reached the end of the parade ground, I saw about six Japanese soldiers who appeared to have been machine-gunned down. Walking down, I saw another six Japanese soldiers who had also been machine-gunned. We continued down the road about one hundred feet, when Sergeant Hoover yelled at us to go back, because the gunfire was very heavy. You could see the dust fly when the bullets hit the road. We retreated to the parade

---

31. Castillo, letter to author, July 1986.

ground and proceeded to go into the bush and down the cliff. The enemy fire was still very heavy, and I was called up front to pepper the trees around us with machine gun fire.

I set my machine gun on the edge of a mortar shell hole. Kneeling in the hole, I was able to fire in a semi-circular pattern. After a bit, my gun jammed. Pulling back on the cover, I inserted a new cartridge belt and began firing again. The third time it jammed, I pulled back the bolt to insert a new cartridge belt, but it would not drive in. Lifting the lid, I raised my head about three inches to see what was jamming the chamber. That was the last thing I saw, for at that moment I felt a blow on my right cheekbone, as if someone hit me with a hammer. Everything turned black, but I was still conscious. I yelled, "I'm hit," the medics gave first aid, and two troopers walked me back to the CP. There the doctor told me my Army days were over, that I was on my way home.

For the rest of his life, Jesse Castillo never saw another thing.

On the eighteenth, Colonel Postlethwait's troops on and around Malinta Hill were holding their own. The 2d Platoon of A Company of the 34th ran a gauntlet of fire from the ice-house near the Engineer Dock to the top of Malinta Hill, carrying badly needed water and rations and ammunition to the beleaguered troops of L and K companies astride Malinta Hill. On its way down, the platoon brought out K Company's casualties. I Company spent the day cleaning up pockets of resistance around the North Dock.

L Company used the precision fires of the Navy ships offshore to clean out the caves and minor tunnel entrances on the southeast side of Malinta Hill. These fires blasted three naval guns and one monstrous 14-inch howitzer. The fact that the eastern side of Malinta Hill bristled with guns of heavy caliber, brought in and emplaced by the Japanese, led Colonel Postlethwait to conclude that the Japanese had expected a landing east of San Jose Point rather than near South Dock. If the landings had been made to the east, the Japanese would have had a field day shelling the vulnerable landing craft as they tried to make their way ashore.

As it was, the Japanese guns could not be brought to bear massively on the South Dock landings because of the ridge that separated South Dock from San Jose Point.

Engineer Point was still in Japanese hands. The air controller with the 34th called in an air strike on the afternoon of the eighteenth, and the Air Corps planes blasted it with napalm and high explosives but did not eliminate all of the enemy.

In the late afternoon, just before dark, Colonel Postlethwait sent I Company, with a detachment of heavy machine guns from M Company, to relieve the decimated K Company on top of Malinta Hill. M Company also sent three heavy machine gun squads to bolster the firepower of L Company. The relief of K Company and the reinforcement of L Company considerably strengthened the forces atop Malinta. For the night of the eighteenth, the Japanese seemed to leave the 34th to their own devices except for K Company's 3d Platoon, which was still holding out on Malinta Point. The platoon did lose communications again with the rest of the 34th, and for all intents and purposes, it was cut off from the rest of the battalion. But the platoon continued to hold.

The night of the eighteenth and morning of the nineteenth may have been quiet for the 34th; it was a night to remember for the 503d.

Lieutenant Endo's command to his forces on Topside to charge at 0600 on the nineteenth—the dark hour before the dawn—apparently reached a large number of his scattered units. The Imperial Marines began forming for the attack during the hours of darkness on the night of the eighteenth, principally in the area near Wheeler, Cheney, and Crockett batteries. Wheeler and Cheney were in the sector of the 2d Battalion of the 503d, and Crockett was in the 1st Battalion's.

Capt. William T. Bossert had set up his A Company, 503d, command post in a shattered concrete officers' quarters a few hundred yards north and inland from Breakwater Point. At about 0130 on the nineteenth, Bossert and his men were rocked by an earthshaking explosion in an ammunition storage tunnel directly beneath the building in which they had set up. The blast was so powerful that the rest of the 503d in perimeters around Topside heard and felt it. A football-size rock came through the roof of the 503d command post and landed a few feet from Colonel Jones. Twenty of Bossert's men from his Headquarters Company were killed or wounded; twenty of the forty Japanese who were in the tunnel below were killed. The twenty Japanese who survived, however, must have felt a sense of failure in the mass effort to kill themselves. The survivors of the blast emerged from the tunnel and, to the consternation and shocked disbelief of some of the paratroopers who could make them out dimly in the dark of the night, squatted in a circle outside the tunnel entrance and chanted a number of slogans. Then almost at a command, they pulled pins from hand grenades, held them to their stomachs, and ritualistically blew themselves up. Major Levine reported that the number was twenty minus one, "One at the last moment got 'cold feet.'"

By the afternoon of the eighteenth, the 503d perimeter stretched in a rough circle whose center was the concrete shell of the old Topside Barracks. The various rifle companies had been deployed around the barracks roughly to a distance of two or three hundred yards from the barracks center. But beyond the inner circle of companies, Major Caskey had moved two of his companies forward of the perimeter to break up any "strong points the Japanese might use for assembling." By late afternoon, Lieutenant Turinsky had worked his D Company along a ridge as far as the high cliffs on the western head of the island. Caskey ordered Turinsky to set up his own self-contained perimeter on the ridge so that he would be ready for additional patrols to the west and south in the morning. Turinsky realized that his position was hazardous because he was completely on his own, cut off from the battalion by a deep ravine and backed up on the brink of a 200-foot cliff that dropped behind the company directly to the sea. Caskey, however, reasoned that by pushing out along the cliff, D Company could break up any attack the Japanese might launch from the vicinity of Wheeler Battery.

Caskey put F Company around Cheney Battery, also on its own. Both Lt. William T. Bailey, F Company commander, and Lieutenant Turinsky had instructed their platoon leaders to draw in as close as possible within their assigned areas. By nightfall, the men had eaten their K-rations, had dug in or found shell holes to fight from, had their weapons cleaned and loaded, and had laid grenades beside them in their holes. Water supply was low, their uniforms were dirty, but they were ready. Every few minutes the pack-75 artillery shells would whistle overhead and thump into the ravines, and occasionally the men could hear the mortars firing from positions near Topside Barracks. Few of them slept during the night.

At about the time that the Japanese contingent blew up the tunnel under A Company, Endo led a force of some six hundred Imperial Marines out of Cheney Ravine and Wheeler Point. For the next few hours the Japanese Marines infiltrated the perimeters of the 2d Battalion, principally the area between Cheney and Wheeler batteries held by D and F companies. During the hours of darkness, Endo's men made a series of feints and strong, probing attacks.

Late on the night of the eighteenth, Pvt. Lloyd G. McCarter of F Company left the security of his foxhole on the F Company perimeter atop a small knob and moved downhill to a more ex-posed position from which he could take under fire any Japanese coming up the slope through the draw. During the night, whenever he heard movements in the draw, he fired repeatedly at the enemy with his Thompson submachine gun. When that jammed, he used a BAR, and then an M1. He kept chatting with his buddies behind him, asking, "How are you doing?"

The enemy tried repeatedly to knock McCarter out of his position. By 0200 on the nineteenth, all of the men near McCarter had been wounded. McCarter would not give up his forward position. Repeatedly, he crawled back to the perimeter to get more ammunition, and then he returned to his one-man outpost.

While McCarter was singlehandedly defending his position near F Company and causing Endo's attack in that area to stall, D Company, deployed around the rim of Wheeler Battery, came under intense pressure from another segment of Endo's forces. D Company bore the brunt of Endo's attack during the dark of the early morning hours. Endo managed to move his marines around both sides of Wheeler Battery and had D Company almost completely encircled. In the middle of the night, the paratroopers knew that it was almost fatal to move their positions because it was a well-established truism that anything that moves at night is the enemy. Nonetheless, S. Sgt. Nelson Howard managed to work a machine gun crew close to the main point of Endo's attack.

From this position, Howard and his team littered the ground around them with enemy dead. But the Japanese attack took a very heavy toll on D Company: during the night, the company lost twelve men killed, including one of Sgt. Howard's machine gunners, and the company commander, 1st Lt. Joseph A. Turinsky, who was killed when a Japanese threw a hand grenade into the plotting room of Wheeler Battery where Turinsky had set up his command post. A dozen more men of D Company were wounded during the assault.

Just before dawn, as he had planned and in spite of his losses, Endo had his troops in position for a banzai attack. His men, perhaps influenced by saki, which the 503d had been finding in large quantities around the buildings on Topside, came screaming out of Cheney Ravine and the area near Wheeler and Crockett batteries, carrying whatever weapons they were able to procure: grenades, rifles, and even bayonets on sticks. They stampeded in a frenzy of almost diabolical fervor. Simply by the weight of their numbers, they raced past the foxholes and machine gun positions on the forward perimeters of the 503d. The paratroopers fired volley after volley, but some of the racing, screaming enemy soldiers managed to get through the outer perimeters.

At dawn, McCarter was still in his exposed position in front of F Company's position. When Endo began his attack, McCarter stood up, in full view of the enemy, to try to find the location of the enemy's supporting machine guns and mortars. A Japanese saw him and hit him in the chest with a rifle shot. McCarter fell down, but he had located the fire bases he was looking for. He yelled the location to the squad behind him, who, in turn, put mortar fire on the Japanese machine gun and knee mortar locations. Then McCarter allowed himself to be evacuated from his forward position. After daylight, McCarter's squad mates found thirty-five Japanese bodies in front of McCarter's position and a hundred more massed in a cut below the draw, where McCarter had spotted them.

S. Sgt. Chris W. Johnson of F Company said later that "if Private McCarter had not stayed in that dangerous position, we would have had many more men killed and possibly lost the hill."

McCarter was eventually evacuated from Corregidor and taken to a hospital. At one point, he passed out from loss of blood but woke up to find an MP standing near his bed. McCarter looked at the MP and said, "What have I done now?" George Jones says that this comment "rather characterized Private McCarter— he was a terrific fighter but was frequently in trouble when we weren't in combat."

In the fall of 1945, after he had recovered from his wounds, McCarter received an invitation to visit the White House, where President Harry Truman presented him with the Medal of Honor. There were undoubtedly other heroes worthy of winning the Medal of Honor in the fight for Corregidor, but McCarter was the only one so rewarded.

One of the surgeons on the 503d staff wrote later about the banzai attack:

The Japs came sometimes in bunches, sometimes in individual groups, sometimes by ones and twos; and when the leaders were shot down, more pressed on, yelping from behind. For the most part, our Tommy-guns and M-1s held them off; but at times groups of them succeeded in plunging through. Some of them were tossing grenades as they came; others were jabbing in front of them with steel-pointed banzai spears—the old samurai fanaticism pitted against the deadly armament of America's picked fighting men. In the worst moments, it seemed as though the overbearing numbers of the wild Bushido savages might sweep our men away. Eight or ten of them charged right across the pit where our machine gunners lay, and raced up to the cliff's edge. Some tripped and hurtled over the brink, while others were blown to the hell they came from by our grenades. At one time a whole squad of them climbed onto the top of the round-house [part of Wheeler Battery], and one forced his rifle through the slit window from which our men had been firing. He was killed by a medic who fired his carbine point-blank through the narrow embrasure. The Japs on the roof were shot down by a Tommy-gunner who aimed from below at their darkly silhouetted forms. One of these, mortally wounded, rolled off the roof and lay moaning on the cliff's edge 'til one of our men kicked him over. In spite of repulse after repulse, the Japs kept returning; and though their numbers grew smaller, they seemed to gather from nowhere to continue their sporadic assaults. For hours this continued. No one who took part in the fight was able to describe just how or just when or just why the Japs were finally beaten off.

Inevitably, with an attack of this sort, hand-to-hand fighting breaks out. One very uneven hand-to-hand engagement pitted Pvt. James J. Edgar of Battery D of the 462d Field Artillery Battalion against an energetic and perhaps crazed Japanese marine. Edgar was manning a .50-caliber machine gun near the Topside barracks. The marine grabbed the barrel of the machine gun and attempted to wrest it away from Edgar. As Hoot Gibson reported, "Private Edgar squeezed the trigger, which ended the brief tug-of-war."

Bennett Guthrie of H Company, 503d, describes the hand-to-hand combat this way:

> Primitive hand-to-hand combat was unavoidable. The clank of steel on helmets, the rattle of bayonets on bayonets, the cries of the wounded as trench knives were driven home, and the shrill voices of unit commanders of the opposing forces directing their combatants in this din of hell were terrifying. But the stoic, grave, and steeled troopers held their ground.

The Japanese attack flowed to its highwater mark at the Topside barracks. There, three Japanese had infiltrated as far as the 2d Battalion command post and the regimental supply office in Topside Barracks. One of the three tossed a grenade into the supply office, wounding four of the supply section men. Capt. Robert M. Atkins, the regimental supply officer, gathered a few of his men and led them to the third floor of the barracks. From that vantage point, he and his men sniped away with their carbines at whatever Japanese they could find loitering about the barracks area. Colonel Jones accounted for three of the enemy who ventured near his command post area.

By 0845, Endo's banzai attack was spent. Most of the few Imperial Marines who were still alive vanished from Topside's plateau "as abruptly as the tropical night." But others hid out in buildings and had to be dug out one by one. Behind them they left scores of bodies all over the top and sides of Topside. The battlefield was a gruesome sight. The paratroopers estimated the enemy dead by "counting the arms and dividing by two." One Japanese marine lay only ten feet from the side of Topside barracks.

Endo's banzai charge cost him some four hundred men, dead or wounded; the 503d lost thirty-three killed and seventy-five wounded. It was a lopsided score, and Colonel Jones could attribute the results to the fire discipline that his men knew and observed. Lieutenant Flash put it this way:

> In the Pacific we had fire discipline for two good reasons. One, they were out looking, and you exposed your position if you did fire. Secondly, you conserved your firepower in case they did decide to attack banzai style. Movement at night was restricted. None of my men moved from their positions throughout the night as they knew they could become a casualty by their own men if they did.

During Endo's banzai attack, the pack 75-mm howitzers of the 462d fired at maximum rates of fire from their hub-to-hub positions on the parade ground on Topside. They accounted for many of the enemy dead in the draws and ravines. The Navy helped too by keeping the area lit with parachute flares, which they launched about every fifteen minutes over Topside.

USAFFE Board Report No. 308, dated 16 May 1945, summarized Endo's banzai attack: "From that time on the Jap could read the 'off limits' sign on Topside, and contented himself with life (and death) in the caves and ravines. Individuals infiltrated and sniped without material effect."

When the firing subsided, Colonel Jones directed that his units thoroughly and carefully look over every square foot of their areas of responsibility. This meant every building, every ravine, every hole. The mopping up proved to be very dangerous work. Hoot Gibson said that "we had to inspect every building to make sure that no Japs were hiding in them, and many were found holed up under stairs or in dark cellars." Some of the supposedly dead marines were not dead at all. As a patrol passed, one would rise up and throw a grenade at the tail of the patrol. Such incidents forced the Americans to take no chances with seemingly dead Japanese.

In the aftermath of the banzai attack, the 503d did manage to capture three Japanese. For the first time, Capt. Francis X. Donovan, George Jones's S-2, was able to get some reasonably "hard" information on the number of the enemy who had been on Corregidor at the start of the campaign. The prisoners reported that about three thousand Japanese had been stationed on Topside and that another two thousand or more were in the area from Malinta Tunnel eastward. This information gave George Jones pause. He realized how vulnerable the paratroopers of the 503d had been during the first hours after the first drop. Jones thought only briefly that if the Japanese had made a concerted effort in those initial stages of the operation, he and his troops would have been in trouble. But they had not, and Jones passed the thought from his mind. He had much work to do.

The Japanese may have had equally faulty intelligence, and that may have accounted for their peculiar tactics after the first parachute landings. With the 3d Battalion of the 503d already on the ground, the Air Corps and the Navy could not fire the massive suppressive fires that had pounded Corregidor before the first jump. This firing pause should have given the Japanese an opportunity to overwhelm the scattered and still-disorganized paratroopers of the 3d Battalion. Fortunately, the Japanese stayed underground during the vulnerable, initial assault of the paratroopers.

Donovan's interrogation of one of the POWs captured during the 19 February banzai attack revealed a startling piece of information: Endo had another banzai attack scheduled for the night of 19–20 February, but this time with one thousand marines. Donovan quickly relayed the information to Colonel Jones.

Colonel Jones met with his battalion commanders and instructed them to tighten their perimeters in anticipation of the attack. It did not materialize. The troopers on the line accepted the lack of another banzai with mixed emotions: on the one hand, a banzai attack can be terrifying; on the other, it does serve the very useful purpose of getting the enemy out of their holes and exposed, making them fairly easy targets, provided they do not overrun a position with massive numbers. When he heard about the possible second banzai attack, one F Company philosopher reasoned: "If it's true, let 'em come. We'll get it over with one big banzai."

On the nineteenth, the 503d units on and around Topside took care of their dead and wounded, distributed ammunition to the gunners and riflemen, reorganized their platoons and squads, and fanned out from their perimeters to continue digging out the remaining live Japanese. The task was formidable because there were still thousands of live enemy soldiers hidden in large and small groups all over the island.

Just to the west of North Dock, in a deep ravine, the prewar Americans on Corregidor had built a power plant and cold-storage facility. Like most of the buildings on the island, the "icehouse," as the building came to be known, was built of reinforced concrete. It was so located that anyone occupying it could command the road from Bottomside to Topside, could deliver fire on troops of the 34th on top of Malinta Hill, and could also fire to the south and west on G Company of the 503d, which was in position halfway down the slope on Middleside. The Japanese occupied it and had converted it into a "formidable fortress," according to Lt. John H. Blair III, who was one of John Erickson's staff officers.

Since the icehouse was in Erickson's battalion's zone of responsibility, it fell to him to reduce the "fortress," whose occupants made life hazardous for anyone trying to move up the road or expose themselves on the top of Malinta Hill. Erickson assigned Capt. Joe Conway and his H Company the mission of reducing the obstacle.

Conway decided to attack the icehouse with a traditional maneuver: he had one platoon lay down a barrage of fire aimed at the front gun ports, thus keeping the enemy inside occupied, while he maneuvered another platoon around the flank and rear of the building. The platoon in the rear was then able to climb on top of the icehouse and pour captured oil and gasoline down the ventilating shafts. They also found some rubber tires that they set afire and stuffed them down the shafts. Colonel Jones remembers that "the foul-smelling smoke and possibly deadly fumes from the burning rubber forced the Japanese defenders out of the ice plant, and the attackers killed or captured them as they ran from the plant."

While two of Conway's platoons were attacking the icehouse, a third one, some distance away and protecting the attacking platoons from an enemy attack from the outside, received a heavy volley of fire from a large cave. After a time, however, the Japanese inside realized the futility of their situation and set off a powder magazine that killed them and one officer and three men of the 2d Platoon, H Company. The blast was so devastating that the bodies of the four paratroopers were never found.

With the reduction of the icehouse minifortress, the road from Topside to South Dock was now clear, and the 503d could evacuate its casualties and get supplies without subjecting themselves to sporadic Japanese fire.

The other companies of the 503d methodically went about their business of eliminating the Japanese defenders on Topside and in the ravines and cliffs that bordered the high ground.

Lt. Bill Blake, the 503d demolitions expert, was getting even more adept at his job. One of Erickson's companies was trying to knock out one of the reinforced gun positions near Battery Point. The mouth of the position was protected by double steel doors. Two hundred yards back from the doors was a ventilator. The 503d S-2, Captain Donovan, had warned Blake that the position might be a powder magazine. Nonetheless, the infantrymen blasted open the first door with a bazooka round and then went inside to blast the second door. They beat a hasty retreat because once inside the Japanese threw grenades at them through a couple of small air openings in the wall. The company commander and Blake decided that the best way to seal the position would be to blast the area above the door, causing a rock slide which would block the door and then use the ventilator shaft access to kill the enemy inside.

When Blake studied the situation, he came up with what became known among the 503d paratroopers as the "infernal machine." He and one of his men, Sergeant Hill, took a five-gallon GI can and filled it with napalm. Then they taped eight WP grenades to the outside of the can. Around the grenades, they looped six turns of prima cord (an explosive cord) and added a couple of blocks of TNT on each side of the can. To the prima cord, they attached a 15-minute fuze, so timed to permit the men to get to a safe place before the charge blew. Blake planned to drop the "machine" down the ventilator shaft. But then he had misgivings. If he dropped the whole thing down the shaft with a 15-minute fuze on it, the Japanese would have plenty of time to disarm it.

He solved the problem by tying the can above the shaft with prima cord with a fuze that was only three seconds longer than the one on the can. Thus, the first fuze would pop and drop the can into the shaft; three seconds later the whole thing would explode. The ventilator shaft was a cupola about five feet above the ground. It had barred windows on three sides and a steel door on the fourth. Through the windows, Blake could see a ladder going down into the shaft. He decided to cut the bars from one of the windows with prima cord so that he could get to the padlock on the inside of the steel door. He put a couple of turns of prima cord around the bars, lit the cord, and then stepped back. After it went off, he went back to the shaft and there, he says:

> I got the surprise of my life. From down in the shaft came these words in English: "I wouldn't do that if I were you; there is very much dynamite down here."
>
> I called back and said, "Hi ya, Nip."
>
> "Very much dynamite down here. You will blow us all up."
>
> "OK, Nip."
>
> "Ho Kay," was his reply.
>
> He continued to jabber with some others in the hole while we proceeded to blow the lock so that we could get the door open. When this explosion took place, the Nip engaged me in conversation again.
>
> "Don't blow this one, or you'll blow us all up."
>
> "Well, come out then," I told him.
>
> "I can't come out, but don't blow this up. There is very much dynamite down here."
>
> "How much dynamite, Nip?"
>
> "Eighty thousand pounds, very much," he answered.

"OK, Nip, if you won't come up the ladder, stay where you are, and we'll send you to your ancestors," was my parting shot.

His was a simple OK.

Blake was afraid now that the Japanese below might be able to climb up the ladder and disassemble the "infernal machine" before it had a chance to drop down the shaft. So he figured that if the enemy were made to think that he and his team were still working above them, they would stay below. To encourage that thought, Blake and his men prepared a string of fifteen half blocks of TNT and put different time-length fuzes on each one. They scattered these around the ventilator shaft and lit the main fuze. Then Blake lit the fuze on the "infernal machine," and he and his team took off at a dead run to get as far away as possible, feeling that the Japanese and Captain Donovan might have been correct about the eighty thousand pounds of dynamite in the underground room.

I could fairly hear the pop of the prima cord and shortly after a deep roar and a huge cloud of black-and-white smoke belched up from the general area. We waited and waited for the Nips' 80,000 pounds of dynamite. It didn't go off. After a couple of hours we decided to give a look. When we got back to the vent there were still flames and smoke coming out. There was the crackling of some small arms ammo burning and a few explosions that may have been grenades, but no sign of the big dynamite. We checked the entrance that we had closed the day before. It was still closed, and smoke was seeping around the door jambs and out of the holes from which the Japs had tossed their grenades. As a coup de grace, we blasted the little cupola down into the shaft and sealed it up, and I guess Nip went to his ancestors as he didn't answer when I called to him this last time. But that alleged 80,000 pounds of dynamite gave me quite a few anxious moments, for that *still* is a lot of dynamite!

For the next few days, the 503d on Topside continued to mop up the remnants of Endo's forces and constantly expand their perimeter across the entire top of the head of Corregidor. I Company, under Capt. Lyle M. Murphy, was operating in a sector around Ramsay Battery, with patrols checking the area to the east as far as South Dock. Down near the beach, along the water's edge, one of Murphy's patrols found five large caves that had been carved into the near-vertical cliff. Inside, the patrol found Japanese Q boats, promptly dubbed "suicide" boats by the paratroopers. The patrol found nineteen of the boats, and "some of them were in excellent condition." One of the 3d Battalion staff officers described the caves and the boats:

Within each cave were tracks which when laid down to the water, would easily launch the boats. These boats were made of plywood and would have the space between the hull and the engine rigged up for the charges of dynamite. The object was to launch the boats from Corregidor or surrounding shores and have them ram into a naval ship which would present a point target.

Before the Rock Force had invaded Corregidor, Itagaki had used thirty of Lieutenant Commander Koyameda's Shinyo, or Q, boats against the landing craft that had been anchored in Mariveles Harbor on the night of the fifteenth. Only a dozen of the small craft succeeded in reaching the harbor, but in pairs they rammed themselves suicidally at four patrol boats guarding the harbor. Three of the patrol boats sank immediately, and one was damaged. Fortunately, the crew of LCS (1) 27 spotted the Q boats and sank at least five.

Why Itagaki did not use more of the Q boats against the landing craft in Mariveles Harbor lined up for the next day's invasion is a mystery. Perhaps he intended to use the remainder against the amphibious attack that he expected would be launched the next day. At any rate, after Murphy's men found the caves and the Q boats, they destroyed them.

By 20 February, the 503d had accounted for 1,453 enemy dead and the 34th, 388.

According to the 34th historian, 20 February "was a quiet day." Colonel Postlethwait moved his units around to the best advantage and sent I Company to clear off the northern end of

Malinta Hill. Using their flamethrowers and supporting rifle fire, the company cleaned out the remainder of the enemy by afternoon. Other companies sent platoons to reinforce their outlying positions, sent patrols out for rations, water, ammunition, and other supplies and called in air and naval support when they ran up against unexpected opposition.

L Company, for example, sent a patrol to Engineer Point. The patrol had nearly reached the patrol objective "when a naval air observer informed them that they were walking into a Jap ambush. His observation was perfect. The patrol withdrew, and the guns of a supporting destroyer blasted the position. The patrol accounted for four Japs who tried to sneak around them."

Twenty February might have been a "quiet day" for the 34th, but 21 February made up for it. Colonel Jones and Colonel Postlethwait knew full well that there had to be a large number of the enemy in the Malinta tunnels. The many Japanese who harassed their positions, mostly at night, had to be hidden somewhere. And the vast, underground labyrinths of Malinta would obviously be the place of refuge.

L Company's commander tried to flush the Japanese out of the underground maze of tunnels under Malinta Hill using smoke grenades. He sent a patrol to the east entrance armed with a number of WP grenades. His plan was to have the patrol throw the grenades into the entrance, and he hoped that the rising smoke would drift out of the air vent servicing the tunnel. Then, he reasoned, he could block the vent, and suffocate the Japanese inside.

The patrol dutifully went about this mission, throwing its grenades, killing "a Jap or two," and retiring. The smoke unfortunately stayed in the tunnel.

Later on the twentieth, Colonel Postlethwait ordered K Company back up on top of Malinta Hill. This realignment of the 3d of the 34th would complete a solid line across the battalion objective and would reestablish physical contact with K Company's 3d Platoon.

The commander of A Company, 34th, sent a squad from his first platoon to replace the elements guarding the west entrance to Malinta Tunnel.

Later, on the afternoon of the twentieth, during a naval strike, destroyers fired 5-inch shells into the eastern entrance to Malinta Tunnel. The bombardment caused a landslide that closed the tunnel from the east. By now, and with the east exit blocked, the Japanese inside must have felt that they either had to break out of the tunnels or die of thirst. The commander of what elements were left in the tunnel decided to take drastic action: he would explode some of the huge stores of ammunition in the tunnel, thereby stunning the Americans and blasting aside the landslides. Then his massed troops would march out of all exits, race to Topside, and annihilate the enemy.

Colonel Postlethwait's men had captured a Japanese manifest detailing the staggering amounts of ammunition stored in the tunnel. His engineer, armed with his slide rule, predicted that that amount of explosives was sufficient to blow the hill, and I and L Companies atop it, "sky-high" and "leave a canal through the island where it had stood." Colonel Postlethwait kept the dire prediction to himself but worried about it nonetheless.

On the twenty-first, "the scene was quiet as night fell," reported the 34th's historian. The quiet was not to last. At 2130 that night, "Corregidor rolled like a ship at sea, but the Bataan Peninsula reverberated and trembled, so great was the explosion. Flames poured from all the tunnel entrances. There were landslides and casualties, but the question that had been in the minds of all for days was answered: Malinta Hill survived."

A few minutes after the explosion, about fifty Japanese, in a column of twos, "marched out of the west entrance as if they were on parade." The A Company squad guarding that entrance allowed them to move about fifty yards and then "opened up with everything, cutting them down like grain. A few minutes later, Japs started trying to infiltrate out of the tunnel by ones and twos. They were picked off as they appeared. It was one of those irreconcilable Japanese acts. It netted them nothing but corpses."

After the explosion, captured Japanese admitted that the detonation had in fact been intentional, that they had tried to control it, but that it had gotten out of hand and had killed many of the men inside. In spite of the horror of the explosion and the confusion that must have resulted inside the various tunnels, some six hundred of the enemy did make their way out of the eastern exit, which had been blasted open by the fury of the explosion, and moved to the tail of the island. They would be heard from again.

The 3d Platoon of A Company of the 34th had been deployed along the road that ran to the south of Malinta Hill toward and beyond San Jose Point. The road had been carved from the face of a cliff as it went around the point; a bank of the cliff overhung the road. Six men of the 3d Platoon had been guarding one of the caves that had been hacked out of the bank. The tunnel explosion crumbled the hill on top of them in a massive landslide. The 34th's historian reported that a "sudden, inescapable landslide threw men to the ground, cutting and bruising them, isolating A Company's roadblock detachment [the 3d Platoon] and burying alive the six men who had been guarding the cave."

A Company's commander began immediately after the explosion to rescue his men who were trapped on the other side of the landslide. PT boats tried to help by coming into the bay below the blown-out road. Most of the wounded unfortunately were too seriously injured to permit lowering by rope to the boats. Besides that, a heavy concentration of enemy machine gun fire from the east made movement difficult.

The company commander had to wait until daylight to finish the rescue of his men. Only six men on the other side of the blown-out cave were in fit condition. They maintained the roadblock during the night. The historian reported:

> At the crack of dawn, a rescue party was led to the other side of the slide by the commander of Company A. Guide, advisor, director, chief rescuer of the party was a corporal whose profession prior to the war had been mountain climbing. His tireless work and deft skill were the greatest factors to the extraction of the isolated men, wounded and well alike.

> By 1030, February 22, the casualties had all been brought out, and the rescue party had completed its mission. During the rest of the operation, A Company had no 3d Platoon. The platoon leader and all but 6 men had been either killed or wounded. Those 6 who came through whole were distributed among the other platoons.

On the twenty-third, Colonel Postlethwait decided to open up the North Shore Road in preparation for the Rock Force's eventual attack toward the eastern tail of the island. His 81-mm mortars fired a preparation, and his infantrymen moved out to a knob above the old enlisted men's beach at Engineer Cove. A platoon moved out first, accompanied by a tank that blasted the hospital entrance to the tunnel. Some diehard Japanese tried to banzai out of the entrance, but they were cut down summarily by the infantrymen. The tank fire drove the rest back into the tunnel. The infantrymen then sealed the entrance by piling rocks and debris against the entrance doors. K Company's lonely 3d Platoon, after eight days of isolation, was now back in touch with the rest of the battalion.

One of the most vicious of the company-size battles pitted Capt. Hudson C. Hill ("perhaps the outstanding company commander of the Rock Force on this operation," according to Colonel Jones) and his E Company, 503d, against the Japanese defenders between Searchlight and Wheeler points. After his battle for James Ravine, Hill's company numbered only 4 officers and 71 men. The normal complement would have been 6 officers and 137 enlisted men.

On the afternoon of the twenty-second, Hill reported to Major Caskey in the 2d Battalion command post on the west end of Topside Barracks. Caskey gave Hill his mission: "At 0630 on the twenty-third, relieve C Company, 503d, near Searchlight Point and destroy the enemy in the area between Searchlight and Wheeler points." Late that afternoon, Hill and Lt. Larry Browne, the battalion S-3, went to the cliff edge overlooking Wheeler Point. Lying on their stomachs, they carefully searched the area between Searchlight and Wheeler points. "It was about 1800 hours, and the rapidly setting sun cast an ominous mixture of dark shadows and a red glow over the entire area," Hill reported later. "The scene below the cliff edge sent a cold chill running up and down my back."

What caused Hill's "chill" was the fact that the only two routes through which he could move his company to attack Wheeler Point were along the remains of a narrow, bomb-cratered roadway about halfway up the cliff face and the beach. The beach itself was only about fifty feet wide at its greatest width below Searchlight and Wheeler Points. He could see no cover along the road, and he realized that the Japanese along the cliffs could "lay fire on every inch of ground" between the points of land. When it got too dark to reconnoiter further, Hill and Browne went back to Hill's command post and studied in detail the oblique photos of the area, which had been taken only two days previously.

The photos revealed that there were at least seven caves and concrete fortifications in the area and a fortified tunnel entrance that opened into Wheeler Point and led far back into the underground magazines of Crockett and Wheeler Batteries. The bombing of the area before the jump had at least blown off the heavy tropical growth that had previously covered the caves and the tunnel. Hill concluded, accurately, as the next day's events were to prove, that the tunnel was clearly the strongest position.

The 503d S-2 estimated that there were about 175 to 200 Japanese marines in the area. Hill was deeply impressed with the difficulty of his mission. His company would be supported by one destroyer offshore, his "naval artillery," and demolitions and heavy weapons sections from regimental headquarters. He would also have a detachment from the 592d JASCO and the 6th SAP to direct naval fire support and air attacks.

At 0630 on the morning of the twenty-third, after issuing ammo, one-third of a K-ration, and water, Hill and his company left the area of the parade ground and moved out toward Searchlight Point. At 0655, the company passed through C Company. Capt. John Rucker, commanding officer of C Company, told Hill that each time he had tried to move around Searchlight Point the first man had been killed by the large volume of fire from Unknown Point. The body of a man who had been killed not fifteen minutes earlier lent grim emphasis to that observation.

Using fire, maneuver, caution, and ground-hugging tactics, Hill managed to move his lead elements around Searchlight Point and to bring Unknown Point (between Searchlight and Wheeler) under fire from the destroyer. He sent Lieutenant Crawford and his platoon down to the beach and had him move north toward Unknown Point. Crawford set up a light machine gun and from there could bring fire to bear on one of the caves that had been holding up Corder's platoon on the road on the middle of the cliff. Whenever the Japanese opened up with fire from the caves, Hill had machine guns and grenade throwers ready to take the enemy under fire.

One of the caves nearer the beach was especially troublesome. Lieutenant Crawford had his machine gunner and riflemen pour fire into the cave entrance to cover him. Then he worked his way up to the cave and tossed two WP grenades into the cave's mouth. Then, using his submachine gun, Crawford moved across the opening of the cave, firing short bursts into its mouth as he moved. Crawford got across to the other side, but the Japanese still continued to fire from the inside. At one point, the enemy threw a shower of grenades out of the cave; then eleven Japanese marines raced out. Crawford's men killed nine of them. Later, Hill wrote:

> Of the two who managed to survive thus far, one was killed when he grabbed the barrel of a BAR with both hands. It proved to be a very foolhardy step to take. The other Jap was knocked down with a butt-stroke by one of the riflemen, and his skull crushed when the man followed his butt stroke by smashing down on the Jap's head with his rifle butt. This Jap proved to be the last Jap alive in that cave.

When Hill's men examined the cave, they found a total of forty-seven bodies, forty-one rifles, and a badly damaged heavy machine gun. His own casualties were five slightly wounded men. By 1105, he had cleared the area between Searchlight and Unknown points. But the neutralization of Wheeler Point itself remained. It would not be an easy task.

Hill decided to attack Wheeler Point in much the same way that he had moved from Searchlight Point to Unknown Point—rely on fire and maneuver and use the destroyer's pinpoint accuracy when needed. Hill started his attack at 1255 with a ten-minute preparation by the destroyer, shelling the caves near the Wheeler Point tunnel and the tunnel itself. Then he used his light machine gun to cover Lieutenant Corder's platoon as it advanced by squads in file toward the entrance to the tunnel. The shelling had had some effect on the Japanese in the caves and the tunnel because Corder and his men received no fire until they reached a point about five yards from the outer wall around the tunnel entrance. Captain Hill wrote:

> Then all Hell broke loose. Nine Japs charged out of the tunnel entrance hurling hand grenades as they charged. A machine gun started firing from the side port of the concrete emplacement [near the tunnel entrance]. The men moving in on the tunnel entrance had cautiously been advancing by bounds. Consequently, all but one of the men were in the prone position, and only the man standing was hit.
> Apparently the Japs were blinded somewhat by coming out of the dark tunnel into the bright sunshine. Most of their grenades were thrown over the cliff. Also, as they charged straight out of the entrance and ended up at the outer wall, there was a moment's confused milling around. The full blast of the machine guns and the lead squad's weapons hit the Japs. All were killed in a moment's time.

The Japanese continued to fire from the tunnel, and Corder's squads continued to maneuver around the opening, firing their rifles and machine guns into the opening as rapidly as possible. But Corder's men could not gain an advantage because "the Jap fire from the tunnel was so intense that it was impossible to gain an opening." Even throwing grenades into the tunnel had little effect.

Hill decided that because he was running seriously low on ammunition, and for which he faulted himself, he had to make a decisive move. He went to the entrance of the tunnel and had the BAR men from Corder's platoon as well as the submachine gun men from the squads work their way forward and around an outer protective wall that wound past the tunnel entrance about five yards from the mouth. Once these men were in position, he planned to have all the other men throw grenades, cover the tunnel with fire, and thus try to break the deadlock. The first attempt failed, and Hill lost a man to the Japanese. He wrote:

By crawling around and coaching each man in front of the tunnel to throw his grenades just over the wall across the tunnel entrance and to direct his fire low and deep into the tunnel, a second attempt of the plan was set up.

With all men watching for the signal, I raised my carbine over my head, and the men threw their grenades almost as one man. At the same time, they stood up, pouring very heavy fire into the tunnel. Jap fire slackened perceptibly, and much shouting and chattering could be heard through the momentary breaks in the firing.

Suddenly, the Jap firing stopped. This resulted in a slowing down of our fire. Two men, Pfc. W. A. Brown and Private Jandro, moved cautiously toward the entrance and were almost to the wall across the entrance when 14 Japs came swarming out of the tunnel. We had been nicely "suckered in."

The Japs grabbed the two men, and a Jap officer started hacking at Pfc. W. A. Brown with his saber, using short choppy strokes. The men outside the wall moved in, firing from the hip, and engaged the Japs hand to hand. The advantage was ours, in having weapons. The Japs had charged with only hand grenades, and the officer, with his saber, had the only weapon. A tug-of-war took place between the men of the 2d Platoon and the Japs for possession of Jandro and Brown. This scrap lasted nearly 10 minutes. It ended when Jandro and Brown were retrieved, and the Japs were dead or wounded. Brown was seriously wounded [he died of wounds on 25 February],[32] but Jandro wasn't seriously injured, [although he] was considerably battered up by his own helmet, which the Japs had used as a bludgeon. Most of the other men had received a few hard knocks but not serious enough to impair their efficiency.

Hill was reorganizing his men when the Japanese fired intense bursts again from the tunnel entrance. The Japanese banzaied

---

32. Brown may have been one of a very few men who were killed in a combat situation by a Japanese officer wielding a samurai saber.

once more. Hill's men killed seventeen of the enemy this time. Hill described the action:

It was at this time that I noticed Lt. Emory Ball in the firing line, and immediately I ordered him back to his mortar platoon. As Lieutenant Ball departed to the rear, the Japs mounted another banzai charge. It was preceded by a shower of hand grenades, most of which went over the heads of the men outside the tunnel and over the cliff. . . . Seven Japs charged but were killed as soon as they broke out of the tunnel entrance. Several men were hit by small grenade fragments, including me. Two of the men were sent back to the road cut and told to send two more men forward. Unnoticed by me, one of the men to come forward was Lieutenant Ball.

Silence from the tunnel followed the last banzai. The men prepared for another charge. All were beginning to feel the strain of the past two and a half hours. Time was now about 1530.

There were about five minutes of waiting, punctuated by an occasional shot from the tunnel, which was immediately answered by a burst of fire from the men outside the tunnel.

The buildup started. First, there were a few scattered shots, which steadily grew in violence. Private Jandro, of the hand-to-hand skirmish, was hit five times and was killed instantly. Lieutenant Ball was hit twice in the chest and staggered over and fell in front of me. (I will never forget the mixed emotions I felt, seeing one of my men die in front of my eyes as a result of disobedience of my orders.)

Almost on the instant of Lieutenant Ball's death, the Japs charged, 22 strong. Two Japs charged with such violence that they leapt over the outer wall and tumbled over the cliff. Their efforts carried Private Jones over with them. Jones, however, managed to grab the stubble of a bush and saved himself. Another Jap succeeded in grappling with Pfc. Kirkpatrick, who killed the Jap with his trench knife. The rest were killed by small arms fire.

By this time, Hill and the men on the firing line near the tunnel were nearly out of ammunition. Hill decided to evacuate the area. Most of Corder's platoon moved out first, carrying Brown and Pfc. McBride, who had been wounded in the last banzai attack. T/5 George A. Chuises, Hill's radio operator, was hit in the hand. Another shot hit his radio, putting it out of commission. Hill ordered the light machine guns to spray the tunnel with their remaining ammunition. Then he ordered Corder, his radio operator, and the few men remaining in front of the tunnel "to make a run for it." Hill then fired a clip of ammunition from his submachine gun and raced for safety behind the men he had already sent around the cliff.

In pure unemotional militarese, Hill wrote that "the time of withdrawal recorded by the 1st Sergeant was 1615. The company had been fighting approximately 9 hours to cover a distance of about 700 yards."

When Lieutenant Browne, the battalion S-3, saw the company start to withdraw, he called for an LCM to meet the company south of Searchlight Point to pick up Hill's dead and wounded. Unfortunately, Hill was not able to bring out the bodies of Lieutenants Ball and Jandro. Patrols the next morning could find no trace of them.

Hill loaded his dead, wounded, and badly fatigued men aboard the LCM and then, with the rest of the company, worked his way back to the perimeter on Topside. As they moved across the parade ground, men from other units walked up to Hill's E Company men, offered a cigarette or a canteen of water or lifted the man's weapon from his shoulder and walked silently beside him. Hill said of his men, "Although tired beyond reason, they held their heads high."

At a later date, writing a paper for the Infantry School, Captain Hill succinctly and knowingly appraised the value of the TSMG (Thompson submachine gun): "TSMG is unequaled in close combat and is outstanding in its effectiveness in cave and hand-to-hand combat."

By the evening of the second, the Japanese had lost a total of 2,466 counted dead and 6 prisoners of war. Uncounted and unknown numbers littered the caves, tunnels, buildings, batteries, and redoubts around Corregidor. The Rock Force, including the 503d and the 3d Battalion of the 34th with A Company of the 34th attached, had lost 118 men killed in action and 314 wounded or injured.

After Hill's company had neutralized the Wheeler Point area, Colonel Jones could begin to plan the rest of his campaign to win back all of Corregidor. He knew full well that not all of the enemy on Topside had been killed but that enough of them had been put out of action so that he could leave a part of his force to continue clearing Topside and use the bulk of his troops to reduce the eastern half. He knew that hundreds of the enemy were still alive and able to fight for the remainder of Corregidor. He had never underestimated their strength; he was not about to do so now. And events would prove him right—the enemy on Corregidor as of the evening of 23 February 1945 was far from beaten. In the days ahead, the Japanese would still banzai, snipe, machine-gun, grenade, bayonet, and detonate huge underground stores of powder and ammunition. Corregidor was far from clear.

CHAPTER XIV
The Mop-up

Twenty-four February marked the turning point in the Rock Force's reconquest of Corregidor. On that date, Colonel Jones initiated the attack to clear the eastern end of the island—from Malinta Hill to East and Hooker points—a distance of about four thousand yards. Historians, looking at this portion of the battle for the rest of The Rock, might call the operations of the next few days a "mop-up"; in the larger context of the overall battle to retake the Philippines, it undoubtedly was. But to the men of the Rock Force, the mop-up was a brutal, dirty, slugging match with a still-indomitable enemy, who, even when cornered in the most dire, desperate, and hopeless of circumstances, not only refused to surrender, but was determined to take with him as many as possible of his enemy through any diabolical device or unconventional means available.

Throughout the war against the Japanese, the American and Allied soldiers had frequently run into the kind of fanaticism that the Japanese routinely displayed on Corregidor. But when the Japanese realized they were losing, their Bushido spirit, stressing loyalty and self-sacrifice for the Emperor and for one's honor, came more obviously to the fore. Bushido fostered the kamikaze attacks, the banzai assaults, and the hara-kiri (belly-cutting—referred to by the Japanese as "seppuku") suicides of individuals and groups when capture or death was imminent. The Bushido spirit caused a man to fight to his last ounce of energy—and never surrender.

One PT boat commander reported that he saw a Japanese soldier trying to escape to Mariveles by swimming through the three miles of shark infested waters from Corregidor by clinging to a bamboo pole. When the PT boat went to pick him up, the Japanese pulled a carbine from the pole and fired one shot at the boat. The PT boat commander did not rescue him.

The Navy reported that in spite of the tides, the distance, and the sharks, scores of Japanese tried to swim from Corregidor to Mariveles. "Our PT boats kept patrolling all night," a naval officer reported. "With the moonlight and star shells we could usually see what was going on; and we sometimes 'jacked' them with our own lights. I guess there were fifty or maybe more swimmers every night or so for five or six nights running. They didn't get many through, though."

Weldon B. Hester was the Red Cross field director with the 3d Battalion of the 34th. On one of the occasions after he had backpacked cigarettes to the men of the 34th on top of Malinta Hill, he stood talking to one of the soldiers. He remembers that he "chanced to look around and spotted a Jap some thirty to thirty-five feet away trying to get the stuck pin out of a hand grenade. My reactions were perfect—I yelled and dove behind a rock. Someone else shot and wounded the Jap, who struggled to the cliff's edge and dove off, refusing to surrender."

Hoot Gibson was at his artillery observation post one afternoon when he spotted a Japanese in the water hanging onto a log and swimming away from the beach. "A machine gun opened up on him, but he seemed to survive," Gibson wrote. "I asked fire direction center (FDC) for permission to fire one round at this target. FDC agreed. I fired one round, which landed in the water with a splash but no explosion. I felt sorry for the Nip and cancelled the fire mission."

But a P-47, circling overhead, spotted the Japanese and strafed him with .50-caliber machine guns blazing. "The water boiled around the log, and the figure disappeared," wrote Gibson. "I thought about the incident many times. We expended a lot of ammo on one poor frightened Japanese soldier who was desperately trying to survive by swimming away. He never had a chance."

Colonel Jones's operational plan for the final attack to clear the tail of Corregidor was fairly simple: Major Caskey and his "hard-hit" 2d Battalion, 503d, would remain on Topside and continue to mop up that area; Colonel Postlethwait and his 3d Battalion, 34th, would remain in blocking position across the waist of Corregidor from San Jose Point on the south to Malinta Point on the north; Pug Woods and his 1st Battalion, 503d, would lead the attack across the narrow width of the island and along the tail; Colonel Erickson and his 3d Battalion, 503d, would follow the 1st; the 462d Parachute Field Artillery Battalion would support the attack from positions on the parade ground.

To support the attack on the eastern half of the island, the artillerymen of the 462d simply had to turn their howitzers around 180 degrees, face them to the east, and register them on a point on the eastern end of the island. The artillerymen found this situation unique. Ordinarily in combat, the artillery shoots in front of the infantry and then moves forward as the infantry advances. But on Corregidor, the island was so small that the pack 75-mm howitzers could cover the entire length and breadth of the island from their gun positions on the parade ground in front of Topside barracks. And because by now there was no threat of enemy mortar, artillery, or air attacks, the 462d could enjoy the luxury of lining up their howitzers hub to hub—which made the battalion easier to control and the concentrations a little more precise and compact.

On the afternoon of the twenty-third, Colonel Jones, Colonel Postlethwait, Colonel Erickson, and Major Woods met on top of Malinta Hill. From that vantage point, they could see the entire eastern half of Corregidor all the way to Hooker Point. They studied the terrain, looked for possible enemy strong points, and planned the attack. Colonel Jones pointed out to his battalion commanders the general route of the 1st Battalion. He told Pug Woods that he wanted one company of his battalion to move down the east and south side of Malinta Hill to secure the road in that area. He told him to move the rest of the battalion through the 3d of the 34th and move out along the northern side of Malinta and along the northern half of the tail. He also told Postlethwait to assign his two remaining serviceable tanks to Woods's battalion.

Colonel Jones told Postlethwait to hold and block the terrain he was currently occupying but to move part of his battalion around the north side of Malinta Hill to secure the high ground in the vicinity of Engineer Point. Which part of the battalion, Colonel Jones left up to Postlethwait.

Colonel Jones told Erickson that he wanted his 3d Battalion to follow behind the 1st, mopping up the "small islands of resistance" that the 1st might bypass, leaving the 1st free to move along the tail as rapidly as possible.

Colonel Jones ended his orders to his battalion commanders by telling them that before the assault began the next morning, air, naval, and artillery fires would soften the area. He did not need to tell them that the ever-present Navy was waiting offshore to attack any targets that were hard to reduce and that the "air" could be on target in a very short time. By this time, the infantry knew that they could count on both the Air Force and the Navy for accurate, timely, and heavy assault fires whenever and wherever they needed them. All troops of the Rock Force agreed that the air and naval support on this operation were simply superb—quickly responsive, accurate, deadly.

That same afternoon of the twenty-third, Hoot Gibson, on orders from his battalion FDC, went to the top of Malinta Hill and set up an observation post, ready to adjust the battalion and then concentrate artillery fire where needed to support the infantry moving east. He established radio contact with the FDC and then with his radio operator settled down for the night atop Malinta Hill within the lines of K Company of the 34th, who were back on top of Malinta. "During the night," wrote Hoot Gibson later, "the Japs inside the tunnel began to explode ammunition deep inside the mountain. The hill rumbled, and smoke and fire erupted from the many air vents all over the mountain. I thought the whole hill was going to blow, and we got no sleep that night. It was scary!"

What Gibson and the men of K Company of the 34th heard and felt were the Japanese, trapped in the tunnels of Malinta, committing suicide. Seven separate and deafening explosions rumbled through the dark hours of the morning of the twenty-fourth. The 34th Regiment's perceptive historian later wrote:

During the night of 23–24 February, the enemy made his most serious attempt to demolish Malinta Hill. In the early morning hours, seven explosions, all in quick succession, threatened to tear the hill asunder. Foxholes crumbled, flames belched from every hole in the central and northern portions of the hill, and with it belched parties of Japs—either corpses blown out by the blast, or men driven out into American fire and death.

It was devastation—stark, awe inspiring, terrifying. But for the Jap—not for the intended victim.

One of the 503d's regimental surgeons wrote:

It was not only the failure of their banzais that had driven the Nips to this bit of hara-kiri. Our men had been busy from the start with demolitions activities wherever they could approach any of the side entrances to the great tunnel system; and the Navy gunners had contributed a major share in sealing off openings that lay within range of their guns. Furthermore, our patrols on the summit found the air vents which came from the great corridors below, and dropped phosphorous grenades down them "like nickels in a slot machine." The sum total of these various measures must have added up to a terrific ordeal of terror, even for a Jap. Their comrades were being slaughtered in banzais, their tunnel entrances were caving in, their ventilation was fouled with choking smoke fumes, and the rock corridors were quaking under the heavy blasts of bombardment—yet they did not surrender. By day the vigilance of our air corps kept them from moving in any numbers, and they had to stay underground, like moles when hawks were overhead; but at night, they made use of a rear entrance that was sheltered from direct fire, and they filtered out toward the eastern end of the island, or else they took up nearby positions to launch fresh banzais.

At first light the next morning, the twenty-fourth, the battalion FDC called Gibson and asked him to register the battalion. For a base point, Gibson selected a concrete water tower in the middle of the tail of the island near the old airfield. He registered one howitzer on the tower. From then on, for the rest of the campaign, the water tower was the 462d's base point.

Gibson later wrote that after he had registered the battalion, the 462d

> laid down a rolling barrage with the entire battalion all along the tail. Our forward observers with the assault infantry also called for specific fire on targets of opportunity. We also used smoke shells to mark the forward units because the two destroyers offshore were firing their 5-inch guns at any targets of opportunity they could observe. The fighter cover overhead made low-level sweeps and dropped bombs and strafed targets. It was a classic demonstration of a perfectly coordinated attack. We were all in perfect radio contact. From our OP, we had perfect visibility on the action going on in front of us.

Pug Woods led his battalion across the line of departure behind the rolling barrage at precisely 0830. At that same time, the final air attack hit Engineer Point after ninety minutes of other preparation by the mortars, machine guns of the 503d and the 34th, and the fires from the destroyers offshore. It was an especially heavy preparation. In the morning's attack, Capt. William T. Bossert led his A Company of the 503d down the east side of Malinta Hill. By midafternoon, A Company had reached Camp Point, just short of Water Tank Hill. So far, so good. The enemy was holed up in caves along the shoreline, and the infantrymen could attack them from the rear. In addition, the Navy spotter with the 1st Battalion brought the destroyer fire accurately on targets that held up the company. Captain Bossert said, "It was an exhilarating luxury to have a destroyer attached to a rifle company."

He also had the use of P-47s that eased his advance with numerous strikes using 500-pound bombs and napalm. Before he reached Camp Point, Bossert and his men accounted for 101 Japanese dead. On one occasion, Bossert reported, "A Japanese officer waving a samurai sword, screaming courage into a group of grim-faced men, who then dutifully staggered forward over the rubble directly into our aimed fire."

But the Japanese were far from finished in front of A Company. When Bossert tried to move his 2d Platoon to the top of Water Tank Hill before nightfall, the platoon bogged down about fifty yards short of its objective even though it had strong mortar support and direct fire from a couple of the 462d's howitzers, which had moved down from the parade ground. The 2d Platoon had two men injured, and Bossert withdrew it to join the other two platoons in a perimeter just below the hill.

Across the ridge from A Company, B and C companies of the 503d, plus L Company of the 34th, jumped off to attack Engineer Point. These companies had the luxury of two Sherman tanks, from the detachment of the 603d Tank Company, which had come ashore with the 34th, to precede them along the northern shore toward the holed-up enemy on Engineer Point. The tanks blasted the mouths of the tunnels on the northern slope of Malinta Hill, which kept flanking fire off the advancing infantrymen. "The momentum of the shock attack was never lost. The Japs were wiped off Engineer Point and the attack mission completed at 1100 hours," reported the 34th's historian.

But the enemy was far from defeated. Strong Japanese opposition developed at Infantry Point, about eight hundred yards farther east along the north shore. After nightfall of the twenty-fourth, some six hundred Japanese attempted to assemble about three hundred yards south of Infantry Point for a counterattack. A Japanese survivor reported later that his commander fully intended to reach Topside. At about 2100, the enemy began firing his mortars and rained heavy and accurate fire on the perimeter of the 1st Battalion, which was dug in along a line roughly from Infantry Point to Camp Point. The mortar fire would prove disastrous to Pug Woods, the 1st Battalion's commander, some of his staff, and his company commanders.

Colonel Jones had visited Pug Woods during the late afternoon of the twenty-fourth and saw that the battalion had made considerable progress. Jones wrote later:

Just at dusk, I was with Pug in a shell hole some several feet wide, which he was using as his CP. He had several people with him, including his radio operator and one or two others. The plan called for his battalion to take a defensive

position for the night and resume the attack at daybreak
the next morning. Pug insisted that I spend the night with
him and be present at daybreak when the attack would continue. I told him that I couldn't do that because I had to
get back to my CP to find out what a general officer was
doing there, and to find out what he wanted. [The general
officer, Maj. Gen. William Marquat, had appeared at Colonel
Jones's CP in the morning.] Pug cautioned me that it was
getting dark and that by the time I got to Topside, I ran a
good chance of being shot by one of our own sentries. I
told him that I had to take the chance because I had to
return to confer with the general officer. My enlisted aide
and I made it back to the CP in record time. It was only
about 20 minutes after I arrived back that I received word
over my radio that a mortar shell had exploded in Pug's
CP, which I had just left. Pug was killed.

Colonel Jones did confer with General Marquat, who was a
senior staff officer on General MacArthur's staff. He confided in
Colonel Jones that he was on Corregidor to make plans for General
MacArthur's return to Corregidor.

When the Japanese mortar round landed in Pug Woods's command post, the bomb crater, he was having a meeting of his
staff and company commanders relative to the attack for the following morning. In addition to Woods, the battalion S-2 and two
radio operators were killed. Of the thirteen present at the meeting,
only two were untouched. Capt. John P. Rucker, commanding
officer of C Company, almost lost an arm. The battalion executive
officer, Maj. John N. Davis, took over command of Pug Woods's
battalion. Major Davis thought that he had seen the worst of it,
but for the 1st Battalion, 503d, the worst was yet to come.

From his observation post on top of Malinta Hill, Hoot Gibson
"could see and hear mortar flashes and explosions." What he
was witnessing was the Japanese mortar barrage that killed Pug
Woods and was the prelude to another all-out banzai attack by
the six hundred men who had assembled south of Infantry Point.

The forward observers from the 462d who were with the frontline companies of the 1st Battalion brought down heavy concentrations of artillery fire on the Japanese forming up for the attack.

The infantry fired their machine guns and mortars at maximum rates of fire. For the men firing the defensive fires in front of the 1st Battalion, it was more than they could have hoped for. A prisoner later reported that the artillery and mortar barrage caught the Japanese at the worst possible time—as they were assembling in the open and out of their caves and tunnels. The Japanese commander, stubborn and resolute in a hopeless situation, refused to disperse his men and let them find cover even after the American fire landed in his ranks. As a result, some three hundred of the six hundred were killed before the attack even began.

Notwithstanding his terrible losses, the Japanese commander ordered an attack. He had regrouped his survivors, fired what mortars and machine guns he still had operational, and threw his force against the defensive line of the 1st Battalion. The dug-in infantrymen did not yield an inch. Their defensive fires were perfectly adjusted to enfilade the attacking Japanese and the artillery and mortars, previously adjusted in front of the infantry's defenses, further decimated the ranks of the diehard enemy. By 0400, the battle was over. The remnants of the force, about 165 men, withdrew toward Cavalry Point and the tunnels under Monkey Point, dragging their wounded with them.

Early on the morning of the twenty-fifth, the 1st Battalion, following another heavy artillery and mortar barrage, moved out through the terrain over which the Japanese had tried their attack only hours previously. In spite of their horrendous losses, the Japanese were still able to put up a fight. The resistance was stiff, including some small banzai charges near Monkey Point. Davis's battalion attacked Water Tank Hill at 1045. In the approach to the hill, the Japanese killed Pvt. John C. Pace and two men near him when the enemy rushed from a small tunnel dug into one of the ravines.

Major Davis decided against a frontal attack on Water Tank Hill and sent one company around the east flank of the hill and another company to the west. By dark of the evening of the twenty-fifth, Davis had positioned his battalion on a line roughly from Cavalry Point on the north shore southeast some seven hundred yards to the south shore at Monkey Point. By 1800 on the twenty-fifth, the 1st Battalion held all of the high ground, and the troops could see Kindley Field just a thousand or so yards down the trail. The end was literally in sight; it was, but tragedy would strike again the next day.

On the twenty-fifth, the Rock Force lost the services of the 3d Battalion of the 34th. Postlethwait's division, the 24th, had been ordered to Mindoro for operations in the southern Philippines. In ten days of fighting on Corregidor, the 3d Battalion of the 34th Infantry Regiment had killed more than 800 Japanese; the battalion's losses were 38 killed in action, 150 wounded, 10 injured, and 5 reported as missing. Postlethwait's battalion combat team was replaced by the 2d Battalion, 151st Infantry Regiment of the 38th Division. The 2d of the 151st moved over to Corregidor from Mariveles. Fortunately, Postlethwait left behind his two M-7 self-propelled 75-mm howitzers and two M-4 Sherman tanks. By the time the 3d of the 34th left the island, the entire Rock Force had counted 3,703 enemy dead and picked up a total of 16 POWs, most of whom had been caught as they tried to escape from the island.

The night of 25–26 February passed rather quietly for the 1st Battalion. With more than three thousand Japanese killed and scores more shot by the Navy as they tried to escape the island, the troopers of the 1st Battalion thought that there could not be many more of the enemy left alive on the island. Unfortunately, the few enemy who remained would almost wipe out the 1st Battalion as an effective fighting unit on the morrow.

Just northeast of Monkey Point was a little ridge under which was an underground network of tunnels; before the war, it had housed the Navy's Radio Intercept Station. The 1st Battalion launched its attack toward Monkey Point at 0800 on the twenty-sixth and met strong resistance—mainly from automatic fire—from the vicinity of the tunnel entrance. But with the help of the artillery (A Battery of the 462d was on the road leading to Monkey Point) and the destroyers sitting in the bay on a "Let us fire basis," the 1st pushed forward and drove the Japanese underground. The two Sherman tanks assisted the 1st Battalion in closing the tunnel entrances. Major Davis ordered his companies to throw a perimeter around the entire Monkey Point knoll, effectively covering all entrances. The paratroopers had bottled up the Japanese once more—and once more the cornered enemy resorted to fanatical violence.

A Company was atop the small ridge on Monkey Point, directly above the Japanese in the Radio Intercept Station below; B Company was down the slope toward the south guarding a lower entrance; C Company was to the north; A Battery of the 462d had moved along the shore road just past the tunnel entrances to a position where they could deliver direct fire into some caves in the rocky cliffs beyond. One infantry platoon had moved out along the flank of the ridge to reconnoiter what lay beyond and around Monkey Point.

All of the approaches to the tunnel were now secured. Major Davis brought the two tanks forward and had them prepare to fire on the approach to the tunnel to blast its doors open.

At a little after 1100, Major Davis was standing on a knoll on top of the concrete upper entrance of the tunnel, watching the artillery and air strikes preparing for his final attack down toward Kindley Field. Ten troopers of the 1st Battalion were resting on top of the ridge and below it watching the air and artillery preparation and getting ready to move out. One of the Sherman tanks was firing its 75-mm gun into one cave after another below the ridgeline. The whole atmosphere in the 1st Battalion area was relaxed; the troopers felt that the worst had to be over. After all, they could see the tail of the island, their ultimate objective. Once there, Corregidor would be rewon—the island secure. But the Japanese in the tunnel under Monkey Point ridge were not quite finished.

At about 1105, one of the tanks had fired its main tank gun down into the sloping revetted entrance into the Monkey Point tunnel. Occurring almost simultaneously with the explosion of that shell against the door of the tunnel, a violent underground detonation lifted the top off the ridge over the Radio Intercept Station in the Monkey Point tunnel. The blast, according to survivors, was more violent than the one that detonated in the Malinta tunnels.

The explosion sent Japanese and paratrooper bodies, arms, legs, and torsos flying into the air. The entire island was shaken as if an earthquake had struck. Both of the 35-ton tanks were tossed into the air like toys, and one of them tumbled end over end for nearly fifty feet down the ridge, trapping the crew inside. Incredibly, rescuers later found that one man inside was still alive. They borrowed an acetylene torch from a Seventh Fleet destroyer and cut open the tank to save him.

A destroyer that was more than two thousand yards away in the bay was hit by a large chunk of rock. Another huge rock hit a man a mile and a half away on Topside.

Hoot Gibson was at his observation post atop Malinta Hill. "The troopers were resting on a hill near the water tower, and a Sherman tank moved up and was firing at caves and bunkers, when, all of a sudden, the entire hill went up in a huge explosion. Bodies were flying through the air, and we could not believe our eyes. The forward observers reported that the Japs had set off ammunition stored in the hill."

One of the regimental surgeons working in the aid station in the barracks on Topside reported:

I was busy in the Regimental dispensary a mile and a half away. Even here we were shaken by violent tremors, and heard such a terrific blast that we thought the whole of Malinta Hill must have blown up. The concussion was so great that its reverberations reached as far as ten miles away. We soon received telephone messages: "Prepare for a lot of casualties. The 1st Battalion has been caught in a big explosion and we are sending all the trucks we can get down to pick up the wounded." Fortunately, there were three medical officers with their aid stations close in the vicinity. They were men who had learned by hard experience, that branch of the surgeon's art which is not taught in any medical school, the art of improvised first aid under the shattering conditions of a combat disaster. Dead bodies lay all about, some of them half buried; and among them, others dying or severely injured. It took them an hour and a half of fearful effort before the last casualty had been treated and tagged and loaded into a truck for the hospital. "Then I realized what a strain I had been under all this time," one of the surgeons explained to me afterwards. "As soon as I got all of the casualties off, I sat down on a rock and burst out crying. I couldn't stop myself and didn't even want to. I had seen more than a man could see and stay normal. Right after coming out of the daze of the explosion, I looked up and there was one of my own men with a tank blown over on top of him, and just his head and chest squeezed out from under it. It was like that everywhere. When I had the cases to care for, that kept me going; but after that, it was too much."

The explosion flung into the air huge rocks and boulders that crashed down on the troopers in their foxholes and in the open. A giant hillslide covered the platoon-size patrol that had gone around the flank of the tunnel complex on reconnaissance. Bennett Guthrie reported, "I observed one man, along with a tree, blown so high in the sky that they nearly disappeared from sight."

The main explosion was followed immediately by four smaller ones. Pieces of concrete, steel, boulders, trees rained down on the defenseless troopers. A thick and blinding pall of dust engulfed the area. One man reported that the blast was so big and intense that it blocked out the sun and that for a moment the sky was dark.

Colonel Jones was not in the area when the blast happened, but he immediately hurried to the 1st Battalion's scene of carnage. Recently he wrote:

When I arrived shortly after the explosion, I observed many of the people lying about who had been killed by the concussion of the blast but who appeared to be still alive.

This was by far the saddest moment of my military career. I have more than once "clammed up" when relating this incident. Just thinking about it still brings me grief. Of course, the 1st Battalion was completely knocked out as a fighting unit, but I ordered the 3d Battalion to move through the 1st Battalion and continue the attack.

As soon as the extent of the Monkey Point disaster became known to Maj. Tom Stevens, the 503d regimental surgeon, he made certain that every aidman and doctor on the island was pressed into service either at the site of the explosion or in the dispensary in the barracks on Topside. He radioed the destroyers offshore, who sent medical corpsmen and doctors to help with the casualties. The Navy doctors and corpsmen were on the scene a half hour after the explosion. Colonel Jones sent what trucks he could find and any ambulances to the scene to evacuate the wounded.

The dead were wrapped up in ponchos and lined up along the dusty North Shore Road, ready for evacuation by ship. Bennett Guthrie remembered seeing them along both sides of the road "perhaps an arm's length apart, their feet pointing toward the tracks of the roadway. The line of bodies probably extended more than a hundred feet."

The explosion threw Major Davis through the air for 20 to 30 feet but only knocked the wind out of him and stunned him momentarily. "I have never seen such a sight in my life—utter carnage—bodies lying everywhere, everywhere," he remembered. And just a few feet from where he had been standing near the concrete tunnel entrance, there was the edge of a huge crater 130 feet long, 70 feet wide, and 30 feet deep. "The crater left by the great upheaval," wrote the regimental surgeon, "was big enough to include an area the size of four or five tennis courts and was as deep as a house." Where once there had been a ridge-line, now there was a jagged, rock-strewn crater. "A ravine was created where a hill had been."

When the 503d surgeons and commanders had finished sorting the dead and wounded, to their horror they counted 54 dead and another 145 wounded, some grotesquely. More than 150 Japanese were killed. For once, the Japanese had inflicted more death and destruction on the Americans than they had on themselves.

The cause of the explosion is difficult to define. Obviously, from the size of the blast, it is clear that the Japanese had stored huge quantities of explosives in the Radio Intercept Station tunnel, moving shells, ammunition, Bangalore torpedoes, and TNT from Malinta when they recognized that the Americans were pushing them relentlessly toward the tail of the island. Some of the men of the 503d think that the tank round fired into the mouth of the tunnel caused the explosion. The round from the tank did

hit and explode just before the huge detonation. But Lt. Edward
J. Callahan, who commanded the platoon of B Company guarding
the lower entrance to the tunnel, noticed smoke seeping from
the entrance just a few moments before the explosion. He quickly
ordered his platoon down the hill, away from the entrance, but
he and his radio operator remained near the entrance. When
the explosion came, he remembers, "Suddenly I dove for protection out of reflex action. . . . Everything was pitch black." Callahan was knocked out, and when he regained consciousness, he
was lying on his back, injured and covered with a layer of debris.

From Callahan's experience, it seems probable that the Japanese blew the tunnel and its vast store of explosives on purpose.
The Radio Intercept Station was the last bastion between the
Americans and the tip of the island. And a naval ship had reported
to the 503d earlier that one of her lookouts had seen about two
hundred Japanese crowding into the tunnel as the 1st Battalion
had pushed eastward from the east side of Malinta Hill. One
must assume that this "final, suicidal tour de force" was just that.
This was a last gasp, a Bushido-inspired attempt at self-destruction.
Even given the horror of the blast, not all of the Japanese died.

Major Davis gathered up the remnants of his battalion and
led them back to a perimeter near Water Tank Hill for the night.
The company commanders counted their men and reorganized
their platoons with what they had left over. Captain Bossert's A
Company was the hardest hit: On 17 February he had landed
on Bottomside with 6 officers and 126 men. On the evening of
26 February, he had two officers and 42 men left. His was the
hardest hit of any company that had fought for the recapture
of Corregidor.

By shortly after noon, Erickson had pushed his 3d Battalion
through the lines formerly held by the 1st. Captain Murphy had
his I Company in the lead down the middle of the tail, with
Captain Doerr's G Company on the north and Captain Conway's
H Company on the south. By dark on the twenty-sixth, part of
the 3d Battalion had reached Kindley Field and had de-mined
it. For the night, the battalion went into a perimeter defense
around Kindley Field.

The next day, Captain Doerr cleared the area north of the
airfield down to the water's edge and back toward Cavalry Point.

Captain Conway's H Company worked over the area south of the airfield down to the shoreline and back toward Monkey Point. Captain Murphy and his I Company continued east, down the middle.

I Company ran into some difficulty because it had to follow the ridgeline that ran down the center the length of the tail. It could move only along a single path that traced the ridgeline. The company suffered a few casualties from some enemy who had hidden out along the edges of the tree-lined path. But the company succeeded in driving the enemy from the ridge down to the shorelines, both north and south, where G and H companies could eliminate them.

Toward the end of the ridgeline, Captain Murphy decided to split his 1st Platoon and send half down the south shore and the other half down the north shore toward the farthest point on the tail, East Point. On its way east, the platoon succeeded in killing a number of the enemy in caves along both shorelines.

It was not easy. S. Sgt. Ernest J. Debruycker attempted to flush some of the Japanese out of a cave by tossing in a WP grenade. The Japanese inside threw the grenade back out, where it exploded and seriously injured Sergeant Debruycker. Undaunted, he took another grenade, pulled the pin, held it for a few seconds, and then tossed it into the cave. He killed four Japanese marines. Pfc. Stanley C. Crawford of I Company was not so lucky. He was mortally wounded as he tried to clean out another cave in I Company's sector.

By 1600 on the twenty-seventh, Murphy's 1st Platoon had fought its way to East Point. Amazingly enough, this was still not the end of the enemy on the most eastern point of Corregidor. Hooker Point was a small island a few hundred yards still to the east of East Point. A group of Japanese had waded out to the island at low tide and had set up a defensive position on the tiny, rocky, narrow spit of land. The 1st Platoon did what the enemy had done: it waited for low tide and then waded out to the reef where it made short shrift of the enemy. As one of the doctors with the 503d put it: "The island had now been combed from end to end. Probably many skulking Jap fugitives were still hiding out, but in substance the fighting was over." Unfortunately, more men of the 503d would be killed before the island would be secure.

Twenty-seven February marked another significant occasion for the men fighting for Corregidor. On that day, for the first time since 23 January, there were no aerial strikes because the 503d and the 2d Battalion of the 151st Regiment were deployed over the length and width of the island. The infantrymen did, however, continue to call in naval gunfire on the shorelined caves and tunnels.

The Japanese seemed to realize finally by the twenty-seventh that they had lost Corregidor. In the preceding days, a number of the enemy had tried to swim, float, or paddle behind a log or a raft to reach Bataan. On the twenty-seventh, however, a great many of the survivors slipped down from their caves and tunnels along the shore and made the attempt to escape. The Navy had at first attempted to pick up some of the enemy but were frustrated when the Japanese fired at them. As the regimental adjutant of the 503d, Maj. Lester Levine, put it: "To avoid loss of American lives in attempted rescues, strafing was authorized. Fighter planes, naval craft, and even liaison planes armed with hand grenades and rifles allowed few survivors to reach Bataan. About two hundred enemy were killed in this fashion, but that number is not included in RCT totals, in that the RCT neither killed nor counted them."

Lt. James R. Thomas was the 462d Field Artillery Battalion's liaison officer—aerial forward observer—who flew a Piper Cub from the old parade ground, which had been cleared sufficiently for him to land his small, two-seater airplane. He joined his big brothers in the Air Corps in hunting down the escaping enemy soldiers. He flew his Cub over the shoreline, and when he found the Japanese trying to escape, he strafed them, firing a Thompson submachine gun out his side window.

Lt. Donald E. "Abe" Abbott was the executive officer of E Company of the 503d. Forty years after his experiences on The Rock, Abe remembers the smell and the flies:

Speaking of smell, two of the most vivid memories that stand out when one remembers the experiences connected

with the retaking of The Rock are related to the smell and
the flies. We were told that men on the ships that entered
Manila Bay after we had secured the island would get sick
from the smell even from a distance of several miles out in
the bay. For us, it was ever present, something we could
not escape. You cannot shut out the smell by ducking your
head under a poncho or blanket when there are hundreds,
even thousands, of dead bodies around. We finally got so
we didn't notice as much. Flies were so thick that a person
would have to eat his jelly- or Spam-covered cracker with
one hand holding the food and the other hand brushing
off the fifty or one hundred flies on the surface. The flies
got in your eyes, your ears, and in your mouth, not to mention
all over your body. We had noticed that the flies were bad
when we landed because the Japanese santitation was apparently pretty bad, but the thousands of bodies supplied them
with plenty of breeding places and really brought them out
after a few days of fighting. One time, at about the ten-day
point, a C-47 flew over and dusted the whole island with
DDT, killing nearly every fly. It was almost as if a miracle
had happened. After that a fly was an oddity, and we were
left with only the pervasive smells. I often thought of how
effective that dusting was when people after the war com-
plained of the environmental effect of the use of DDT. If
they had been faced with the number of flies we had been,
they would have been as glad as we were to see DDT used.

After the twenty-seventh, the Rock Force did in fact go into
a "mop-up" mode. The 2d Battalion's area of responsibility was
Topside. Even then, the battalion ran into heavy opposition, especially around the ruins of Wheeler Battery. In one attack near
Wheeler Point, D Company lost three men killed and five more
wounded. Bennett Guthrie reported that "near the large cave, a
patrol was pinned down so tightly by enemy fire that it had to
be evacuated from the beach by one landing craft while another
fired into the cavern entrances to keep the enemy in recess." In
all, during their attack on the island, the Rock Force had sealed
more than four hundred caves and tunnels, using more than
seventeen tons of explosives.

The 3d Battalion continued to rout the Japanese out of the caves and tunnels to the east of Malinta; the 2d Battalion of the 151st worked the area around Malinta Hill; the 1st Battalion was in a perimeter around Topside, licking its wounds and attempting to reconstitute and reorganize itself.

The mopping up of the island proceeded apace because the 503d had been alerted to return to Mindoro base camp no later than 10 March in order to make ready for its participation in an operation to clear the southern Philippines. That was one reason for haste in cleaning up The Rock; the other was the impending visit to Corregidor by General MacArthur on 2 March.

By 2 March, General Hall, the XI Corps commander, and Colonel Jones decided that the "mopping up had progressed to the point that they could set a date for the official termination of the operation," wrote Robert R. Smith in his book, *Triumph in the Philippines.*

Casualties, including those from the parachute drop, numbered over 1,000 killed, wounded, injured, and missing. The Japanese losses—actually counted—numbered about 4,500 killed and 20 captured. An additional 200 Japanese were estimated to have been killed while trying to swim away, and it was thought that at least 500 might have been sealed in caves and tunnels; a few remained alive in various hideaways.

Retired Brigadier General Jones wrote recently of his preparations for General MacArthur's return to Corregidor, the event that would fulfill General MacArthur's promise in the dark days of March 1942: "I shall return."

After Major General Bill Marquat's visit we became very busy making plans for General MacArthur's visit, completing the clean-up of Corregidor, and getting ready for redeployment back to Mindoro.

On Topside, in the old barracks, we had the Headquarters of the Rock Force, the Headquarters of one battalion, Headquarters Company of the 503d, Service Company of the 503d, the Dispensary, which I guess was the portable surgical hospital which was attached, and some other miscellaneous units. At any rate, it was very crowded on Topside. On the small parade ground in front of the barracks we had all of the 75-mm pack howitzers of the 462d Field Artillery Battalion because that was the only level and clear place on the island to put the guns in position. We had artillery ammunition, mortars, hand grenades, and all sorts of other ammunition stored right out in front of the barracks; there was really no other place to store them.

In anticipation of MacArthur's visit, I wanted the troops in formation to look their best, so I was overjoyed when my supply unit received a large supply of new field uniforms. I can remember also that I was the proud possessor of a Japanese jeep that was sitting alongside the supplies and ammunition. I wasn't much for war trophies, but I did hope somehow to get that Japanese jeep back to the United States.

Among the ammunition piles were a number of white phosphorous grenades and approximately ten tons of TNT which our demolition platoon had been using to close caves and for other purposes.

The sun on Corregidor gets pretty hot. Just after midday, several days before MacArthur was to arrive, someone yelled that there was smoke coming from the white phosphorous grenades. A couple of men from the demolition platoon attempted to segregate the white phosphorous grenades to prevent them from setting off other munitions in the area. The men got their hands burned in the attempt, and they were unable to isolate them completely from other munitions. The fire spread, and we had mortar and artillery shells and other rounds exploding like fireworks—set off from the heat of the white phosphorous grenades. I suddenly realized the danger of the fire spreading to the stockpile of TNT and, accordingly, ordered all the barracks cleared. My chief interest was the Dispensary, which was within 100 or 150 yards of the center of the fire. Within a short time all units had been cleared from the barracks. The last person ahead of me had just gone through the door when the expected happened— the fire got to the TNT. The resulting explosion blew down three or four sections of the concrete barracks walls. Fortunately, there were about three barracks walls between the explosion and the room that I was walking through on the ground floor of the barracks. The concussion pushed me as if someone had put his hand in the small of my back and shoved. My helmet flew off, and I landed flat out on my stomach, about two yards away.

The result of the fire and explosion was that the Japanese jeep was burned up and nearly all of the new field uniforms were ruined. Many of the munitions were spent, along with the white phosphorous grenades and, of course, the TNT. Best of all, though, there was only one injury, and that was very minor.

Thinking back it seemed like this "big bang" was very much in keeping with everything else that had been going on before, only this time the Japanese had nothing to do with it.[33]

Two March 1945 was an eventful and historic day in the history of Corregidor. After the munitions-dump fire in front of Topside Barracks, Colonel Jones directed his unit commanders who were on Topside to "police" the parade ground as best they could. He was well aware that it was impossible to clean up the area to any semblance of its previous condition. But because they could not dig graves in the granitelike soil of Corregidor, the troopers threw the Japanese bodies over the cliffs.

At 1000 on 2 March, a day that the troopers of the 503d remember as a bright, clear day with a fresh breeze, General MacArthur returned to Corregidor in the same way he had left it nine days short of three years before—he landed in a PT boat at South Dock on San Jose Beach. His PT boat, No. 373, commanded by Lt. Joseph Roberts (USN), carried eleven members of his staff. Other PT boats carried Lieutenant General Krueger, commanding general of Sixth Army, Lieutenant General Hall, commanding general of XI Corps, key members of their staffs, and a large contingent of naval officers and newsmen. The fleet of four PT boats was commanded by Lt. Henry Taylor. As the

33. Jones, letter to author, 11 June 1985.

PT boats docked at South Beach, twelve P-47s were in the process of dive-bombing Fort Hughes, just a few thousand yards to the south in the bay. The Air Corps show may or may not have been coincidental with General MacArthur's return.

After he stepped out of his PT boat at the battered South Dock, Colonel Jones reported to General MacArthur, who then greeted Vice Adm. Daniel E. Barbey, commander of the Navy's amphibious forces in the Southwest Pacific. MacArthur then strode ahead, walking straightforwardly over mounds of rubble thrown into Bottomside by the Malinta Tunnel explosions. One tunnel exit high on the rocky hillside still belched smoke from the still-smoldering interior of Malinta Hill. The stench of decaying Japanese bodies permeated the air. To no one in particular General MacArthur said, "Well, gentlemen, it has been a long way back."

Colonel Jones had assembled as many operational jeeps as he could find and had them lined up near the dock at Southside. He escorted Generals MacArthur and Marquat to the first jeep on the line, identified on the passenger side by a number 1 twelve inches high. On all the jeeps, the windshield was tied down flat on the hoods and the tops were missing; they had long since disappeared. General MacArthur got into the first jeep, and General Marquat and Colonel Jones climbed into the same jeep from the rear. The rest of the entourage found spaces in the rest of the jeep column. The visitors were all dressed in khakis, low-cut shoes, and visored officer caps, in sharp contrast to Colonel Jones and his men who were in fatigues, dusty jump boots, and well-worn steel helmets—and carrying weapons. With MacArthur were these members of his old staff who had left Corregidor with him three years before: Lt. Gen. Richard K. Sutherland, chief of staff; Maj. Gen. Spencer B. Aiken, Southwest Pacific area signal officer; Maj. Gen. Hugh Casey, engineer officer; Maj. Gen. William F. Marquat, antiaircraft officer; Maj. Gen. Richard Marshall, commanding U.S. Army forces in the Far East; Paul Stevens; Brig. Gen. Charles E. Willoughby, assistant chief of staff for intelligence; Brig. Gen. LeGrande A. Diller, public relations officer; Colonel Sidney Huff, aide-de-camp; Lt. Col. Joseph A. McMicking; and Lt. Paul Rogers, MacArthur's secretary.

MacArthur directed the procession of jeeps around the east

side of Malinta Hill, dismounted, and walked inside the tunnel, at the mouth of which he had had his command post in a tent, three years previously. MacArthur spied some Japanese who had been burned to death with flamethrowers. "It was bad enough for us when we were here," he said, "but it has been worse for them."

The jeeps then headed for Monkey Point, now a jagged, rock-strewn crater. MacArthur next headed up the north road to the ruins of the houses where he, the late President Manuel Quezon, and American High Commissioner Francis B. Sayre had lived temporarily after they had evacuated Manila. MacArthur walked up the three steps covered with rubble and said, "Well, I'm home again."

Colonel Jones then led the column of jeeps up the dusty roads that wound through the rubble and the bombed-out vegetation of the once-lush growth that had covered the island in its more peaceful days. The column of jeeps snaked its way past the ice-house, the hospital, the Middleside barracks, the post exchange, the theater, and finally halted on the parade ground in front of the "mile-long barracks." MacArthur then asked Colonel Jones to take him down to Wheeler Battery. There, MacArthur walked through the ruins of the once-formidable coastal guns. Now they were rusting hulks. There were probably live Japanese in the concrete emplacement. General MacArthur stopped, put his hands on his hips, and gazed silently over the South China Sea and across to the lofty mountains of Bataan. Then he got quietly back into his jeep, and the motorcade made its way up to the parade ground, arriving there at about 1100.

On the parade ground, Colonel Jones had assembled an Honor Guard of 336 men from both the 503d and the 34th Infantry Regiments. The 34th contingent had returned to The Rock for the occasion and consisted of Lt. Col. Postlethwait, his company commanders, and a number of the battalion's NCOs. The troops formed a rectangular block with the Rock Force staff in a line in front of the formation. The fatigue-clad troops had their backs to Topside Barracks and were facing the old flagpole. The khaki-clad visitors and newsmen were aligned on the other side of the flagpole, facing the troop formation. Parachutes still festooned the trees and the ruins of the buildings around the impromptu ceremonial site.

Colonel Jones called the Honor Guard to attention and then turned to face General MacArthur. Standing tall, with his elite and properly proud troops standing at attention behind him, Colonel Jones saluted General MacArthur and said, "Sir, I present you the Fortress Corregidor."

General MacArthur paused only momentarily and then said in a voice obviously accented with deep emotion:

> Colonel Jones, the capture of Corregidor is one of the most brilliant operations in military history. Outnumbered two to one, your command by its unfaltering courage, its invincible determination, and its professional skill overcame all obstacles and annihilated the enemy. I have cited to the order of the day all units involved, and I take great pride in awarding you as their commander the Distinguished Service Cross as a symbol of the fortitude, the devotion, and the bravery with which you have fought.[34] I see the old flagpole still stands. Have your troops hoist the colors to its peak, and let no enemy ever haul them down.

Colonel Jones made an "about face" and gave the command, "Present Arms." The troops, General MacArthur and his staff, and all the observers saluted while Buglers Cpl. Michael L. Meedkins and Tech. Sgt. Cyril Schneider sounded "To the Colors." The flag rose slowly, snapping briskly in the usual Corregidor wind. MacArthur's eyes followed it all the way to the top. Then General MacArthur returned Colonel Jones's salute, and he and his entourage mounted their jeeps and rode down the winding, rocky road past Malinta Tunnel and reboarded the PT boats that had brought them to Corregidor. Within minutes after the party left the dock, the 503d killed a sniper near Malinta Tunnel.

In his *Reminiscences,* General MacArthur wrote movingly of his visit to Corregidor.

---

34. Later, General MacArthur recommended, and the War Department approved, the Presidential Unit Citation for the entire Rock Force.

There are moments of drama and romance in every life, and my first visit to recaptured Corregidor was one of these. I borrowed four PT boats from the Navy and gathered all those who had originally left Corregidor with me. We went back to The Rock the same way we had left it. We had departed in the darkness of a somber night. We came back in the sunlight of a new day. In the background, the ragged remnants of our parachutes dangled from the jagged tree stumps, the skeleton remains of the old white barracks of "Topside" gleamed down on us, and a smart-looking honor guard rendered us its salute.

I was greeted by Colonel George Jones, the young man who had commanded the troops that had so recently retaken the island in such gallant fashion. I congratulated him and decorated him.

The regimental surgeon of the 503d also recorded his impression of the emotional, flag-raising formation.

On the bright, breezy afternoon of March 2, the colors were run up in an official, flag-raising ceremony on the same staff from which the Japs had dragged them down three years before. It was a picturesque spectacle. The rooftops and balconies of battered buildings all around the parade ground were crowded with soldiers who had taken part in the combat and who were now enjoying the historic occasion. A particular friend of mine, named Pete, had insisted that we scramble to our vantage point on the top of the old barracks, from which we had so often in the last eventful days looked down on the progress of the various patrols and ships and planes. A wry fellow was this Pete, deeply emotional at heart but always masking his feelings with a salty curtness. Even on occasions such as this he was not one to let sentiment run away with him. After the Stars and Stripes had rolled out in full glory from the peak of the staff, I felt my nerves tingling; but beside me Pete dropped his salute and commented, "Well, that ends the story of Corregidor—the true story. From now on it's a legend and belongs to the scenario writers. They'll make comic-strip heroes out of the real men who fought here. I'm glad we saw our part. They can have theirs."

The flag-raising ceremony, impressive, poignant, and historic as it was, was over in seven and a half minutes.

In twelve days, Corregidor had been retaken from a tenacious, determined, unyielding enemy of some 6,000 men by 2,700 paratroopers (including 600 field artillerymen and engineers), and 1,100 standard infantrymen. The RCT suffered 165 men killed and 615 wounded or injured; the attached units lost 45 men killed, 175 wounded, and 5 men missing.

On 6 March, Lieutenant General Hall returned to the island and at another ceremony presented Silver Stars, Bronze Stars, and Purple Hearts to the heroic men of the 503d.

For the next few days, the 503d continued to patrol the island's caves and cliffs, still looking for the enemy who had proven so obstinate and single-minded. Between 2 and 7 March, the Rock Force killed an additional 118 of the enemy. Four 503d men were killed in this mop-up operation before the regiment left the island.

While the mopping up proceeded, the bulk of the regiment made ready to leave. They packed their gear, fired off some more artillery and mortars at suspicious locations (and to use up ammunition), and cleaned up their bodies and uniforms. The last of the wounded were evacuated by ship to hospitals ashore.

On 8 March, Navy LCIs backed into Black Beach, and the regiment marched down from Topside, moved back from the tail, and loaded up. The 2d Battalion of the 151st remained behind to garrison the island. The 503d headed for its base camp at Mindoro to get ready for another tough battle: the cleanup of Negros Island.

After April of 1945, a lone Quartermaster Graves Registration Team remained on Corregidor searching for the American dead of both the 1942 and 1945 Corregidor battles. One rifle company protected the QM Company against any possible remnants of the Japanese force on the island. In September, an official survey team headed by Col. Reingold Melberg came to The Rock to inspect for any salvageable remains of the 150 million dollars' worth of prewar coastal defenses. The survey party's conclusion was pretty obvious: nothing left worth salvaging.

The Graves Registration outfit continued about their grim task but with a dawning sense of uneasiness that there were other than Americans alive on the island. By day, they saw suspicious, fresh footprints around the dusty trails, and at night, they heard unusual noises out beyond the guard posts. They began to suspect uneasily that some of the Japanese who had been sealed in the caves had somehow survived.

Sgt. James "Moon" Mullen was one of the NCOs assigned to the Graves Registration Company. On 1 January 1946, he was going about his business near the company command post. He looked up at a noise and was startled to see a formation of some twenty Japanese marching in formation toward him, waving surrender flags. The group was led by a young Japanese army officer. Sergeant Mullen noted that the soldiers appeared to be "exceptionally soldierly," from which he concluded that they had not been suffering from their long underground confinement. The young officer bowed to Sergeant Mullen and presented to him a paper written in excellent English that contained their offer of surrender.

After the commanding officer of the Graves Registration unit had interrogated the Japanese, he found out that they had not learned of Japan's surrender until a few weeks prior to their capitulation when one of them had found an old American newspaper during one of their nightly, water-search forays out of their hiding places. The Japanese then debated among themselves as to the proper and honorable course of action. They decided that it was their duty to surrender and that surrender would be according to the will of the Emperor. Then they decided that before surrendering they would check the island for other survivors. Their search paid off: they found two sailors in another cave. After their search, they cleaned up, shaved, put on their best uniforms, and marched in to surrender.

Corregidor today is a jungle-covered pile of rock and ruins. The Pacific War Memorial, which the U.S. government built in

1968 to memorialize all of the Allied dead in the Pacific campaigns, is itself neglected and timeworn. But on one wall of the memorial is carved a poem that speaks words of sorrow and mysticism:

> Sleep, my sons . . .
> Sleep in the silent depths of the sea,
> Or in your bed of hallowed sod,
> Until you hear at dawn
> The low, clear reveille of God.

The tiny island, now lost in the waters of Manila Bay, with no tactical or strategic significance, fades in memories. But if it could speak, if it could rerun its history, sometimes glorious, sometimes dark and calamitous, it could tell a tale that would place it in a unique niche in the annals of military history. But it cannot speak; this will have to suffice.

BIOGRAPHICAL DATA
What They Do Today

Abbott, Donald E. Retired after a career as a computer programmer with a large forest products company; lives in Santa Rosa, CA.

Atkins, Capt. Robert M. "Cracker." Colonel, Infantry, U.S. Army, Retired 1971. Second career as a pharmacist, Student Health Service, Univ. of Florida. Retired again in June of 1986. Lives in Gainesville, FL.

Bailey, Lt. William T. Earned an M.D. after the war; now retired from the U.S. Public Health Service; lives in Richmond, VA.

Blake, Lt. Bill. Became Adjutant General of West Virginia and retired from the National Guard as a Major General; also a newspaper publisher; lives in Fairlea, WVA.

Bossert, William T. Captain, AUS, Retired; commercial artist with *New Yorker* magazine; lives in Mt. Kisco, NY.

Britten, Lt. Col. John W. Promoted to Colonel; Army aviator; died in 1957; last assignment, commander of Army Aviation Detachment, Fort Belvoir, VA.

Browne, Lawrence. Promoted to Colonel of Infantry; retired from the Army in October, 1972.

Burt, Lt. Robert E. Retired from the Army as a Lt. Colonel, Engineer Corps, October, 1965; now lives in Sacramento, CA.

Callahan, Lt. Edward J. Retired from the Army with a physical disability; now lives in Atlanta, GA.

Caskey, Major Lawson B. Retired from the Army as a Lt. Colonel; died in 1967.

Castillo, Jesse S. Totally blinded on Corregidor; made a career in real estate and restaurants; now retired; says that "Fortunately, I do not have to rely on social security benefits"; lives in Pomona, CA. Married in 1945 to his World War II fiancee who said that if he didn't marry her, even though blind, he "would get awfully tired with me sitting in your lap." Four children of the marriage: eldest son Daniel with the LA County Sheriff's Dept.; Jim in the Army as a pilot with the rank of CW 4; Elizabeth a homemaker in Indiana. Jesse says that his eight grandchildren are "all the apples of their Grandpa's plastic eyes."

Clark, Ernest C. Retired from the Army as a Lt. Colonel in 1964; died in June 1986.

Conway, Joseph M. Retired as a Colonel, USA; lives in Estill Springs, TN.

Corder, Lt. Roscoe. Currently living in Pasadena, TX.

Corregidor. After the war, the U.S. built an elaborate Pacific War Memorial and Museum on Topside. Today, that Memorial and all of Corregidor are in a state of abject neglect. The Philippine Government has appropriated no funds for the Island's upkeep. Scrap dealers have illegally cut up and removed the guns, howitzers, and even the reinforcing rods from buildings, hastening the collapse of the bombed-out structures. A DAV report from the National Commander's visit to Corregidor says that the Memorial and the Museum are a disgrace to those who fought and died there. There was a large "gaping hole in the roof of the Memorial" and "the marble interior walls of the memorial were also covered with moss and mildew." "Corregidor is one vast untended jungle that chokes the island's shattered defenses, obliterates paths and roadways, and invades the crumbled remains of buildings like tropical growth in a once great Mayan metropolis," reported William Graves in the July 1986 issue of *National Geographic*.

Crawford, 1st Lt. Donald A. Retired as a Lt. Colonel and died in April 1980.

Crawford, Lt. Lewis B. Currently living in New Iberia, LA.

Davis, Major John N. Retired as Colonel of Infantry in September 1965; died March 1983.

Dean, Lt. Leonard M. Post-World War II career generally unknown; one source believes that Dean was one of three 503d officers killed in a plane crash while flying to a 503d reunion in Boston in 1947 or 1948.

Debruycker, Sgt. Ernest J. Association has no record of his post-503d career.

Doerr, Capt. Jean P. Retired as a Lt. Colonel in 1962; died in February of 1985.

Donovan, Capt. Francis X. No record or information.

Eddleman, Brig. Gen. Clyde D. USMA Class of 1924; rose to four-star rank as the Commanding General of Army forces in Europe in 1959; served as Vice Chief of Staff of the Army, 1960–62; retired in 1962; currently living in Arlington, VA.

Edgar, James J. No record or information.

Eichelberger, Lt. Gen. Robert L. USMA Class of 1909; commanded the Eighth Army in Japan from 1945 to 1948; retired as a Lt. General in 1948; died in September 1961.

Erickson, Lt. Col. John R. Died in 1967 while serving as a Colonel and PMS and T at the University of Wyoming.

Eubanks, Sgt. Roy E. Killed on Noemfoor Island in 1944 while assaulting an enemy position; was awarded the Medal of Honor; plaque honoring Sgt. Eubanks is in the National Infantry Museum at Fort Benning, GA. A memorial honoring his memory was placed on the lawn of the courthouse in his home town of Snow Hill, NC in 1985.

Flash, Lt. Edward T. Retired as Lt. Colonel in January 1972; currently a "gentleman farmer/rancher" near San Antonio, TX.

Fraser, Jimmy. No record or information post-503d service.

Gibson, Capt. Henry W. Retired from the Army as a Colonel in Military Police Corps in September 1973. His wife, Patricia, ferried planes across the Atlantic in World War II; currently living in Port Townsend, WA.

Graves, William. No record or information.

Grochala, Stanley. No record or information.

Herb, Chaplain Robert E. Episcopalian priest; life-long bachelor;

currently physically disabled and confined to a wheelchair; lives in Homestead, FL.

Hester, Weldon B. Spent post-World War II years as YMCA Director of Boys' Work and Camping; has collected, bound and indexed thousands of articles and military reports, 90% of which are on World War II, including 125 items on Bataan and Corregidor; currently retired and living and expanding his collection in Riverview, FL.

Hill, Capt. Hudson C. Retired as a Colonel of Infantry in October 1968; died in November 1984.

Howard, S/Sgt. Nelson H. Currently living in Santa Rosa, FL.

Homma, Lt. Gen. Masaharu. Brought to trial in December 1945 charged with the responsibility for the Bataan Death March; convicted on 11 February 1946; executed by a firing squad at Los Baños, Luzon on 3 April 1946.

Hovis, Capt. Logan W. Practiced medicine as anesthesiologist and operated a school for nurse anesthesiologists; retired in 1985; lives in Vienna, WVA.

Johnson, S/Sgt. Chris W. No record or information.

Johnson, Major Harold K. USMA 1933; Chief of Staff of the Army, 1964–68; retired disabled as a four-star general in 1968; died September 1983.

Jones, Colonel George M. USMA 1935. After the war had many important and interesting assignments: observer at Bikini Atomic Tests in 1946; member of Eisenhower Advanced Study Group to develop concepts of future warfare in atomic age, 1947–49; commander of Special Warfare Center, 1958–61; promoted to Brigadier General 1962; assistant division commander, 3d Division in Europe, 1962–64; Chief of Staff, Fifth Army, 1965–66; deputy commander of U.S. Army, Alaska, 1966–68; retired from the Army, 1968; MBA, Univ. of Alaska, 1968; MPA Univ. of Northern Colorado, 1978; currently active in civic affairs, financial planning, and investment business in Tucson, AZ.

Knox, Major Cameron. Retired from the Army as a Colonel of Infantry in 1961; reported to have earned a PhD. in ichthyology and taught at the University level after his retirement from the Army.

Knudson, Major Melvin R. Left the Army as a Lt. Colonel in

May 1946; for next fifteen years, served as Director of Research
for the St. Regis Paper Co.; currently a management consultant
for universities and corporations and owner of a travel agency;
currently lives in Tacoma, WA.

Krueger, General Walter. Retired from the Army as a four-star
general in January, 1946 at the age of 65; published his memoirs,
From Down Under to Nippon, in 1953; died in Valley Forge, PA
on 20 August 1967.

Lackey, Lt. Col. John H. Served on the staff of the Armed Forces
Staff College in early fifties; died in 1956 while on active duty.

Levine, Major Lester H. Retired from the Army as a Colonel in
the Ordnance Corps in 1968; lives in Sun City, FL.

McCarter, Pvt. Lloyd G. While recovering from his wounds in
Letterman Hospital, Presidio of San Francisco in 1945, he received an invitation to the White House; President Truman
decorated him with the Medal of Honor; he was discharged
shortly thereafter because of constant pain from a bullet which
lodged too close to his heart for surgery. Bennett M. Guthrie
in *Three Winds of Death* said that "In February 1956, greatly
depressed by the recent death of his wife and suffering constant
pain from his war wounds, Lloyd did what the Japanese could
never do: he took his own life." Plaques honoring McCarter
are placed at his home of record and at the National Infantry
Museum, Fort Benning, GA.

Mitchell, Major Harry T. Sr. Retired from the Army as a Lt.
Colonel of Infantry in January of 1963; retired from Director
of Civil Defense, Huntsville, AL in 1977; currently lives in
Huntsville, AL.

Murphy, Capt. Lyle M. Killed during the Negros Campaign which
followed the Corregidor operation in April of 1945. General
Jones reports that Captain Murphy "was probably the outstanding company commander in the 503d at the time of his death
on Negros Island."

O'Boyle, S/Sgt. Bernard. After the war, worked for the Department
of Public Works in Chicago, IL; retired in 1984; currently lives
in Oak Lawn, IL.

Powers, Father John J. Went to work for the Veterans Administration at the end of the war; promoted to Monsignor; devoted
his life to the service of the veterans; retired from the VA in

1980 because of "health reasons"; currently lives in Palo Alto, CA.

Postlethwait, Lt. Col. Edward M. USMA Class of 1937; after the war, became a paratrooper; retired from the Army as a Colonel of Infantry in 1967; worked as financial manager in Fayetteville, NC after retirement; died in April of 1985.

Pugh, Lt. Col. John R. USMA 1932; POW 1942–45; rose to Major General; commanded the 3d Armored Division, 1962–64; commanded 6th Corps, 1964–66; retired 1966; currently lives in Little Fiddlers Green at Round Hill, VA.

Rucker, Capt. John P. No information or reports; currently believed to be living in El Paso, TX.

Shaw, 1st Sgt. Carl N. Currently living in Waverly, VA.

Smith, Lt. Magnus. Retired from the Army as a Colonel of Infantry in 1972; employed as a Hospital Personnel Officer until his death in November of 1982.

Smithback, T/5 Arthur O. Cracker Atkins reports that he is "Still a great tenor singer and bachelor; attends every national reunion; arrives early and stays late; currently living in Stoughton, WI.

Stevens, Major Thomas. Died in 1961.

Swing, Lt. Gen. Joseph M. USMA 1915; commanded 11th Airborne until 1947; promoted to Lt. General in 1950; Commandant of the Army War College in 1950–51; commanding general of 6th Army 1951–1954; retired in 1954; appointed by his classmate, President Eisenhower, to be Commissioner of Immigration in 1954; retired from that position in 1961; died in San Francisco in December 1984.

Templeman, Harold M. Red Cross director with the 503d; qualified as a paratrooper by the 503d; wrote *Return to Corregidor*, a book reporting the 503d assault on Corregidor; employee of the State Department 1945–75; currently lives in Quarryville, PA.

Thomas, Lt. James R. Discharged as a 1st Lieutenant in 1946; earned an M.D. degree and practiced in Port Arthur, TX until the time of his death. His widow, Gina, lives in Port Arthur, TX.

Tolson, Lt. Col. John J. III. USMA 1937; Commanded 1st Cavalry Division in Viet Nam in 1967–68; commanded 18th Airborne

Corps, 1968–71; retired from the Army as a Lt. General in 1973; served as Director, North Carolina Department of Military Affairs from 1973–77; currently lives in Raleigh, NC.

Wainwright, Gen. Jonathan M. USMA 1906; POW 1942–45; Medal of Honor; promoted to General in 1945; served as commander of 4th Army, 1945–47; retired 1947; died San Antonio, TX, 2 September 1953, age 70.

Whitson, Lt. Joe M. Jr. Owner of a large lumber company in Nashville, TN.

Williams, Lt. Dick. Owns and operates a commercial communications and photographic business in Gulf Breeze, FL.

Woods, Major Robert C. KIA Corregidor, 24 February 1945.

Bibliography

Abbott, Donald E. Letter to author, 13 July 1986.
———. Article in *The Static Line*, July 1985.
"American Military History, 1607–1953," ROTC Manual 145-20 Department of the Army, July 1956.
Baldwin, Hanson W. "Corregidor: The Full Story," *The New York Times*, September 1946.
Ballard, Carl. "Chronological History of Company F, 503d Parachute Infantry, *The Static Line*, 1986.
Belote, James H. and William M. *Corregidor—The Saga of a Fortress*. New York: Harper & Row, 1967.
Blair, John H., III. "Operation of the 3d Battalion, 503d Parachute Infantry Regiment in the Landing on Corregidor, PI 16 Feb–2 Mar 1945." Monograph, Fort Benning, Ga., 1950.
Castillo, Jesse S. Letter and telephone call to author, November 1986.
"Combat Over Corregidor." Undated but probably written in 1945.
Devlin, Maj. Gerard M. *Paratrooper*. New York: St. Martin's Press, 1986.
Dewey, George A. *Autobiography of George Dewey*. New York: Scribners, 1913.
Drews, H. J. Letter to author, 5 November 1986.
"Drop on Corregidor," *Far East Air Force Magazine*, June 1945.
Elfrank, Warren W. Tape to author, July 1986.
Evans, Nancy. Letter to author, 2 October 1985.

Flanagan, Edward M., Jr. *The Angels.* Washington, D.C.: Infantry Journal Press, 1948.

———. "Squash on the Rock," *ARMY,* September 1958.

Flash, Edward H. Lesson plan. Fort Benning, Ga., February 1946.

———. Letter to author, 15 March 1985.

Gibson, Col. Henry W. (Hoot), U.S. Army Ret'd. Letter to author, August 1986.

Graves, William. "Corregidor Revisited," *National Geographic,* July 1986.

Gray, Joseph L. Four letters to author, dated June–July 1986.

Guerrero, Leon MA. "The Fall of Corregidor," *Philippine Review,* July 1943.

———. "The Last Days of Corregidor," *Philippine Review,* May 1943.

Guthrie, Bennett M. Letters to author, 1986.

———. *Three Winds of Death.* Chicago: Adams Press, 1985.

Hardman, Maj. Thomas C. "Drop on Corregidor," *Coast Artillery Journal,* July–August 1945.

Helbling, Maj. James J. "Combined Assault—Fortress Corregidor," USCGSC student paper, March 1971.

Hennessy, William F. Interview with author, 22 May 1986.

Hester, Weldon B. Eight letters to author, 1985 to 1986.

Hill, Capt. Hudson C. "The Operation of Company E, 503d Parachute Infantry Regiment at Wheeler Point, Corregidor, 23 February 1945." Monograph, The Infantry School, 1958.

Hodak, Paul. Letter to Joseph L. Gray, June 1986.

Hovis, Dr. Logan W. Three letters to author, 1986.

Howard, Brig. Gen. Samuel, USMC. Letter—subject: Report on Operation, Employment, and Supply of the Old 4th Marines from September '41 to Surrender of Corregidor, May 6, 1945, to commandant of the Marine Corps, 26 September 1945.

Jones, Brig. Gen. George M., U.S. Army Ret'd. Eleven letters to author, with lengthy enclosures, 1986.

Kelly, Frank. "MacArthur Sees Flag Rise Again on Corregidor," *New York Herald Tribune,* 2 March 1945.

Krueger, Gen. Walter. *From Down Under to Nippon.* Washington, D.C.: Combat Forces Press, 1953.

Lackey, Col. John H. "The Rock Operation or the Return to Corregidor." Monograph, Armed Forces Staff College, 1948.

Landes, Karl H. Letter to author, 1986.

Lee, Ron. Letter to author, 1986.

Levine, Maj. Lester H. "The Operations of the 503d Parachute Infantry Regiment on Corregidor." Monograph, Fort Benning, Ga., The Infantry School, 1948.

Linnell, Lt. Col. Frank H. "The Re-taking of Corregidor, February 1945." Monograph, Marine Corps Amphibious Warfare School, 1948.

MacArthur, Gen. Douglas. *Reminiscences.* New York: McGraw Hill, 1964.

Mitchell, Lt. Col. Harris T., Sr. Letters to author, 1986.

Morris, Eric. *Corregidor, The End of the Line.* New York: Stein and Day, 1984.

Morton, Louis. "The Fall of the Philippines," USGPO, 1953.

Mulligan, Hugh A. " 'Rock' Lives Again for Both Sides," AP, undated.

"On Top of Malinta Hill." Unknown author, but a member of K Company, 34th Infantry. *Infantry Journal Press,* August 1945.

"Operation Corregidor Island," history of 2d Battalion, 151st Infantry on Corregidor, 1945.

"Operation M-7." Book II, "The Rock," history of the 3d Battalion, 34th Infantry, December 1945.

Pater, Edward F. Letter to author, 25 July 1986.

Postlethwait, Lt. Col. E. M. "Corregidor Coordination," *Infantry Journal,* August 1945.

Powers, Rev. Msgr. John J. Letter to author, 26 July 1986.

Russell, Lt. Col. John T. Letter to author, 6 December 1984.

Sellinger, I. Letter to author, 1986.

Shutt, Thomas L. Letter to Joseph L. Gray, 6 June 1986.

Smith, Capt. Magnus L. "Operation of the Rock Force in the Recapture of Corregidor." Monograph, Infantry School, 1950.

Smith, Robert Ross. "Triumph in the Philippines," USGPO, 1963.

Smithback, Arthur O. Letter to author, July 1986.

Spector, Ronald H. *Eagle Against the Sun.* New York: Macmillan, 1985.

Steinberg, Rafael. *Island Fighting.* Alexandria, Va.: Time-Life Books, 1979.

————. *Return to the Philippines.* Alexandria, Va.: Time-Life Books, 1979.

Templeman, Harold. "The Return to Corregidor," 1977.
Tolson, Lt. Gen. John J. Four letters to author, 1985 to 1986.
USAFFE Board Report No. 308, dated 16 May 1945.
Williams, Dick. Three letters to author, 1986 to 1987.
Wilson, Mrs. Wanda K. Letter to author, 11 April 1986.
Zich, Arthur. *The Rising Sun.* Alexandria, Va.: Time-Life Books, 1977.
Ziler, Don. Letter to author, 3 December 1986.

Index